DIRTY DISHES

DIRTY DISHES

A RESTAURATEUR'S STORY OF
PASSION, PAIN, AND PASTA

PINO LUONGO
and ANDREW FRIEDMAN

BLOOMSBURY

New York   Berlin   London

Published by Bloomsbury USA, New York

All papers used by Bloomsbury USA are natural, recyclable products made from
wood grown in well-managed forests. The manufacturing processes conform to
the environmental regulations of the country of origin.

Portions of chapters 5 and 7 appeared in somewhat different form in
Don't Try This at Home, edited by Kimberly Witherspoon and Andrew Friedman.
They are reprinted here by kind permission of Inkwell Management.

LIBRARY OF CONGRESS CATALOGING-IN-PUBLICATION DATA

Luongo, Pino.
    Dirty dishes : a restaurateur's story of passion, pain, and pasta /
Pino Luongo and Andrew Friedman.—1st ed.
        p.   cm.
    ISBN-13: 978-1-59691-442-1 (hardcover)
    ISBN-10: 1-59691-442-4 (hardcover)
    1. Luongo, Pino.   2. Restaurateurs—New York (State)—
New York—Biography.   I. Friedman, Andrew, 1967–
II. Title.

    TX910.5.L86A3 2009
    647.95092—dc22

                                                    2008034860

First U.S. Edition 2009

1 3 5 7 9 10 8 6 4 2

Typeset by Westchester Book Group
Printed in the United States of America by Quebecor World Fairfield

Contents

To my wife, Jessie, and my children, Marco, Jacobella, and Lorenzo—you are the backbone of my up-and-down life—and to all the people who, intentionally or not, entered my life or my restaurants—I hope you enjoyed yourselves.

—Pino Luongo

Foreword

Dirty Dishes is either a classic restaurant morality tale of what happens when you fly too high and too close to the sun—or a spiritual journey, a cycle beginning and ending with the simple good things of Italy. It's either the memoir of an ambitious, creative, food-loving kid from Tuscany who grows up to be a successful New York City restaurateur—or the redacted confessions of the Dark Prince of Italian fine dining, a man loved and hated with equal fervor by the wide swath of New Yorkers left in his wake.

Its author, Pino Luongo, is either the perpetrator of some of the greatest and most hubristic follies in the recent history of the American restaurant business—or another victim of circumstance, of his own success, of a notoriously cruel and crowded marketplace, and of the caprice of the dining public. Or he's the happy, self-actualized owner-proprietor of Centolire, an excellent Upper East Side restaurant.

Personally, I think all of the above statements are true. Pino's like that: a complicated man. It's only fair that this foreword remain largely speculative, as so many thousands of hours have been spent by so many trying to figure Pino out. He may love simple, straightforward things with genuine passion, and he has always been frank (to say the least) about his likes and dislikes. But one underestimates him at one's peril.

What is clear and inarguable is that he was instrumental in creating the template for what we now take for granted as acceptable Italian food in New York City (and, increasingly, across the country). He was a proponent of menu items which then were unthinkable to serve, but are now standard and much-loved fare. His was the first restaurant to show me, for instance, what a properly sauced pasta could be—how important the pasta itself was. He turned everything I thought I knew about Italian food—all the conventional wisdom of the time—on its head and woke me up to an entire world of food and culture. My Francophilic roots were shaken to the core and have never recovered.

That I have recently married into a large Northern Italian family I blame in no small part on Pino. That during the last World Cup finals I betrayed my French roots and rooted for Italia. Pino's fault. That I now crave slowly braised ragùs, Sardinian flatbread, focaccia pizza with robiola cheese and white truffles, osso buco . . . His fault. That I even know what *spaghetti alla chitarra* is? Him. Again.

Did I mention yet that the bastard fired me?

When I met Pino for the first time, shortly after I'd been hired as sous chef at his excellent Le Madri, he was at the very peak of his powers and influence. I was summoned to his lair above Il Toscanaccio, a sleek, dimly lit room surrounded by offices and conference areas where terrified minions clacked away on keyboards or hunched over their telephones, passing along his orders in hushed tones. Somewhere across an ocean, boats were being loaded with wheels of aged parmesan and cold-pressed olive oils—fuel for the ever-expanding empire. All across town, chefs twitched involuntarily every time their kitchen phones rang. Would it be Pino, calling from his car, mandating an immediate menu change? Managers sharpened their knives, ready to plunge them into their general managers' back should the need arise. Busboys powdered and groomed themselves, fearful of the involuntary flop sweat an unexpected visit from Pino might induce. It seemed, sometimes, from inside his sphere of influence, that the entire world's nervous system was wired to Pino's. He caught a cold? We all coughed.

Yet the man who peered at me from across the desk that day had an amused look on his face. A bit world-weary, for sure—the face of a guy who'd seen a lot. But not the face of a jaded or cynical man. This was unusual in a business where such feelings are almost compulsory. Where the daily grind, the grim realities of feeding and liquoring up the general public, tend to discourage such things as love and idealism. And yet I was looking at . . . an optimist.

Granted, an optimist who gifted me with many such Golden Moments as: "It's good to have enemies. It means you are important."

Or, when asked when his chefs could again begin ordering from a particular company whose owner, Pino felt, had been insulting in his demands for money: "When? *When?* When he crawls across Fifty-ninth Street and sucks my fucking DICK!"

Or, in discussing another restaurateur with a tough reputation: "He's the biggest son-of-a-bitch in New York. And this is *me* talking!"

In spite of this, when I remember Pino, it's always a smiling man who comes to mind. (In fact, I can take issue with only one minor point in this book: He is way too kind to me. I was in so far over my head at Coco Pazzo Teatro, the *Titanic* could have passed over me un-noticed. I was a virtual Opie Taylor surrounded by Medecis.) Remi-niscing about his early days in the business, about his childhood in Italy, about meals eaten, mistakes made, friends and enemies both, Pino always seemed entirely in his element. And it's worth mention-ing here that of the major decisions, restaurant ventures, concepts, and business moves described in this account, nearly all them were brilliant. Coco Pazzo, Le Madri, Il Toscanaccio, Sapore di Mare, and Mad. 61 were all excellent and innovative restaurants. Only a few other projects turned out to be "really bad ideas." It's significant as well that one of the moves for which Pino was most excoriated by the press, the one for which he was ultimately punished, was Tuscan Square, a con-cept he cherished and felt particularly close to.

In the restaurant business, love is often a killer. This is a business where all too often a place where people gather to eat and drink is in fact a "high concept," designed, from the ground up, by committee. Everything from the name on the door to the menu selections are the result of market surveys and conventional wisdom. This is how we ar-rive at big-box monstrosities marrying one demographic's vague fond-ness for Chinese or Japanese food with another's need for brightly colored girl drinks. No one is home in these places. They are designed not for anyone in particular, but instead for a bland cross section of perceived appetites.

This was never the case with Pino's places. His restaurants never lacked for an identity. You *knew* who was talking to you with every dish, with every painting on the wall, with every waiter's gesture. Though a great number of the city's best and most prominent Italian chefs have passed at one time or another through Pino's kitchens, it was Pino's voice speaking to you from the moment you sat down. A man trying to convince friends and strangers both to enjoy the food and the things and the country he loved. With this book, he gets a chance to speak to you directly.

Anthony Bourdain
Venice
September 2008

Introduction

I WANT YOU to take a walk with me to meet Pino Luongo."

"Why?"

"I want you to take over his account."

Fuck me!

"No, David. Really? C'mon. Really?"

The year is 1998. I'm sitting at my desk at the public relations firm of Kratz and Jensen, and my life is complicated enough without the possibility of Pino Luongo being added to it, but that's just what the firm's co-owner David Kratz is doing.

I don't know Pino, but he's a notorious figure in the restaurant community of New York City. There are *stories* about Pino that have circulated and snowballed for years, the way the legend of Keyser Söze did in *The Usual Suspects*. Dude came over from Italy in 1980, not speaking a word of English. Three years later, he opened his first restaurant, pilfering the entire staff of the place where he was once employed as a busboy, or so they say. Within five years he sat atop a burgeoning empire of his own, some of the most influential and successful Italian eateries in New York City history. He is rumored to have a monster temper—to be prone to telling off anyone and everyone, even the most powerful food writers in town, and to firing employees for sport.

I have never met the man, but I have admired his restaurants. In June 1996, I passed a wine-soaked Saturday evening at his Sapore di Mare in East Hampton, celebrating my birthday, and was seduced by the setting—an enormous, spot-on re-creation of a seaside Italian villa done up in terra-cotta tiles and white stucco walls—and the food.

A relative newcomer to fine dining at the time, I was struck by the seemingly effortless meeting of simplicity and sophistication. An orecchiette, or ear-shaped pasta, with broccoli rabe, house-made sausage, shriveled cherry tomatoes, and a dusting of parmesan, was so perfect and profound that I can still capture the whiff of toasted garlic and recall the dreamy lighting of the dining room, the din of the well-heeled revelers surrounding me as I dug in. That same summer, in the enormous parking lot behind his restaurant Le Madri in Manhattan, he staged a series called "Cinema al Fresco" every Sunday night, projecting movies on the wall of a nearby apartment building, and selling food and drink from the restaurant. I went one Sunday to watch *Cinema Paradiso* with some friends. I lingered, sipping espresso at my table, until the last credit crawled its way up the side of the building and past some poor soul's window, but somehow I never caught a glimpse of Pino himself.

I know what he looks like, though. At the agency, we maintain a number of oversized, black-leather-bound portfolios with press clippings about various clients preserved under sheets of crinkly plastic, and I've seen David flip through Pino's greatest hits at more than a few sit-downs with prospective clients. Pino has dark olive skin, and in most of the clips, he looks right at the camera and smiles like a Cheshire cat. The smile is the same from article to article, but the man, who was an actor back in his native Italy, is dressed in a variety of costumes: a black turtleneck for a lifestyle publication, a business suit in another. I remember thinking of Scott Fitzgerald's line about there never having been a great biography of a novelist because "he's too many people if he's any good." Thinking of Pino in all these guises, I wonder if the same principle applies to restaurateurs.

A couple of months earlier, the woman who had been running Pino's account had asked me for some help editing a letter: the food writer for the New York *Daily News* and on-air personality on WOR Radio had savaged one of Pino's restaurants and Pino had dictated the broad strokes of a blistering declaration of war that he planned to send to the critic. It was still in somewhat broken English, but the meaning was clear, and there were some irresistible turns of phrase; my favorite line was how Pino didn't know "what the fuck you think you learned on the Perillo Tour you took to Italy last summer"—implying that the critic, who had just penned a book on Italian food, should remember where he came from (the United States) and where Pino came from (Florence).

I had read it to the bottom, alternately amused and appalled, then had looked up and said what any public relations expert would have said: "He can't send this."

"You haven't met Pino yet, have you?"

"No."

"He'll send it."

A FEW HOURS after he appeared in my doorway, David and I meet Pino for dinner at Le Madri, the third restaurant he opened. He's a broad-shouldered man, with a wide face and pugnacious nose that bring to mind a bull, and this impression is enhanced by a peculiar special effect: he *always*, even when sitting perfectly still, seems to be moving *forward*, to be charging. Maybe it's his eyes, which are constantly darting around. In time, I will learn that Pino likes to meet people almost exclusively in his own restaurants, on his turf, and he is forever looking for a waiter to correct, a longtime customer to greet. And so the eyes are always moving, searching, and the man never seems still.

Despite his reputation, I find Pino to be utterly charming. As we sip wine, he regales us with stories about the goings-on in his various restaurants and enterprises—vividly acting out a series of vignettes about moronic waiters and shifty lawyers and city bureaucrats and high-maintenance diners. After about thirty minutes of this, I'm firmly on his side: "No wonder he's always getting into fights," I think, "the man is clearly surrounded by idiots!"

I take on Pino's account, though neither I nor any of the associates who work for me really get to know him very well because he has a marketing team in place and we deal mostly with them. But I have recently co-written a cookbook with another client; and Pino, who has written two himself, hires me to write the proposal for his third, and, presumably, to write the book as well. At Le Madri, we sit and talk about what the book, which he has decided should be called *Simply Tuscan*, will be exactly. We get to comparing notes about our favorite foods and Pino says, "You know what I love: tuna, grilled, thinly sliced, with Tuscan fries. You ever have that?"

"No."

He waves over the nearest waiter: "Tell the kitchen I'm going to make grilled tuna and fries. Set it up!"

The waiter nods and a few minutes later, Pino leaves the table, returning, sweaty from the stove, with two plates of charred sliced tuna, ruby red on the inside, practically blackened on the outside. Next to the tuna is a mound of fries, tossed with crispy herbs (they went into the fryer with the potatoes) and piled so generously high that a few have tumbled onto the fish. It's the ideal summer meal, and we eat and resume our brainstorming on the book. At one point, after I clarify a point he has just made, Pino clasps my wrist with his hand and says, "I'm going to use you a lot. You know why? Because you know how to *listen*."

The moment is a revelation for me: walking around the Flatiron District a few days later with David Kratz, I say, "I think I figured Pino out."

David smiles wryly. "Oh, yeah?"

"He doesn't suffer fools very well."

"You know, Andrew," David says. "That's true. I've always gotten along great with Pino. I know what people say, but we've never had a problem." David paused as we walked along, his hands in his pockets. "But you haven't figured Pino out."

WORKING ON THE proposal was highly entertaining; interviewing Pino often felt like attending a theater performance for an audience of one. But no sooner did we sell the project to a publisher than Pino disappeared. I went on with my life as a marketing executive. I didn't hear from him for months, and I more or less assumed he had decided to hire another writer—which would have been bad form, but not unheard of. Then, about a year later, Pino's assistant called me out of the blue. With just eight weeks left before his publishing deadline, he was ready to "get started" on the manuscript. I chuckled and made an appointment.

When I showed up at the executive offices of Pino's company, Toscorp, three floors above Le Madri, I was struck by the unmistakable signs of crisis, beginning with the fact that I was kept waiting for nearly an hour outside the conference room, where he had all of his managers and accountants holed up for a meeting. Every few minutes, the door would open and one of his lieutenants would emerge, panic dancing across his face, and scurry off around the corner, dashing back a moment later with a file or a piece of paper that I surmised had some bearing on the goings-on behind the door.

Once Pino and I were alone, it was immediately clear that something was very much amiss in his professional life: he seemed never to stop sucking down cigarettes, and there were aluminum take-out containers with half-eaten cheeseburgers on his desk, a far cry from the porcelain plates streaked with tomato and olive oil and the drained wine glasses I had seen on earlier visits. And yet, when we sat down to work, he was able to compartmentalize whatever it was that was going on and give me his complete attention. We'd meet in the conference room and interview for hours, often wandering off on a tangent, never to return to the work at hand. The picture he painted of Tuscany was pure magic: a dreamscape of sunflowers and vineyards in the summer; a darkly romantic hill country hugged by rolling fog in the autumn. He spoke of food, especially his mother's, in a way that I had never heard anybody speak about food, describing everything from after-school snacks to New Year's Eve feasts with a passion that made me feel diminished to have been raised anywhere else.

At some point in every evening, Pino would call down to the restaurant and minutes later we'd hear the elevator bell ding and a runner, dressed in black pants with a white shirt and black vest, would arrive in the conference room holding a dinner tray aloft: two orders of spaghetti AOPP (shorthand for *aglio, olio, pomodoro, e peperoncino* or garlic, oil, tomato, and pepper flakes—it's one of Pino's signature dishes, a simple pasta that can be made, start to finish, in the time it takes for the spaghetti to cook), and vodka martinis, which the waiter would pour into chilled glasses, leaving each of us another martini and a half, milkshake-style, in the shaker.

It was about this time that David *did* have a problem with Pino, who had begun falling months behind on his public relations bill. I would later learn that in order to finance his dream project—a combination restaurant, retail store, and marketplace in Rockefeller Center—he had folded his handful of successful restaurants into a larger venture that was failing before the ink on the paperwork had dried. This was no small development: his restaurants—Le Madri in Manhattan, Sapore di Mare in East Hampton, and Coco Pazzo in both New York and Chicago—were trend-setting goldmines in the late 1980s and early 1990s, and putting them on the line was a perilous roll of the dice. As we shot the breeze over martinis and pasta, and he painted his big, broad brushstrokes of Tuscany, he was holding an astonishing amount of heartbreak and fear at bay. It wouldn't be until much later that I would learn the full extent of the dark seas he was navigating in those days, of how close he came to losing his entire empire.

What follows is the story of Pino Luongo, from his childhood in Tuscany through his days as an actor in Rome, emigration to the United States, and rise and near-total fall as a restaurateur in New York City. For the record, it was *his* idea to pull his collaborator out from between the lines of the text and have his story told in the way it's laid out here, with snippets of the meal we shared as he first told me his story. Maybe it's because he recognizes that he's larger than life and, like paintings of a certain size, can only be fully absorbed from a distance. Or maybe it's that, like the novelists of whom Fitzgerald wrote, Pino understands that, for better or worse, he isn't a single person but many, and that any attempt to neatly package him, or to tell his story strictly from the inside out, was doomed to fail.

Or perhaps it's simply that he best expresses himself in the kitchen or at the dinner table—settings that, as you are about learn, have been the two constants in his life and are the only places where he truly feels at home.

Andrew Friedman
New York City
September 2008

ONE

The Fugitive

OR ME THE journey was always about food.

Whenever I made the drive from Rome, where I lived and worked as an actor in my twenties, to Grosseto, a sleepy Tuscan town about one hundred kilometers southwest of Florence, in the flatlands of Maremma, my mother's cooking came to mind, which was nothing unusual; I thought often of her food because I had yet to discover a restaurant in the Big City whose offerings compared to what Má turned out in her modest home kitchen.

Zooming back there in early October 1980, in my four-door 1968 Lancia Fulvia sedan, I would have loved nothing more than to be headed for a routine family dinner, but that was far from the case. I didn't know quite how this visit would end, but I was certain that there would be pain, and that it was the last time I'd be able to see my hometown for the foreseeable future, perhaps forever.

Nevertheless, as I drove, I kept my fondest memories in mind for as long as possible, most of them centered on my mother and her love of food.

MY MOTHER, MAFALDA, was and remains a brilliant and intuitive cook. A strong and striking redhead (friends likened her to Rita Hayworth), she came from a large family: legend had it that my grandmother, who married at sixteen, gave birth to twenty-one children.

Piecing together the family's oral history, I can only come up with a
dozen, but her number may be right: some of her kids died heart-
breakingly young, while others were killed or assassinated by Mussolini's soldiers during World War II. In any event, by the time I was
born, my mother had six surviving siblings. As they tell the story,
when they were younger, the only two girls were my mother and her
sister, Marcella. As the boys matured and took up the family fishing
business, Mafalda and Marcella were educated in the kitchen so they
could help their mother prepare dinner every night. They received fish
dripping wet from the family nets, and the lone means of preventing
perishables from spoiling was keeping them on ice, so the teachings
were thorough: they learned how to butcher and clean just about every
variety of fish, as well as how to preserve, cure, and smoke it. Because
they ate a lot of eels and bluefish, my mother developed an un-shy
palate, and because the kitchen was comically small—four burners
were clustered tightly together on the stovetop, the oven was narrow,
and the counter space was limited—she learned how to be ruthlessly
efficient, whittling recipes down to their essence and producing the
most flavor with the fewest possible ingredients and steps.

Má never worked in a professional kitchen, but by the time she became a parent, cooking was such an extension and reflection of her life,
it became a natural means of self-expression, right down to how she
demonstrated her love for her children. One of my first memories is of
sitting at the kitchen table in the early mornings. I suffered from colitis
as a toddler, and she served me the home remedy of the day, barley coffee. I remember sitting there, dwarfed by the adult-size chair, letting the
smell of coffee and toast wash over me, and watching her strut her stuff,
readying breakfast and lunch for everyone, and sometimes prepping
dinner as well. Two of my earliest memories are those smells and the
cool, creamy ricotta cheese that I spread on the warm toast before eating
it. I'd dip the bread in the coffee, and when I drained the last sip from the
cup, there would be a pile of bloated crumbs resting there. There was a
kind of simple perfection down in the bottom of that cup, and it never
failed to enthrall me.

My given name was Giuseppe, but from earliest memory I was
called Pino, a shortening of the common nickname for kids with my

name, Giuseppino. Mothers rule in Italy, so once my mom took Pino as a term of endearment, everybody else quickly fell into line and adopted it. My father was a medic in the Italian air force, so we moved every few years. When I was born, we lived in Florence. In 1961, when I was eight, we moved near Lago di Garda, another small town, this one in the north of Italy, then returned briefly to Florence in the mid-sixties, and then in 1965 we moved to Grosseto. My favorite room in each of the four apartments we lived in was the kitchen. Come to think of it, we never used the dining rooms, which became dusty and neglected spaces to do homework or the family bookkeeping. I guess we all wanted to be as close as possible to where my mother did her cooking, maintaining a kind of umbilical relationship. Má always told us that she cooked because having family around the table twice a day was the most important thing in life. The kitchen was her domain, and she wanted everything to be *perfect*, so much so that if we got into a protracted argument, or began punching each other or throwing food as little kids are wont to do, she'd slap us. But that rarely happened; we all respected her table because . . . well, how can I explain the sound of people laughing and making noise and being together and eating?

Most Italians passionately love our native cuisine. It's a source of personal passion and communal pride. I say "native" rather than "national" cuisine because Italy is only truly understood as a collection of twenty regions, each with its own dialect, legends, and culinary customs. For example, generally speaking, Piedmont is the home of truffles and relatively rich food (translation: lots of dairy), and of little ravioli called *plin*; Naples is the place for pizza and for pasta *sciue' sciue'* (a quick dish in which partially cooked pasta is finished in a mixture of pureed tomatoes and olive oil) and *zuppa maritata*, the famous "marriage soup" with escarole and tiny meatballs; Sicilian food is infused with the flavors of North Africa and Spain, reflecting the genealogy of the people who live there; and so on.

Our region was Tuscany, and Tuscan cuisine is known for its use of beans, vegetables, and mushrooms, its soups and fish stews, its game in the inland areas, and its shellfish along the coast. Thanks to Má, I revered Tuscan food even more than most kids my age did, even more than my siblings did.

I never questioned my attraction to food; it was just part of who I was. I could watch my mother do anything related to cooking, even mundane prep work, all day long. There was nothing my mother couldn't make. She was a great broth and stew maker, whether it was capon broth or the fish stew called *cacciucco*, which was a window into her upbringing: she'd procure fresh fish from the local monger and clean it herself, first cutting off the tail and head and then reaching inside and jerking out the guts before filleting the fish and portioning it out. She sautéed the head and tail with olive oil and garlic, added tomato and basil, then water, and let the mixture simmer. She processed this aromatic concoction through a food mill, and it became the base for the stew. To complete the dish, she wiped out the pan, heated some olive oil and sliced garlic, then lay slices of bread in the oil and toasted them on both sides until crisp and golden. She topped the bread with the filleted fish, then with the milled sauce, and set it to simmer until the fish was cooked and the flavors had mingled.

My favorite seasons were fall and winter, when the windows were closed, trapping the aromas in our home. The dishes of those seasons require a longer preparation and she would begin early in the morning. I'd see her braising *cavolo nero* (black cabbage) or making *ribollita*, a twice-boiled soup that you cooked the day before, refrigerated in the pot, and reheated the next day, when the vegetables would all have broken down and integrated. *Ribollita* demonstrated my mother's love of individual ingredients and attention to detail. Most cooks would simply simmer the vegetables together in the broth, but she sautéed each one on its own to coax out its full flavor before adding it to the pot.

The winter also brought the holidays, when it seemed my mother had no life outside the kitchen; she was there when we woke up and there when we went to sleep. The night before Christmas, she'd make a sweet dough called *cenci* and a semolina dough for pasta. After dinner, my father would go to bed, and the rest of us would stay up late watching television, but we'd still hear her rustling about in the kitchen. When I arose on Christmas morning, the air would already be dense with the sugary scent of the *cenci*, which she fried in strips then drained on towels and kept on hand to serve visitors along with glasses of syrupy, sweet *vin santo* ("holy wine"). Next came the scents of meat, wine, and herbs as she began making lamb stew. I'd scamper into the kitchen and find her sautéing lamb in an enormous roasting pan that she rented every December and that covered all four burners of the stove. It didn't fit in the oven, so once we were all awake, my father and I bundled up in our coats, scarves, and hats and carried it a few blocks to the local bakery, where they'd cook it in their oven for her. Then we'd drape a towel over it to keep it hot, lug it back home, and serve it with the rest of the meal, a classic Tuscan affair that combined regal and rustic: *brodo di cappone* (capon broth) with *stracciatella* (ribbons of egg that cook in the broth) served alongside a *crostino* of chicken liver paté spread over warm bread; spinach and ricotta ravioli sauced with a meat ragù; the lamb stew, with bitter broccoli rabe and roasted potatoes alongside. For dessert, there was *panettone*, a classic Christmas sweet bread stuffed with raisins and candied fruits, or *panforte*, a very hard, thick, fruit-and-nut cake of the Siena area, depending on what struck Má's fancy that year.

I was my parents' first son after three daughters, so my mother had a soft spot for me. When I became interested in cooking, she was happy to teach me, and some of my first lessons came during New Year's Eve, when she prepared dinner for about thirty people in her little kitchen. She'd show me how to hand-roll pasta, flouring the rolling pin and work surface to keep the dough from sticking and rolling in tight, short strokes followed by longer, looser ones to ensure a uniform thickness. We'd roll one sheet like this, top it with little mounds of filling—usually ricotta cheese flavored with a sweet liqueur—then lay another sheet on top, letting the pasta conform to the mounds. We'd then cut the ravioli using the lumps as a guide and seal the edges with a fork. When we'd add them to hot oil, she'd say, "When you put them in, they are floating like little boats about to sink. When they just begin to bob, they are ready." She also let me help her stuff pork chops, slicing a pocket into one side and filling them with lentils, then showing me how to pan-sear the chop on the stovetop and finish it in the oven.

Spring and summer brought their own touchstones. With the annual thaw came fava beans (the quintessential way to eat them in Tuscany is raw, right from the pod, with a loaf of bread and a chunk of fresh, soft pecorino Toscano cheese on the table for slicing as accompaniments), peas, asparagus, and of course baby lamb, which was always the centerpiece of Easter dinner. Early summer brought zucchini blossoms, which Má lightly battered and panfried, and late summer of course meant tomatoes, which had endless applications: you could make them into a *bruschetta* (diced tomatoes and garlic served on a toasted crouton), fashion a quick salad with red onion and blue cheese, toss them cold with hot pasta as a *salsa cruda* (uncooked sauce), and can them for cooking in the winter. My mother also had a trademark use for tomatoes that spoke to her independence and creativity: she would cut them open and rub them on slices of country bread until the juice dampened it. Then she'd refrigerate the bread slices and have them waiting for us as an afternoon snack. I don't know whether or not she was inspired by the components of gazpacho, but once the tomato-tinged bread was in your mouth, the flavor and textures were similar.

That's the way in our home: we never knew what Má would serve next, and every day brought a family classic or a whimsical surprise that deepened my appreciation of food and cooking.

AS WAS THE case in just about every city and town in Italy until the 1970s, there was a farmers' market twice a week in each of the places we lived, and my mother took full advantage of it. My favorite one was in Grosseto. Even to this day, Grosseto remains a fairly medieval town with walls around it. Back then, on Wednesday and Friday, there was a produce and fish market in the square just inside the enormous old city gates, where farmers, each specializing in one or two items or types of items, set up carts and tents. Fish was displayed on ice, vegetables were piled high on long tables or in crates or baskets. On Fridays, just outside the gates, there was another, larger market like a bazaar where you could buy glassware, chinaware, and kitchen gadgets. It was so big and drew so many people that the roads in and out of the square were closed for the day.

I usually accompanied my mother on Friday, especially in the summer when school was out. We walked to the market because the bus was sporadic, and if you missed one it was just as quick, about twenty minutes, to get there by foot. Má taught me that you have to touch and smell everything you buy. With peaches, you had to ensure the skin was velvety and deeply hued, and that they were firm but with a little give. She also warned me to never buy the big ones because they could look ripe on the outside, but be rotten at the pit. Pears were about the stem: if it was firmly embedded, that was a sign of freshness. She had advice like this for everything: Always choose the skinnier zucchini because "the fatter they are, the more water there is" (same for eggplant). Buy tomatoes when they are light red or orange-green, unless making soup, in which case you want them bright red and cracking open from ripeness.

Her ability to evaluate fish had been so well imparted by her mother that she needed do little more than look at one to know how fresh it was. She'd haul a sea bass out of its ice by the gills and look it in the eyes like a police interrogator. If the eyes were clear and bright, the fish was good. With shellfish, such as clams, she showed me how to check that they were sealed tight and were heavy with captured liquid, both of which indicated the mollusk inside was alive.

My parents had relationships with many of the farmers that dated back to the end of World War II. In our tight-knit community, if one of the farmers or his family was sick, my father would discreetly take them some of the medicine he had access to as a medic. In return, they'd point my mother to the best fruits and vegetables: zucchini, green beans, and tomatoes were her favorites. She often took me along on trips to the actual farms, where we'd load up a plastic bag from home with anything we wanted and they never charged us. My mother loved that no money changed hands, not because she was cheap or expected anything in return for my father's kindness, but because she felt it kept her relationship with the ingredients pure.

BACK HOME, IN the kitchen and at the table, my mother educated my palate, explaining what made each dish work, and also taught me the basics, even how to butcher everything from chicken to rabbit, which she had picked up as a young housewife in Orbetello. But perhaps the most valuable gift Má passed on was the ability to wrest great flavor from a handful of basic ingredients. In many ways, the seemingly more complicated French cuisine is more easily mastered than ours because Tuscan cooking depends less on techniques and formulas than on muscle memory and intuition. You can't truly appreciate this until you try to make a salad from nothing but shaved baby artichokes, lemon juice, olive oil, and parmesan shards; *fegato alla salvia*, thinly sliced calf's liver with brown butter and sage; or *pappa al pomodoro*, a dense tomato-and-bread soup made from late-summer tomatoes and stale bread—it's a Tuscan staple, with the tomatoes, bread, garlic, and olive oil fused into a savory porridge. Another of my favorites was *uova all'occhio di bue*, which translates directly to "eggs, cow-eyes style," our way of referring to sunny-side up, which Má made by heating a cast-iron pan over a high flame, then swirling two drops of olive oil in the pan to keep the eggs from sticking. She'd then turn off the gas, crack two eggs in the middle of the pan, making sure the yolks were centered, then sprinkle a scant pinch of sea salt over them. She'd let them cook on the pan, over the turned-off burner, which was a neat trick for making sure they didn't overcook and that the yolks stayed runny. Once in a while, my mother would combine those last two dishes, poaching the eggs gently in the *pappa al pomodoro*—a dish she called *uova alla francesina. Francesina* is a popular expression that Tuscans toss around, but that nobody can actually define; the application made perfect sense, however, because her instincts for naming were as sharp as her palate. It just worked.

She helped me hone a sense of timing: if we were having pasta, then come the dinner hour she'd have the water boiling, and she'd watch out the window until she saw the tips of my father's shoes round the corner at the end of our street. She'd then drop the pasta into the water, prepare or reheat the sauce, and have the pasta perfectly al dente and on the table at the moment he had slipped off his shoes, said his hellos, and taken his seat. (As an adult, I developed a few pasta rituals of my own; for example, the amount of time it takes for spaghetti to cook is just enough for an impromptu tryst in the hallway outside the kitchen. But that's another story.) At the table, she refined my understanding of the progression of a classic European meal. For example, we rarely had dessert; instead, she'd present a piece of cheese, followed by some sliced fruit.

My mother also passed on her frugal nature to me, developing my ability to survey the contents of a refrigerator or pantry and improvise a meal with almost no forethought: leftover pasta would be fried in hot oil before whisked eggs were poured over it to be baked into a *frittata* (omelet); leftover vegetables were finely chopped and tossed with diced boiled eggs (or flaked preserved tuna), cubed mortadella, and sturdy greens such as frisée for a salad substantial enough to be a meal; leftover fruit, such as peaches, became the basis for a sour marmalade, and so on.

Her examples were so firmly etched in my mind that the first time I cooked anything myself, it was as though I'd been doing it all my life: one Sunday morning, when I was about twelve years old, she was behind in her housework. I saw her running around nervously tending to various chores and I thought that I'd take the edge off her day and make breakfast for the family. I decided to make her favorite *frittata*, with potatoes and onion. I par-cooked and sliced the potatoes and lightly sautéed the onions. Then I greased a skillet and started the eggs, embedding the vegetables in them when they began to set. Then came the moment of truth, flipping the *frittata*. I lifted the pan off the heat, and with the image of my mother confidently flipping an omelet firmly in mind, I flicked the pan and the yellow disk did a perfect turn in the air, landing almost silently back in the pan, the top a lovely golden brown. I set the pan out on the table and served everybody breakfast. It was a big moment for me, but they were all decidedly nonplussed, except my mother.

"You made this?" she asked me.

"Yes!" I exclaimed, proud of my accomplishment.

She nodded and said "ah." It was faint praise, but that's the Italian way: you're expected to do good, and a non-criticism from your parents is a compliment in its own right.

FOOD WAS SUCH an integral part of every day of my life at home that, even years later, when I would drive back to visit from Rome I had the feeling that I was following the scent of my mother's cooking, like a trail of bread crumbs to lead me back.

It's pretty much a straight shot from Rome to Grosseto. You head north on a highway called SS1, also known as Aurelia, for about two hours, depending on how fast you drive, which is a significant variable in Italy. As you get farther and farther from Rome, the modern world falls away, and when you enter Tuscany, it goes positively medieval: you can look up and see little villages—each a constellation of centuries-old structures—dotting the craggy hills. As a child, I took them for granted, but as an adult the feeling of hurtling back through time never ceased to surprise me.

To get to Grosseto, just past the village of Ansedonia, you turn off the highway and west toward Orbetello. There's a huge watermelon field there where, as teenagers, my friends and I engaged in a form of oral sex with the fruit: we'd bust the melons open on our knees, stick our heads inside, and devour the sugary flesh, emerging with devilish smiles and dripping-wet faces. After we had our fill, we'd stage a watermelon war, lobbing the orbs at each other in the dark until we were covered from head to toe with juice. Then we'd hop on our scooters and disappear up into the hills to the east, toward Saturnia, where there were warm sulfuric waterfalls. We'd let the spa water cleanse our clothes and skin, then collapse in the grass and stare up at the moon and the stars until we fell asleep.

THESE WERE THE things that I usually thought about whenever I went home to visit my parents.

But this drive was different: it was an angry drive. I whipped around every turn, engaging the clutch with the abandon of a race-car driver.

Darkness was falling around me. The air was growing cold. Passing through the town of Tarquinia, I detected a whiff of chimney smoke for the first time that year, a moment I'd usually savor because it brought its own rush of memories, but not tonight.

Though I was making it quite spontaneously, this visit had been on my mind for months. I had been living in Rome since 1971, when I moved there at the age of eighteen to pursue my dream of being an actor. I studied at the Fersen Acting Studio and went on to land parts with some of the most prestigious theatrical companies in Italy. I was consumed with learning my craft, not just acting, but all aspects of the theatrical profession. Once in a while I'd get to participate in a special project, as during my second year with Fersen, when I was selected to be part of a team charged with creating minimalist sets for an experimental production inspired by Thomas Hobbes's *Leviathan*.

I also loved my daily routine: sleeping late, hanging out with friends, and going to movies in the middle of the afternoon or after midnight. I was crazy for the intimacy and raw emotion of independent films, especially those of Cassavetes, Bogdanovich, and Polanski. Sitting in the dark of a movie theater and savoring instant classics such as *Minnie and Moskowitz, Husbands, The Last Picture Show, Cul-de-sac,* and *Chinatown* was among my greatest pleasures, and it inspired me to be fearless on stage. All my cinematic heroes were iconoclasts, from Orson Welles to a young American filmmaker named Martin Scorsese and his little company of actors like Harvey Keitel and Robert De Niro.

I didn't just love movies; I often related to specific characters. The one I most identified with was the young Vito Corleone played by De Niro in *Godfather II.* I was fascinated by both *Godfather* movies and their fantastical depiction of an Italy that neither I nor any of my friends had ever known, but mostly I felt a strong bond with Vito. I understood that circumstances and a corrupt society forced him into the underworld, and I believed that if I had been in New York City back in those days, relegated to the immigrant ghetto and subject to the will of the local villains, I would have become a gangster to provide for myself and my family, and I'd have done it with no regrets. The movie solidified a personal philosophy that had been coalescing for some time: some people are meant to take it and some people are meant to dish it out. If forced to choose, I'm more of a dish-it-out kind of guy.

It was a thrilling time for a young actor to be living and working in a city like Rome. For nine years, my life just got better and better. I got bigger parts, made new friends in every play, and was earning a good enough living to be comfortable. I had also scored a miracle of an apartment for somebody of my means: an eight-hundred-square-foot unit on the twelfth floor of its building that, thanks to an architectural quirk, was the only dwelling at that level and was surrounded by a four-*thousand*-square-foot terrace, where I kept patio furniture and hosted innumerable parties.

Living on my own, I cooked almost every day, and grew to love it even more than I had back in Grosseto. I re-created dishes I remembered fondly from home, tweaking many of them to make them my own, and also wove in influences from the towns and regions that my work as an actor took me: Italian food is so simple, and the foundation my mother gave me was so strong, that I was able to approximate just about anything I tasted in Rome or on the road based on the memory of eating it. As was the case in my parents' home, my favorite dishes were braised meats and game, because they filled the apartment with potent aromas, offering such an intense sensory experience that it was almost as if I'd eaten them before they were done cooking. I came to see pasta as the most complete of all foods, something that never failed to nourish both body and soul.

I had never been formally trained, but I knew that I'd become a serious cook, and not being schooled at a culinary academy had its benefits: not knowing all the rules, I began breaking many of them to suit my own taste. For example, I stopped flouring meats before cooking them for stews or braises; even though the flour supposedly cooks out, I found that it obscured the flavor of the meat in the finished dish.

My love of food and cooking in general, and pasta in particular, led me to kick off a tradition among my acting circle: after Saturday night's performance, always the last one of the week, we'd gather at one member's apartment and have a pasta carbonara party. Each week a different person would make their version of this quintessentially Roman dish that I had come to adore while living there. It's wide open to interpretation: the basic ingredients are pasta, egg yolks, pecorino cheese, onions, and some type of Italian bacon, such as *pancetta* (salt-cured pork) or *guanciale*, made from spiced pig cheeks or jowls. Though some of my friends preferred fresh fettuccine, my version, perfected over years of tinkering, was always prepared with dried pasta, usually spaghetti. I'd sauté diced onion until golden, sauté *guanciale*, then toss the pasta with them, the yolks, and grated pecorino. It was a Roman dish, but it called on all my skills: the key was to get the yolks and pasta into contact with each other at precisely the right moment so that the heat of the spaghetti would warm, but not scramble, the egg, forming a silky-smooth emulsion.

By 1980, I had also left behind the bachelor life for a more serious relationship with my girlfriend, Patty, a blonde, free-spirited American from Sheboygan Falls, Wisconsin. We met when I was in Trieste, acting the role of Raskolnikov in a television production of *Crime and Punishment*. She lived in Trieste and was employed by a local marketing company, but she was working as an extra on the production. She spoke five languages, Italian among them, so we had no trouble flirting. She was the exact opposite of any Italian woman I'd dated at the time. The late 1960s and early 1970s might have been known as the era of "free love," but in my opinion it came at a high price: before you could have sex with a woman, you had to engage in a political debate. Patty, on the other hand, was just *fun*. We began a long-distance relationship, zipping back and forth on the train to see each other, until she moved in with me in Rome and took a job as an interpreter. I cooked for her all the time, and even taught her to make some dishes as well, such as a version of chicken cacciatore using garlic, tomatoes, rosemary, black pepper, and red wine, that we usually served over roasted potatoes.

To cap it all off, I had just landed the role of Octavian in a Roman stage production of Shakespeare's *Antony and Cleopatra*. It was, potentially, my big break.

Things could not have been better.

But one afternoon in April 1980, I had arrived home and picked up my mail, and mixed in with the other papers was a pink postcard from the Italian army. It was a draft notice, telling me to report for military service in October in Barletta, in the deep south of Italy.

Upon reading it, I stopped breathing and sweat broke out on my forehead. It didn't make sense. Nine years earlier, when I had turned eighteen, I had registered for Italy's then-mandatory draft; every unmarried Italian boy had to register at that age and take a physical exam. The term of duty could be anywhere from one to two years, depending on the type of service to which you were assigned. I requested civilian service, meaning a year and a half doing social work in a Mediterranean country. I never got a reply from the army, and I went about my life in Rome. We weren't at war, and so I didn't find any need to press the issue, and so much time had gone by that I had forgotten about it. But now, here was a notice to show up for regular army duty, not even civilian service.

There were any number of reasons why it might have happened—some ancient clerk might have been catching up on his filing and unearthed my record; or it might have taken them this long to find me as I moved around a lot in those days and the Italian government has a laconic approach to these things. For all I knew they were sending me a card once a year only to have it come back marked *Indirizzo Sconosciuto* (Address Unknown).

But there was something about the summons that troubled me for months: normally, the *cartolina rosa* ("pink card") comes from your district of residence, which in my case was still, legally speaking, Grosseto. But my card had come from the district to which I was supposed to report. The more I thought about it the more I realized that it had to involve some high-level intervention. The base was in the same area of Italy where my father had served for much of his career, so this led to a persistent suspicion. Most people's parents use their influence to get their kids out of the military, but I had to wonder: had my father, without my knowing it, pulled a string to get me *into* the army?

I would find out, by surprising him with a visit to his home.

And so I was driving to Grosseto, to see Papá, toward a confrontation that had been coming for a long, long time.

MY FATHER AND I had our problems from the very beginning, starting with the day I was born. He was watching the Giro d'Italia bicycle race when my mother went into labor, and by the time he heard the news and got home, where my mother delivered me, I was already napping in my crib.

As I say, Antonio Luongo was a military man. My father's parents died when he was young, and he left the orphanage where he was raised and joined the Italian army when he was just eighteen. He was slight, with tiny black eyes, sculpted hair, chiseled features, and a permanent tan. As they did with my mother, friends compared him to a movie star, too—Tyrone Power—though neither he nor Má was *that* attractive. During the African campaign, he found himself in a POW camp where the conditions were subhuman: the prisoners were treated worse than the pigs that roamed the grounds freely; he had to boil urine to make drinking water, and he often stole potato scraps from the swine to survive.

When the war was over and my father was liberated, he staggered around Greece, eventually finding his way back to Italy and ending up on a small military base in Orbetello. It was there that he met my mother, and they fell in love at first sight. There was just one problem: my mother's family were staunch socialists and her brothers were partisans who lived high in the mountains in perpetual hiding from soldiers like my father. It was a true Capulet-and-Montague situation. Two of my mother's brothers had been killed by fascists, and were anyone in the family to learn that she was in love with one of Mussolini's soldiers, they'd have killed my father, brutally, and probably in public.

So, when word finally did get out, my mother, in desperation, took my father to meet her father, Ettore, a gentle giant of a man with wrinkled leathery skin from his decades in the sun and hands as big as shovels. He was one of the real patriarchs of their village, even though he was just a fisherman. Ettore, also known as Bó, was one of the most simple, honest men I ever knew and he had a wisdom and grace that, even at age fifty-five, still eludes me. He had seen two sons murdered, and because of his well-known political leanings, he had himself been tortured. And yet, after interviewing my father, he was able to put all of that aside and see him as an individual.

My grandfather walked my parents into the center of the village and stood with them before everyone: "This man is not a fascist," he proclaimed. "I do not hold him responsible for what happened to me or to my other children. Yes, he wears a uniform, but only because he had to. He says that he loves my daughter and I believe him. I ask that everyone accept him and leave them in peace."

That was all it took: my parents were allowed to marry and my father was welcomed into the family.

Personally, I always thought that my grandfather gave my father too much credit. He might not have been a fascist in the Mussolini sense of the word, but he was definitely a tyrant in my world. His parental motto was: "Do what you're told. Don't ask questions. Or else!"

When I was eleven, on the verge of manhood, Papá sent me off to a military boarding school. The school, three hours from our home by car, overlooked the Bay of La Spezia. It was a secluded place and when I think of it, the first thing I recall is a bit of graffiti, scrawled on a wall by another boy who suffered there some time before I did: "Abandon Hope, All Ye Who Enter Here." It's from Dante's *Divine Comedy*, but to me it was no joke. A constant reminder of the stifling environment was the uniform I had to wear from sunup to bedtime: made of cheap, stiff material, it always felt like something that enveloped and consumed the real me and made me indistinguishable from my classmates.

But the uniforms were just a symbol of the rules and the officers who enforced them. It was like an entire community populated by clones of my father: When you spoke to an officer, you were not allowed to make eye contact—your gaze was to be directed at the ground or off to the side. You had to say "Sir" before simply saying "good morning" or "excuse me." If you deviated from these rules, you were to extend your hand, whereupon whichever adult you had offended would whack you across the knuckles with a wand.

For all the reminders of Papá, there were no stand-ins for Má. I don't know where the barely palatable gruel they served at school came from, but it sure wasn't lovingly prepared by a maternal figure in the kitchen. Every time the grub was slapped down on my plate by one of the servers, I'd try to imagine the beast who had created it, eventually conjuring the image of a decrepit hunchback clothed in rags, with one leg shackled to the stove. How else to explain such inhumanity?

I had three very good friends at the school: Barbato, Michele, and a third boy, Paolo, whom we called by his last name, Granci. Our bond was formed quickly. Of the twenty-five or so children in my class, we gravitated toward each other and became fast friends, vowing to watch each other's backs.

I also had a nemesis: a senior named Menichetti with bulging biceps, a thick neck, and crooked teeth, who had it out for me from Day One. Whenever he had the chance, he'd knock me on my ass or come up behind me in the study hall and smack me on the back of the head so hard that I'd see spots. I had a rebellious streak back then, but I was only eleven, and I knew that if I tried to fight back, it would only lead to a real beating. One day, my class was marching to the dining hall when I saw him leaning forward on a parapet that surrounded the campus soccer field, watching a game. I broke out of formation and ran up behind him, bringing my boot-clad foot up between his legs and catching him hard in the balls. He fell to the ground in a heap, clutching his groin and wailing. He was rushed away in an ambulance and later that day I was called into the office of the camp commander, where he and his two lieutenants, an officious, bespectacled trio, informed me that my boot had almost severed Menichetti's scrotum from his body and that he would be hospitalized for several days. They proceeded to dress me down for half an hour, then sentenced me to serve time in the brig: after dinner each night, an MP would drive me to a nearby military base the school was affiliated with and I'd spend the night in an honest-to-goodness cinderblock jail cell. In my mind, I'd only traded one prison for another, and I didn't really care. The only thing that weighed on me was that Menichetti would get out of the hospital one day and would no doubt seek his revenge. With this in mind, I asked the commanders for permission to visit him in the hospital and apologize. The commanders, impressed by my maturity and remorse, arranged for me to be taken to see him on my way to jail one night.

When the evening arrived, the MP escorted me to Menichetti's door and waited outside. I went into his room and when he saw me there, his eyes widened in anger. He actually began to lunge out of bed, but the pain was too much and he settled back down.

"Menichetti," I said, speaking loudly and gregariously so the MPs could hear me through the door. "I know you're angry, but I'm here to apologize."

I pulled a wooden chair over to his bed, sat down, and leaned in close. "Listen to me," I said, affecting my best tough-guy impression. "I know that you're thinking of coming for me, but if you do, you better kill me. Because if anything happens to me, then my friends and I are going to come for you in your sleep." Small wonder I'd go on to identify with Vito Corleone.

Menichetti never did come after me, but within weeks I had a new problem to contend with: our hormones were kicking in and there were no girls on whom to focus our romantic attentions. The only real women we came into contact with were the ones who worked in the school's dining hall, most of whom were too old and unattractive to be of interest. But there was one woman, Carmela, who became a shared obsession for me and my crew. She was an almost absurdly voluptuous creature, not unlike what you might see in a Fellini movie. In her early forties, she wore snug uniforms that accentuated her breasts and ass. *Valkyria* ("amazon") we called her under our breath. She was our Brigitte Bardot, our Sophia Loren. When she would come around to clear our table, leaning in to collect our plates and glasses, my friends and I would shift in our seats so our elbows or shoulders would brush her crotch. She never reprimanded us, so when she left the table, we would marvel to each other at how she "wanted it."

Carmela was also charged with sweeping and mopping the dorms during the day, when we were all holed up in the classroom building. There was a strict policy that forbade us from leaving that building during school hours, but there was a twenty-minute recess between the second and third period and after several weeks of mealtime groping, we decided to pay a visit to the object of our affections.

We planned the mission like a prison break. As one of us stood lookout, the other three snuck out through a side window. We ran along the shadows cast by the administrative buildings and in through a window in the dorm that we'd left open that morning. We tiptoed together through the hallways until we found her, mopping the floor of one of the sleeping quarters, her formidable hips swaying from side to side with the movement of the mop. We just stood in the doorway, fondling her with our eyes. Catching sight of us, she giggled and began exaggerating her movement, taunting us until we gave in to temptation and rushed her, all of us at once, and grabbed at her ass, pulling at it like a wad of taffy.

Rather than angering her, this amused her even more, and she began laughing.

"*Voi, siete piccoli, ma che fate. Vi piglio a schiaffi,*" she said. I'm bigger than you all. If you don't stop, I'm going to slap you.

We left and traced our steps back to the classroom. Hormone-crazed idiots that we were, we took her lack of outrage as a half-yes, an invitation to rendezvous with her again at a later date. We were more obsessed than ever. I'd lie in bed at night and imagine her mopping that floor, swinging her hips from side to side, looking over her shoulder at us and winking.

About a week later, my friend Barbato and I made another go of it, again sneaking out between classes. We ran into the dorm, only to find that it was utterly silent. We couldn't find her anywhere. We decided to abort our mission and hurry back to the classrooms, when we heard a noise from the communal shower room. Our eyes almost popped out of our heads. It didn't take more than a quick look between us to confirm that we were both thinking the same thing: she was getting ready to take a shower after a hard, sweaty morning of work.

We ran down the hall and carefully peered around the corner. She was in the shower all right, but she wasn't alone: she had her legs wrapped around one of our schoolmates. As he pounded her against the tiles, she moaned with unabashed delight. We were horrified, especially when they turned around and I saw that the guy who was giving it to her was none other than Menichetti!

We left the building in disgust, betrayed by our darling Valkyria, our Carmela.

Deprived of the one thing that gave meaning to our lives, my gang of four made escaping from the school our mission in life, and we spent every free minute plotting a way out. Over the next year and a half, we escaped a half-dozen times: we'd get off the school grounds and hitchhike to the nearest rail station. Aboard the train, we developed a hobo's knack for avoiding the conductor so we never had to produce tickets. I'd get off at Grosseto and my friends would continue south to their hometowns. But these adventures always ended the same way: the school had phoned ahead to my father and when I got home, he wouldn't even let me into the apartment. He'd drag me by the collar to his car, a four-door light-creamy-yellow Fiat 1100 with green trim, and drive me back to school, whereupon the camp commanders would scold me and sentence me to another week in the brig.

After two years, I was at my breaking point. One afternoon, in the spring of 1966, I was sitting in the second-floor study room when I spied the three school commanders walking down below. I had a milk bottle in my hand and, gripped by an irresistible impulse, I climbed outside the window onto the ledge that encircled the building. I lobbed the bottle in their direction. It landed right in front of them and shattered.

Nobody was hurt, and I got my wish: they expelled me.

BACK HOME IN Grosseto, I took up acting during my summer vacations. Like most things I've been drawn to, it was a way for me to honor my intense need for self-expression. My theater friends became like another family to me: any theatrical production is by nature very intense, and the act of creating an alternate reality on the stage makes for quick and abiding friendships. I found myself spending more and more time outside of our family home, in part to limit my time with my father and in part because I was nurtured by these new friends and by a community so free of inhibition.

Eager to spread my wings and get off on my own, shortly after I turned sixteen, in the summer of 1969, I went to work for my uncle Natalino, who owned a restaurant in a nearby seaside resort town. He had been in the restaurant business all his life, mostly running dining rooms on cruise ships, but when he and his wife had kids, he put down roots, taking over the management of a restaurant called La Caletta (The Little Bay) on the ground floor of a seaside boutique hotel in Porto Santo Stefano, just about forty-five minutes from Grosseto.

He offered me room and board and a small sum of money in exchange for my services, so I headed to his place for the summer. Early one morning, we piled into the family car and my parents drove there, tracing a road that snaked along the coastline. As we approached the beach in Porto Santo Stefano, we passed old homes and just before the road dead-ended, we came to the hotel. I got my duffel bag out of the trunk and we walked through the modest, well-maintained lobby to the restaurant to find my uncle.

La Caletta was a dreamy setting: a smart, sleek space fashioned after Giò Ponti designs of the era with lots of sharp angles and glass. It was an enormous dining room with an adjoining outdoor terrace and a total of about one hundred eighty seats. Situated on the ground floor of the hotel, it was set in among the rocky coastline, seeming almost of a piece with the terrain, and offered a perfect view of the flat, azure water beyond the sand.

My uncle, a handsome, hyperactive chain smoker with cerulean blue eyes and black, slicked-back hair (he looked like he was related to my father instead of my mother), emerged from the kitchen and there followed a quick bout of hugging and cheek pinching. After some family chitchat, Natalino turned to me and, with a twitchy wink, said, "OK, Pino, let's go."

My parents turned to leave, but before they did my mother looked her brother in the eye and admonished him, "He's in your hands, Natalino."

"*Va bene,*" he replied with another wink. Don't worry.

My parents took off and Uncle Natalino walked me through the hotel lobby to the end of a corridor, through an employees-only door, and upstairs to the dorms, located in the attic of a wing far removed from the guest rooms. The accommodations were cramped and steamy and smelled faintly of mold. The only ventilation was a little window, set at shoulder height, looking out onto the sea. There were two bunk beds in my room, and my uncle turned to me and said, "You are the last to arrive, you get the top."

I nodded and tossed my bag up there, and he gave me a quick tour of the hotel, showing me a few of the guest rooms and the various exits out to the beach.

We then returned to La Caletta and Natalino quickly made it clear that there would be no favoritism for his nephew, telling me to sweep and mop the entire restaurant as quickly as I could because lunch wasn't too far off. I did as he asked and, after a quick tutorial, he had me set all the outdoor patio tables, putting a tablecloth, then glasses, napkins, silverware, and a bottle of olive oil on each of them. Once the terrace was set, I headed back inside, stopping to turn around and look over my handiwork. I hadn't particularly enjoyed the past few hours, but when I surveyed the area—perfectly neat and orderly and ready to receive its visitors—I felt a surprising sense of pride, of mastery. Natalino appeared in the doorway, obstructing my path. He peered outside, taking in the results of my efforts, then stepped out of my way and let me pass. He didn't say anything, but just like my mother and that *frittata*, this was a good thing; his silence indicated approval.

It had already been a long morning, but things were just getting started. I donned a white dress shirt and took to the service floor, acting as a busboy for the lunch shift. I learned as I went, taking cues from my co-workers and asking questions when necessary, which wasn't all that often because I found all of this easy if not especially gratifying. I quickly picked up on visual cues that required immediate attention and added to the sense of choreography you see in any good restaurant: empty water glasses needed filling *immediately*, preferably the moment a customer sat down. Same with bread: when orders were taken and menus were confiscated, a basket had to be deposited on the table. And at the end of a meal, dirty dishes were to be removed as soon as it was clear that the customers were finished eating. This last concern was of particular importance to my uncle: nothing pissed him off more than dirty dishes cluttering a table, because they signified the transformation from guests enjoying a meal to people sitting in the company of garbage.

I was a quick study and though I didn't love the work, it only took a few days for my co-workers to become another surrogate family, just like the one I had found in my theater productions back home. After service each night, we'd find our way to a bar, or to somebody's home, and party late into the evening. My first weeks were glorious and liberating. Sometimes, we'd even borrow a scooter from my uncle and visit those watermelon fields, followed by midnight showers in the springs of Saturnia. Whenever I turned the key in the scooter's ignition and zoomed back to La Caletta along those country roads, with the wind in my face and the trees and hills silhouetted all around me, I experienced the ultimate feeling of freedom, of flight.

THE ONLY TRADEOFF for those late nights was contending with one of the more menial and lonely tasks at the restaurant: sweeping and mopping the floor in the morning, which a different busboy was scheduled to do each day. The job did have its charms: you got to look out the big glass patio doors at the beach, with the waves rolling in beyond the shore, and to listen to the radio my uncle provided to keep the morning guy company. One of my favorite songs was the Italian pop classic "Sapore di Sale," which means "Taste of the Salt." It's about a young girl on the beach and the taste of salt on her lips and her skin; it always makes me think of Bo Derek jogging in slow motion in that famous shot from the movie 10. It's a perfect evocation of the pungent smells and tastes of the ocean and of the sexy, summer scene of the Italian seaside, and it was an apt living soundtrack to those mornings.

A bottom-liner, my uncle didn't care if the guy charged with opening the restaurant showed up at ten or ten thirty in the morning, so long as the dining room had been thoroughly swept and mopped and set up for lunch by eleven o'clock. To facilitate sleeping in after all those late nights, when my turn came around, I'd sweep the dining room before leaving at the end of the dinner shift, so when I came in the next morning, I only had to mop it. I sometimes wondered if I could have gotten away with not mopping at all, because I often had the feeling my uncle wasn't paying much attention to any of this. But one morning he was off at the market with his chef, and the boy whose turn it was to do the morning clean-up only swept, skipping the mopping. When my uncle and the chef returned, they went into the kitchen to drop off the vegetables and fish they'd procured, and when they reemerged, my uncle looked down and said to the guy, "What happened to the floor today?" which is a really clever way to put the question because it makes it perfectly clear that he knew what was up, but gave the defendant a chance to twist in the wind a little and maybe make the mistake of trying to lie.

"Nothing," the boy said.

"You didn't mop it."

"I did."

"No you didn't," said my uncle.

The busboy opened his mouth to again insist that he had, but my uncle cut him off: "The mop in the kitchen is dry."

For all of his success, it was at that moment that my uncle became something of a hero to me, when I realized how much he knew, how many little tricks he had up his sleeve. I also loved the theatricality of how he handled the situation and the harmlessly sadistic humor of his method. Plus, he taught me something about disciplining one's staff when he told that guy he'd be mopping every morning for seven days straight.

As I stood there grinning at all of this, and at the thought of sleeping in for a full week, my uncle leaned in close and said to me, "You're a family member. You ever embarrass me by pulling something like that, and it'll be ten times worse."

I WOULD NEVER have the chance to do anything worse, though, at least not as a busboy, because I was about to be promoted. We did a lot of tableside preparation at La Caletta: filleting roasted fish and whisking salad dressings *à la minute* (Italians love their dressings *à la minute*). Because of the skills I'd developed at home, my fingers knew their way around the plate, and I could pick up any technique after just one demonstration. Filleting fish was second nature to me, but I also quickly demonstrated a deft touch at plating *pasta al cartoccio* (pasta and shellfish cooked in parchment paper) and at cracking open the hard exterior of fish baked in a salt crust. After a few weeks of witnessing my plating ability in full flight, my uncle made me his dedicated waiter when he himself worked the dining room.

In this new job, I got to follow the progression of a meal from the front of the house and the back of the house, and it was fascinating: when people ordered wine, he was usually too busy to fetch it, so I'd do that. When he took their order, he'd write it down and hand it to me and I'd hurry to the kitchen, hand it to the chef, and keep a carbon copy. Then I'd return to the kitchen to pick up the food and run it to the table. I was doing this for about ten tables at a time, some just starting their meal, some in the middle, and some finishing, and it was a lot to keep track of, but that's just it: I didn't keep track of it, not in any real way. My mind just naturally took in the necessary information and arranged it in order of priority and practicality that changed from minute to minute.

Those urgencies aside, I focused on each table as its own little dinner party. It was second nature to me to know when the kitchen would need to have the next course ready, or when a wine bottle was nearing completion. I also quickly became adept at visualizing the progression of each table's meal from the moment I had their order in my hand, a guide to the logistics of what cutlery and implements they'd require and of how much time I'd have to spend with them finishing and plating their dishes tableside.

Also, perhaps because of my acting training, I picked up on the slightest indication that people wanted to see a waiter or busboy. I had an auctioneer's eye for discreet gestures: for instance, in most cases, when diners are looking at each other and talking that means that all is well. But when you see customers looking around, it usually means they're seeking a waiter and that you should get over to them and ask if there's anything you can do for them. By July, I had categorized a few recurring types of couples and what each one sought in a dining experience: older married vacationers wanted to dine quickly so the husband could disappear to the lounge and enjoy an amaro or join the other men for a game of cards, young lovers wanted to linger and cuddle in a corner, and so on. I always made sure that each one got what they wanted, often giving them the check before they asked for it.

"Why are you always rushing everybody?" my uncle said to me one day.

"What do you mean?"

"You give them the check before they ask for it."

"*Zio* Natalino," I said, "look at them: the napkins are on the table, the espresso cups are empty, their chairs are pushed back, and their legs are stretched out. If you don't give them a check soon, they're going to forget about paying and just walk out."

As he thought this over, I spotted a young couple with all the same done-with-dinner signs.

"I'll bet you one thousand *lire* that they are ready for the check," I said.

We shook on it and I walked over to the table.

"How are we doing?" I said.

The man and woman looked at each other and then the man looked at me and said, "We're ready for the check."

"Right away!" I replied and as I went off to total their check, my uncle handed me a one-thousand-*lire* bill. This became a recurring contest for us for the rest of the summer, and I usually won the bet, but he was tickled that another family member had instincts on a par with his.

Another method of upping my income was revealed to me one morning when an elderly couple was in the lobby with their luggage, checking out after a two-week stay. The wife saw me coming to work at the restaurant and smacked her husband on the shoulder and said, "*Dagli la mancia!*" Give him a tip!

The husband retrieved a few bills from his wallet and handed them to me, and from that day forward I would make a point of complimenting the older wives in the restaurant. It always produced that same sentence on their last day with us: "*Dagli la mancia!*"

Between my little bets with Natalino and my talent for flattering the dowagers of Porto Santo Stefano, I added substantially to my haul for the summer.

THOUGH I WON the lion's share of our little wagers, there was no question that my uncle was the master and I was the pupil. By observing him, I also learned about the *business* of the restaurant business. He wasn't looking to have one or two Michelin stars; he was looking to have six or seven figures in the bank. His practicality rubbed off on me, as in my method for earning more tips. But my mercenary intentions soon gave way to a self-discovery: I *loved* interacting with the customers. And I took the responsibility of being the face and voice of the restaurant very seriously. My goal was to add to each and every guest's

experience: to describe the food lovingly, present it beautifully, and ensure that every need was anticipated and met. I also took great pleasure in learning about the guests, where they came from and what
they thought of the town and the beach, even playing concierge by offering suggestions on where to go after dinner or where to find the
best cappuccino the next morning, or even the perfect places to watch
the sun rise and set.

I couldn't wait to stroll over from the dorms every morning, and the
days and nights flew by. I returned to my uncle's restaurant for another
summer, and when I came home the second year, older and more self-
assured than when I had left, it was difficult to be there. As my siblings
and I grew older, my father tried harder than ever to maintain his control over us. Chauvinist that he was, he insisted that I chaperone my
sisters, Rita, Franca, and Anna, when they went out. We all used this to
our advantage: we'd leave home, go our separate ways, then reconnect
and return together.

Given the hardships of his own life, I guess my father didn't know
any other way. But I didn't have that kind of perspective back then, and
I had simply come to despise him. One day when I was in my final
year of high school, things boiled over and Papá and I got into a nasty
and escalating fight, hurling insults back and forth. At the peak of the
confrontation, I told him he was nothing but "another loser in a uniform." He removed his belt, doubled it over, and raised it in the air as
if to strike me. I caught his hand and when he tried to pull it away, I
didn't let go.

It was then that I decided to leave, for good, and moved to Rome.

I PLAYED ALL of this back in my mind as I drove home on that October evening in 1980. The other reason for the visit was to let my parents know that I was leaving the country. During the summer, I had
hired a lawyer and told him to do whatever he had to do to keep me
out of the army. After doing time in boarding school, there was no way
I'd wear a uniform again; something deep down told me that if I went
into the army, I'd come out a diminished person, a broken soul.

The lawyer's advice was simple: if I wanted to make sure to avoid service, then I needed to get out of Italy until he could work things out.

"Fine," I told him. "I'll go to France or England."

That wasn't good enough. Those countries had extradition deals with Italy and would turn me over if asked to. He told me to get myself across an ocean.

I decided to go to the United States, to New York City. Patty was ready and willing to leave with me, and a friend of her family's had offered us the use of an apartment, though it wasn't in Manhattan; it was in some place called "Queens."

I'd been to New York once before, six years earlier, when I was twenty-one, to experience firsthand the city I'd seen on television and in the movies all my life. I'd felt a connection to America since I was a little kid, and a special bond with New York City. We all did. There were just two television channels in Italy at that time, Channel 1 and Channel 2, and both of them were government controlled. Every night the news began with reports from New York. There were also two reports from Washington, D.C., but I didn't care about that because it was all politics. But New York. Just the name meant so much: New York was Wall Street. New York was Broadway. New York was the ladder of the New World. You climbed in New York. You climbed, and at the top of the ladder, there was money, power, sex, theater, art. Everything you could dream of, or at least everything that I dreamed of. I was so excited to go there that when we landed, I knelt down and, with the roar of departing airplanes rumbling in my ears and the smell of gasoline in my nose, kissed the tarmac. The city was in the middle of its decline back then, and everything seemed extreme. Everybody talked about "don't go here or you'll get mugged," and "don't go there or you'll get mugged," or "I was just mugged for the third time this year." None of that bothered me. I stayed in this cute little apartment on Jones Street, in the West Village. I was twenty-one years old: I wore jeans everywhere and smoked a lot of cigarettes, and everything else available back then, and I had a great time.

And so, when my attorney told me to get across an ocean, I simply didn't know where else to go. Plus a number of my heroes lived in New York, all those filmmakers and actors who I so looked up to, and musicians like John Lennon—one of the ultimate iconoclasts—whom I positively idolized. When I thought of New York, one of the first images that always came to mind for me was the black-and-white Bob Gruen photograph of Lennon in sunglasses and that sleeveless T-shirt with the simple black letters spelling New York City in the middle.

But as much as I loved the idea of New York, this time, obviously, the circumstances were different. It was, in my view, a trip I was being forced to make, and one I might never return from. The more I thought about it, the angrier I got, and by the time I parked outside my parents' building, I was seething.

I ran upstairs to their apartment on the second floor and pressed the buzzer. When my father answered the door, before he could say a word, I waved the little pink card in his face.

"What's the meaning of this?" I demanded.

"Of what?" He was right to be confused; he'd known for months that I'd been drafted.

"Why did they call me up after all these years?"

"I don't know anything about it."

"It was you, wasn't it?"

"What are you talking about?"

"It was you! You told them to call me up. You got your friends to do it."

"You're crazy."

He looked me squarely in the eyes when he said this, as though trying to bore right into my brain and make me believe him. And I *wanted* to believe him. But I couldn't; there was too much painful history between us.

My mother, no doubt sensing that something awful was transpiring in the foyer, came in and tried to change the subject. She knew how to appeal to my better instincts, by raising the promise of one of her home-cooked meals.

"Are you staying for dinner?" she asked. "I made *pappa al pomodoro.*"

Since moving to Rome I had never visited home and not stayed for dinner. We were at the very end of the summer, and more than once I had thought of my mother's *pappa al pomodoro* and looked forward to a visit so I could eat it.

But not this time.

"No," I told her. "I need to go"

She was stunned: "What do you mean?"

I told them I was leaving. That I was going to America until my attorney could work things out with the Italian government.

"What do you mean, you're going to America?" she asked. "Do you have money?"

She touched my arm, as if about to pull at my shirt. I sensed a big scene about to transpire, a lot of screaming and tears.

"*Lascialo andare, Mafalda*," said my father. Let him go.

"*Stai, zitto, Antonio*," she said. Be quiet.

It was one of the rare times that I was in agreement with my father. There was really nothing to say, so I turned and left.

I walked down the street to my car. I wanted to be tough and not give my father the satisfaction of seeing me look back, but I did: my mother was standing on the second-floor balcony, waving sadly at me. Behind her stood my father, emotionless as ever.

I turned away, got in my car, and drove back to Rome.

INTERLUDE

"*GIANFRANCO! GIANFRANCO! TABLE Forty-Six has been trying to get somebody's attention for ten minutes now.*"

We are sitting, Pino and I, where we always sit, at a little table for two at the top of the staircase inside his restaurant, Centolire, near the corner of Madison Avenue and Eighty-sixth Street on Manhattan's Upper East Side. It's an opulent neighborhood, and this restaurant, with its blond wood floors, smartly dressed managers, and sophisticated take on Italian-American cuisine, caters to it perfectly. It's also the ideal location to talk about Pino's life because the restaurant essentially encapsulates it: the name Centolire comes from an old song—it literally means "one hundred lire"—and the lyrics are about a young man asking his mother for just that amount so he can go to America. For those who know Pino, the subtext is obvious: he himself came over with scarcely more than that, and now here he is, almost thirty years later, the owner of a restaurant in one of the most well-heeled zip codes in the United States.

Across the table, Pino watches as his general manager, Gianfranco Cherici—an Old World sort with trousers hiked up to his navel, a short, thin tie, and aristocratic face—whispers instructions to a waiter, who walk-runs to the neglected table.

Pino watches until the waiter has spoken to the customers and departed to attend to their needs. He nods solemnly, satisfied for the moment.

"We should probably order," he says. It's a superfluous comment because I've never sat down with Pino in one of his restaurants and not had lunch

or dinner. The years have done nothing to diminish his passion for food and
wine, and I often learn that he's been pondering what we might eat all day
long.

"I was thinking maybe we split a puntarelle with garlic and anchovy,
and then the lamb stew. It's very good tonight."

I nod. "Sounds great."

Pino rarely orders from one of his waiters, instead waving over Gianfranco and delivering instructions to him in Italian. He does just that, and
Gianfranco takes off to personally put in the order. It's good to be the king.

"Sorry, where was I?"

"You were about to leave for New York."

Pino takes a sip of wine, and continues.

TWO

Abandon Hope, All Ye Who Enter Here

O N MY LAST morning there, I saw the sun come up over Rome. Patty and I spent the entire evening hanging out on my terrace with our friends, then everybody went their separate ways and we watched the city rise up out of the darkness, like the image in a Polaroid. Most of the city was east of the apartment, so when the sun rose, the sky was a perfect, pristine blue. For what might have been the last time, I witnessed the Colosseum and the Vatican emerge, and all the other buildings, especially the churches, which always stood out for me because of the way they pointed up at the sky.

We both dozed off out there, but we were soon awakened by one of my favorite sounds in Rome, the chirping of hundreds of robins as they swept past. I stood up and began my morning routine, making an espresso in my moka coffeemaker, then sat outside again, sipping it and breathing in the aroma of the fragrant citrus fruits that always seem to perfume the Roman air at sunrise.

Will they have good coffee in America?, I wondered. Unsure of the answer, I washed and dried the machine, tucked a bag of Segafredo grounds inside, and packed it in my suitcase.

I took a shower and got dressed. My suitcase had been lying open on the bed for almost twenty-four hours. Though I'd been fully packed I had avoided clasping it shut. Finally, I did, but I was so loath to leave that I couldn't make my feet move for the door. Patty led me, keeping us on schedule. We got downstairs and hailed a taxi.

Like my morning ritual at home, the drive out of the city was chock-full of things I was going to miss, like the little bakery that my friends and I used to walk by after being out all night; its dairy deliveries would be sitting outside in wooden crates and we'd help ourselves to a few bottles of milk and guzzle them as we headed home to bed.

At the airport Patty guided me by the hand all the way through the check-in and right to our seats. When the stewardess pulled the heavy door closed on the airplane and I heard it seal, I was overcome with panic. Should I have run down the aisle and begged them to let me off? Should I have gone back home and made peace with my military obligation, reported to Barletta, and been done with it?

But it wasn't until the plane pushed away from the gate and began the slow crawl down the runway that I began to fully comprehend the possible consequences of my actions. When I failed to return to Italy and report for duty on October 19, I would become a deserter, subject to criminal prosecution, and could be thrown into prison. This wasn't a night in the boarding school brig we were talking about, and it wasn't a scene in one of my favorite movies or in a play I was rehearsing. It was real life.

As the plane took off, I thought back to those nights in Orbetello leaving the watermelon field and soaring along the winding country roads on my scooter, that feeling of freedom that came with the wind in my face. But now, as we climbed higher and higher, the sense of speed was terrifying, and being in flight only added to my feeling of impending doom.

I barely spoke to Patty for the entire trip. I was playing my life over in my mind. Since saying good-bye to my parents, the fight with my father had weighed on me, mostly for the grief it had surely caused my mother. I was old enough by then to know that there are certain things you say in life that can never be forgotten—forgiven, maybe, but never forgotten—and it was sinking in that in some respects my relationships with both of them would be forever altered.

I promised myself that everything would be all right, that the lawyer would come through, that I'd be able to return to Italy in three months, tops. Nobody had ever told me that, but that's what I told myself for peace of mind. Three months.

I spent eight hours thinking about all of this. I didn't drink anything, didn't partake of the in-flight meal, didn't get up to go to the
bathroom.

After all that time, slipping in and out of consciousness along the
way, the plane began its bumpy descent through the clouds, and I became vaguely aware of the east coast of the United States down below.
I didn't really focus on it until the plane got lower and lower and suddenly I could discern the landmarks of New York City: the Statue of
Liberty, the Twin Towers of the World Trade Center, the Empire State
Building.

Almost at the same instant I noted them, the plane's PA system
crackled to life and the opening piano chords of the song "New York,
New York" came blaring through the cabin. Liza Minnelli had introduced it to the world a few years earlier, in the Martin Scorsese movie
of the same name, but Sinatra had pickpocketed it in 1979, making it
his forever. It was Sinatra's version being played on the plane:

Start spreading the news.

I looked around as the other passengers began smiling in recognition and looking out the window and pointing.

I'm leaving today.

It's a corny song. A gaudy song. But it shook me out of my trance.
It woke me up and energized me.

As the song played on, I took in the city, shining in the light of day,
the sun sparkling across the glass and steel of the buildings.

After being afraid for eight hours, I became excited. The song
reawakened in me the sense of America I'd had all my life: that it was,
more than anything, a dream. The dream is different for everybody,
but everybody's dreams have a few things in common, namely freedom and prosperity.

I wasn't coming to stay, but those ideals were enough to momentar-
ily lift my spirits. I put my arm around Patty as the song came to its end.

It's up to you . . .

Maybe everything would be OK after all.

. . . New York, New York.

The plane lurched as its wheels met the tarmac. The song faded,
and the crew made the necessary announcements.

I kept tapping my finger, still hearing the song in my head, ignoring the flight attendants.

I couldn't understand what they were saying anyway.

I didn't speak more than a few words of English.

WE FILED OFF the plane and into John F. Kennedy International Airport. As the Italian passengers scattered in different directions, the familiar sounds of my native language were diluted, and eventually overcome, by English. It was a swift and jarring transition: the air was full of words I couldn't understand. People rushed by in all directions, speaking to each other in a growing cacophony.

Suddenly, I'd been transformed from a confident man—an actor, a person accustomed to strutting on stage and baring my soul (or at least that of my character) to roomfuls of people—to a mute: if separated from Patty, I'd have no means of communication. I also had this odd sense of paranoia that people were looking at me with curiosity. I began to feel like a bit of an animal, like King Kong lashing out at the pop of flashbulbs.

We got our luggage and found our way into a taxi, Patty doing the talking for both of us. The cab screeched its way out of the airport and onto the highway. It was dark outside, and I had no idea where we were. All I knew was that we were going in the wrong direction, *away* from Manhattan and deeper and deeper into Queens. Shadows washed over us as we passed in and out of the range of streetlights, and the terrain kept changing: one moment we were breezing past neighborhoods elevated above the highway on grassy embankments; the next we were passing a desolate stretch of asphalt and concrete with no life in sight. Every time I had my bearings, the environs would change yet again, until we drove past a final cluster of row houses and strip malls, and finally arrived in a community of sad little houses, a world far from the action.

So much for Sinatra. I felt like I was at the end of the Earth.

We got out at the brownstone where we'd be staying and walked up dark stairs to the second-floor apartment Patty's family friend had arranged for us. She turned the key in the lock and opened the door, then fumbled around for the light switch and flicked it on. When the lights came up, my experience took on an entirely new level of unreality. The living room was very simple and clean, with functional furniture, avocado-colored walls, track lighting overhead, and a thick carpet. It reminded me of any American television show I'd ever seen about a police detective, like Kojak, who lived in Queens, on his own, with a parakeet or a dog.

I went into the bedroom and put my suitcase down on the floor, but I didn't open it. Once it was open, I would begin unpacking, and that would be an acknowledgment of my arrival in this new place. As long as it remained closed, I was in transit, with the possibility of moving on, or of returning home.

Lying in bed later with the lights out, I heard all the night sounds of a New York City outer borough: ferocious barking dogs, wailing sirens, rumbling subway trains, and harsh voices that drifted up from the street and through the thin glass of the windowpanes. As my eyes adjusted to the darkness, I could make out the texture of the pressed-tin ceiling, a far cry from the night sky that spread out above my terrace back home. Remembering a trick from childhood, I closed my eyes hard and when I opened them little sparks seemed to be twirling in the air over me, an approximation of the stars over Rome. I kept on doing this over and over until finally, after God knows how long, I fell into a deep, deep sleep.

WHEN I WOKE up the next morning, I didn't move. For the longest time, I just stared at that tin ceiling. Outside it was gray, with rain drizzling, and I passed the entire day just prowling around the apartment, looking out the windows at the dull houses, picking at the green couch we'd inherited. By six o'clock, Patty couldn't take it anymore and she urged me to get dressed so we could go shopping for food.

I hadn't really thought much about sustenance since we'd arrived, but the mention of food gave me a great idea: I'd cook us dinner. Right away, I knew how I'd begin the meal, with *pappa al pomodoro*. By the time I had my raincoat on, my mood had swung and I was giddy with excitement.

We left the building and walked down the road. It was already getting dark and I remember you couldn't quite see Manhattan in the distance, but you could see the glow of its lights, like a carnival over a hill. Until that moment, I had forgotten that we were in New York City. I don't know where I thought I was. I guess it didn't matter. The fact that I wasn't home was all that really counted.

We came upon a supermarket. My first impression was less than favorable: the fluorescent lighting was garish, and once the automatic doors slid shut behind us, there was filthy linoleum underfoot.

I was jet-lagged and disoriented, and I felt like I was suddenly in Eastern Europe. This wasn't what I thought of when I thought of New York. The store was just four or five aisles that seemed to go on forever, and they were understocked, not like the stores we had in Rome, where everything was bountiful.

I followed Patty, pushing the shopping cart, one wheel wobbling, as she casually tossed basics into its depths. She also bought something that she called olive oil, but it looked like it was meant for the engine of a car, and it came in a big plastic jug, shaped almost like one you would buy at a gas station.

Being around food aroused my appetite anyway and I found that I was suddenly starving. I had only been here for about twenty-four hours, but with home so far away, my body was craving something that would reconnect it with the feeling of belonging and of familiarity. I went looking for the produce section, which I thought would be a touchstone, a gateway back, if only through my senses.

I spotted a wall of leafy greens at the end of the aisle up ahead and stepped up my pace, racing past cereal boxes with unfamiliar cartoon characters on them, and bottles of soda with more familiar names—Coke, Pepsi, Tab.

Arriving in the produce section, I looked left and right for *red*, the red of tomatoes, which always stand out among the vegetables. I spotted them on the wall, and beelined for them. But as I approached, it quickly became apparent that something was wrong: the tomatoes were pale and wan and wrapped—*pinned* would be more like it—against a little rectangular Styrofoam tray, encased by taut cellophane. This strange land in which I found myself had just become even stranger. I looked around: it wasn't just the tomatoes. *Everything* was encased in plastic: little culinary condoms covered all the vegetables, from the cauliflower to the corn to the lettuces.

It wasn't until then that I really took in the department around me: it was lifeless, and it felt more like an emergency room than a place to present and sell food; and this feeling was only reinforced by the picked-over bins of onions and garlic and by the absence of fresh herbs. In Italy, even in supermarkets, produce was accorded a certain level of respect; the rest of the store might be sterile, but the produce section was a shrine.

I was overcome with grief. I wanted to drop to the filthy linoleum floor and curl up in a ball. Suddenly, home—which I had planned to conjure up in the kitchen—seemed once again hopelessly far away.

I was breathless, almost panting, and my heart was pounding palpably beneath my chest. I felt clammy and cold and disoriented, almost in a dream state. The people around me—a smattering of single elderly shoppers—seemed strange and otherworldly.

I scanned around for Patty, but she was nowhere in sight.

I began walking, looking for her, tracing the perimeter of the store. Passing the meat department, I was struck that there was no butcher; all of the cuts had already been made and the anemic specimens were wrapped in plastic just like all the fruits and vegetables. If the produce section was the E.R., then this was the morgue, and the dairy section, too, was a horror, with mass-produced cheeses that looked like they were made of rubber.

I had never seen anything so bizarre, so antithetical to my idea of food and cooking—which I was realizing right then and there was the same as my idea of life itself.

I stopped to catch my breath. A thought crept into my head: would wearing a uniform and subjecting myself to military training actually have been worse that what I'd embarked on?

By the time I found Patty, I was no longer interested in cooking or even in eating. I just wanted to get home, to get into bed, to pull the covers over my head and make myself disappear.

THREE

Land of Opportunity

Back at the apartment, Patty cooked for the two of us, making the chicken cacciatore I'd taught her in Rome. I slouched on the sofa, surfing the handful of television channels available back in those days.

To my surprise, I quickly came across a familiar face, the politician Ronald Reagan. It was just a few weeks before the 1980 presidential election and he was making a speech. With his rosy Howdy Doody cheeks, rhythmic nodding, and folksy voice, Reagan quickly lulled me into a trance. I couldn't understand a thing he was saying, but he exuded humanity and warmth and reassured me with his embodiment of everything that I had always associated with America—not New York, but *America*: its promise, its optimism, its open arms and open mind. If you want to understand the appeal of Reagan, you need look no farther than the sight of me, sprawled out on that sofa, an unshaven, unhappy, newly arrived immigrant, already beaten down by the grimy indifference of the city, but suddenly grinning ear to ear. I felt as if I had found an American papá, my own Uncle Sam. He was such a contrast to the archetypical Italian bureaucrat, those shameless shakedown artists who cared nothing for the people they "served."

Just like *that*, my demons were exorcised. I knew that Reagan had been an actor, like me. Maybe not a very good one, but an actor nonetheless. And now here he was, poised to become president of the United States. This could never have happened in Italy. When I decided to become an actor, it wasn't just my father who scoffed. Everybody had had

40

their doubts. That's the way Italians are: you aren't supposed to stray too far from the family tradition, to get too big a head, to try something too ambitious or outlandish. But this guy, this Reagan, was about to become the most powerful man in the world, and it seemed perfectly natural.

Of course, I had no idea how long I'd have to stay here in America, or what I'd do. But that's just the point, I realized: I could do *anything*.

I shook off all the negativity I'd been wearing like a shawl since we'd arrived. I shot up off the sofa so quickly that Patty almost dropped the plates she was carrying to the table. I told her that I was over it, and ready to get on with things.

We made plans to get up early the next morning and go into Manhattan.

THE NEXT DAY, a Monday, was sunny. I woke up excited, thinking, "Today is the day. Today's the day I'm going to New York City."

We boarded the A train. When we got through the tunnel under the East River and arrived on the Manhattan side, I couldn't wait to get to the streets. I wanted to exit at the first station, Broadway-Nassau, but Patty talked me out of it and instead we got out at Chambers Street, near Wall Street. The difference between the Financial District and Ozone Park was like the difference between Kansas and Oz: there were huge buildings of marble and steel and glass that towered so high you almost had to bend your back to see up to their tops. It was one of those October days in New York City when it's summer in the sun and fall in the shade, with the cool air splashing up against your face. In the canyons of the Financial District, the light didn't come through directly, instead tinting the streets a refracted blue. There was steam billowing up through grates in the sidewalk, where it was sucked up by the wind and dissipated into the air. All around us, American businessmen raced to and fro, briefcases swinging at the ends of their arms like pendulums. The spectacle was insane, but I loved it: I had never seen such a pure expression of the power of money—what it can buy, what it can build, how it makes people feel, and how crazy it makes them act. It was a street-level representation of capitalism, of the raw desire and energy required to milk it for all it was worth.

And then there were Patty and I, in our jeans and corduroy jackets. We were very out of place, but nobody cared, and I loved that, too.

We went to see Patty's family friend, a Yugoslavian immigrant I'll call Hadi, who was a director of Bank of America on Broad Street. The lobby of his office building was immense and intimidating. We put on little visitor badges and rode the elevator up to his office. After some perfunctory greetings, he took us to lunch in the corporate dining room. Sunlight flooded the room through the floor-to-ceiling windows and I had the sensation we were floating above the city, with a view unlike anything I had ever seen before. As Patty and Hadi spoke, I kept stealing glances out the window: watching taxis and people glide along the streets and sidewalks, the metropolis playing out its life in miniature. As awesome as it was, I was a bit taken aback. One of the things I'd loved most about Florence was being in a city with great restaurants and museums that was also just a stone's throw from the countryside, a duality that I considered distinctly Florentine. (The closest thing I can think of in the United States is Portland or Seattle, where you have all the electricity of town, but can hop in a car or on a bike, and be hiking up a mountain, or visiting a farm, or gaping at a waterfall in a matter of minutes.) Gazing out over Manhattan from that skyscraper, I was struck that there was no greenery in sight. If you were to put a building this high in Florence, or even in certain parts of Rome, you'd be able to see the countryside beyond the city limits.

Though I didn't speak English, Hadi decided to tell me one thing in the language of America: "Just make yourself at home," he said. "Look at me. I'm an immigrant. I came here and I went through all the steps and now I am what I am."

For emphasis, he gestured at the portrait of the bank's founder, Mr. A. P. Giannini, that hung over the dining room, and with a nod, he added all he thought I needed to hear: "Italian."

WE LEFT HADI and walked north. Within minutes we arrived in the West Village, a neighborhood that made me feel right at home with its

cobblestone streets and nineteenth-century brownstones. All the buildings were old and low and human, and I felt like I could be in Siena, or
Munich, or Amsterdam.

I couldn't believe how many different worlds we had been through
in just a few hours: Ozone Park, Wall Street, the Village. I had a growing sense that New York could be whatever you wanted it to, that time
and space had no meaning—you could snap your fingers and go from
one reality to another.

At the end of the day, we picked up a *Village Voice* and secured a
booth in a coffee shop to go through it and look for apartment listings.
There weren't many, but we mapped them out and scheduled appoint-
ments from the pay phone in the back.

I called my mother to let her know that I was in one piece, and she
said that she hoped the situation would be resolved soon. From her
somewhat guarded tone, I could tell that my father was close by, but I
didn't ask for him and he didn't ask for me.

I also took the opportunity to call my lawyer in Italy and check in
on his discussions with the military.

"They don't want to hear from you," he told me. "Things don't look
good. There's a warrant for your arrest. If you come back, you'll be put
in jail."

I looked over at Patty, sitting there circling apartment listings with
her pen. She was the only person I knew on this side of the ocean, and
all those terrible thoughts came flooding back, all those doubts about
what might become of me here in America, where I had no mar-
ketable skills and didn't speak the language.

OF THE TWO of us, Patty was the first one to get a job, as an assistant
secretary in the private banking department of Bank of America.
Though we were a one-income couple, her salary provided enough
money that by the first week in November, we were renting a small,
one-bedroom apartment at Third Avenue and Seventy-sixth Street on
the Upper East Side. We would rather have been in Greenwich Village,
but we couldn't afford it. This was the only place we could find that had
a living room, bedroom, kitchen, and bathroom for just six hundred

dollars per month. From inside, the unit was charming, with a generous view down Third Avenue from the living room and kitchen. The owner was Italian—a member of the Bari family of Ray Bari pizza fame—and operated a pizzeria downstairs. He had also had the building painted with broad green, white, and red bands, representing the Italian flag, although he must have had a miscommunication with the painters because the stripes were horizontal instead of vertical. I love Italy, but it was a real eyesore.

We were living in the promised land of Manhattan, but I was alone during the day, and I didn't know what to do with myself. I walked the streets for hours, aimless and confused. One day, I was on Eighth Avenue and having one of those moments you have when you first move to New York when you can't tell which way is north and which way is south and haven't yet learned to use certain markers, like the Twin Towers or the Empire State Building, as reference points.

A young guy in an expensive suit was coming my way. "Excuse me," I said, calling on my growing but still meager vocabulary, "I'm lost."

"I'm Alan," he said with a smirk, and kept on walking. It took me a few minutes to decipher what he had said and realize that he was making a joke at my expense. Standing there like an idiot in the middle of the sidewalk, with people moving past me like rushing water around a rock, I felt more lonely than ever.

But the most upsetting aspect of life here continued to be the food. Everything that had to do with food depressed me. I'd walk by restaurants and see what people were eating: in neighborhood joints it was green salads with grilled chicken on top and in fancy eateries it was *nouvelle cuisine*, with its silly kaleidoscopic presentations.

Hungry for home, I decided to visit one of the restaurants in Little Italy downtown, a famous place specializing in seafood that had been there for decades. My walk through the neighborhood caught me off guard: the little souvenir shops with miniature Italian flags and soccer shirts and Frank Sinatra posters for sale—the most superficial, stereotypical depictions of Italian and Italian-American culture. And when I got to the restaurant, I didn't know what to make of it: there were huge fish tanks in the dining room that made it smell like an aquarium.

The food was unfamiliar to me: clams *oreganata* and other Italian-American dishes that had no true antecedent back home. They also served pastas that were overcooked and all seemed to be swimming in the same red tomato sauce, and were presented in huge mounds; in my opinion, even great pasta should be served in portions no larger than one hundred grams.

That indulgence was especially disappointing because I was so broke that I ate most of my meals in diners, or tried to: all I wanted was eggs, sunny-side up. Someone told me that *occhio di bue* translated as "cow's eyes," so I'd take a seat at the counter and, with my thick accent, order "eggs cow's eyes." More often than not, the waiter would look at me like I was crazy and proceed to ignore me until I gave up and left. I'd sometimes come back to our apartment and call my mother to check in; eventually Papá and I began to speak again, as well, but it was always strained.

Fortunately, after some sleuthing about, I was able to reconnect with two old friends from Rome who had come here before me. Oreste, an acting-schoolmate of mine, had chased an American girl to New York. They had gotten married and while he still had his roguish good looks, his acting skills were of little use here and he had taken one of the most common immigrant paths and become a cab driver. The other guy, a James Dean lookalike named Claudio who had come to attend the famous Actor's Studio, had failed in the theater and become an executive with Agip, the Italian oil company.

When the three of us got together and hung out, we reverted back to our old ways, chain-smoking, laughing about our friends back home, and killing bottles of wine in quick succession.

But I could see that they were living very different lives. Essentially, they had become different people. Our get-togethers aside, they had been comprehensively assimilated into American society. In particular, Oreste peppered his conversation, even otherwise Italian sentences, with American slang like "asshole" and "motherfucker." And they dressed like Americans, less conspicuously than they had previously. Maybe they couldn't afford more expensive threads, but they seemed deliberately conformist in their jeans and knit shirts. There was an air of anticlimax about Claudio and Oreste: so alive and creative just a few years earlier, and now resigned to their workaday lives here in the United States, cogs in the capitalist wheel. I adopted a cinematic reference for these guys who looked familiar but were relieved of their vitality: *Body Snatchers*. I had nothing against America, but I liked myself Italian and wasn't interested in becoming an American.

I'd come back to our apartment after spending time with these pod people and sit on the sofa in a stupor that was only partially brought on by the red wine coursing through my veins. I was confronting the specter of my own ambition. Back in Rome, after being cast in *Antony and Cleopatra*, I had been on the cusp of theatrical success. Would I have become a celebrity? Who knew? But the possibility had been there. Now, I was a step away from becoming one of the invisibles who drove cabs and sliced meat at the delicatessen and made deliveries.

To help maintain a strong connection to Tuscany, I'd wrap up my daily vagabonding around New York (job hunting, followed by lunch, followed by wandering the streets) with a trip to the local supermarket, then come home and make dinner for myself and Patty. I felt like my mother, cooking dinner for my father, although the state of supermarkets in America—this was long before the rise of chains like Whole Foods—demanded some creativity to even approximate what we ate in Italy. It was almost impossible to find a good, imported brand of dried pasta (meaning something made from durum), so after one gummy experiment, I gave that up for a time. I began to cook with tougher cuts of meat, punching up the flavor with spices like clove, nutmeg, cinnamon, pepper, and cumin—which isn't Italian but makes a big impact. In time, I developed my in-America repertoire of vegetable soups, stews, and pot roast, and whenever I cooked, I played my cassettes of Italian pop artists such as Venditti, Battisti, and Dalla in the background. In this way, for a few hours each day, it sounded and smelled like home.

JUST AS I was loath to unpack my suitcase when we first arrived, the truth was that I was terrified of committing to a job here for fear that it would set me on the one-way path to obscurity. But eventually I came to grips with the fact that my stay was open-ended and that any self-respecting man had to go to work in the morning and bring home some money at the end of the week. So, with some help from a family connection, I hooked up with the owner of a small men's clothing boutique, another transplanted Italian happy just to be in America. He ran a shop in the East Sixties, near Lexington Avenue, and he hired me as his right hand.

I have no idea how this guy made any money because the shop did precious little business. The mirrored walls were lined with long, steel racks that had men's suits hanging from them, and in the center of the store were additional racks, suspended from the ceiling, on which hung imported slacks and sport shirts. He'd have me occupy myself by sweeping the floors, wiping down the mirrors and windows, and straightening the suits. Once I finished doing it all, he'd make me do it all again, even though sometimes nobody had entered the store since I had begun the endless loop in the morning.

After less than a week of this, I had had enough. On Thursday, I left for lunch and decided that I would never go back.

It was, on its face, an insane decision, but there are times in life when you have to make a change. I had to leave that boarding school, I had to leave Italy, and now I had to leave the boutique. I couldn't quite put words to my rationale. If I would eventually be allowed to return to Italy, who cared how I paid the rent during my brief time here in the United States? And if I couldn't return to Italy, then I might as well make peace with the fact that my acting career was at an end, and that I'd need to at least begin life here with a job like this.

All I knew was that I had to get out of there. I didn't know what I was looking for but I walked south, downtown. I took a right on Fifty-seventh Street and passed Bergdorf Goodman and Tiffany's.

Up until that moment, being in such moneyed neighborhoods had depressed me, but not anymore. The opulent surroundings inspired me, made me hungry for success. My bearing and stride took on more purpose. I stood up straighter, puffed my chest out, held my head high, and *marched* west on Fifty-seventh Street. In those moments I was transformed from a lost soul bobbing through the sea of people into that most classic of New York characters: a striver, somebody looking for his moment, his opportunity, and sure that the city was keeping it tucked away for him somewhere, if he just took the time to go looking for it.

I turned left on Seventh Avenue and headed downtown, past the Theater District, where the theaters were dark in the middle of the day. I kept forging downward, through the Sodom and Gomorrah they called Times Square, through the Garment District and Chelsea and into the West Village. I cut over to Sixth Avenue, the Avenue of the Americas, and, gazing east across it, something caught my eye: just above Houston Street there was a little restaurant with a canary-yellow awning stretched over the door with the name Da Silvano stenciled on it. *Da Silvano* means "Silvano's Place," but in a way that only Italians would understand. It actually means "to Silvano," as in "let's go to Silvano's place."

I crossed the street and walked up to the restaurant. I looked at the menu in its little windowed box outside: it was in Italian, and the food was the stuff I missed, like *fegato alla salvia* (calf's liver with sage) and *cacciucco* (fish stew). This was a real Italian restaurant, like the ones we had back home.

I had never thought of working in a restaurant. Those summers back at my uncle's place were fond memories, to be sure, but I thought of that as just something I had done when I was a kid to get away from home and make some money. But staring at that menu, and looking through the window as the waiters served food to the customers and cleared away the dirty dishes, I suddenly realized that this was where I had been headed when I had left the boutique.

I opened the door. There are two small dining rooms at Da Silvano today, but back then there was just one little room, with a bar in the back corner that looked like a confessional. The size of the room was irrelevant to me: it was the *smells* that sealed the deal: garlic, rosemary, and that sweet, tannic, primal scent of cooked wine and meat.

I identified the manager, a stocky young Italian guy named Delfino whose diminutive size and rigid posture reminded me of a jockey. Speaking in Italian, I introduced myself. He spoke with a thick Southern Italian accent that was a delight to hear. I didn't waste any time and went right ahead and told him I was looking for a job.

I guess it was clear that I was new to the States, because he asked me what I was doing here in New York. I told him I had just arrived.

"*Hai lavorato nei ristoranti?*" he asked me. What restaurant experience did I have?

I told Delfino about my uncle's restaurant. I got a bit carried away, explaining how much I'd done there and how natural I was at it, all of the memories reconstituting in my mind as I relayed them for the first time in ages.

I might have oversold myself, because he said to me, "But you don't speak English. All I can offer you is a busboy job."

I looked around at Da Silvano. It was small, but there was a real attention to detail, an authenticity and familiarity, from the exposed red brick wall to the simple white tablecloths to the espresso machine behind the bar and the pressed-tin ceiling. I didn't want to leave.

"*Va bene, busboy sia*," I said. Fine, I'll be a busboy.

Delfino told me to come back at four o'clock the next day and we shook on it.

On the way out, I took another look at the menu. There it was, under *Antipasti*, third from the top: *pappa al pomodoro*.

I'd come to the right place.

INTERLUDE

W<small>E STOP AS</small> *a waiter brings us our* puntarelle, *a chicory that tastes like a cross between celery and fennel. Pino prepares it after the Roman fashion, cutting it in long strips from the base of the stem and soaking it in ice water, which causes it to curl and become crunchy. He dresses the* puntarelle *with a vinaigrette of minced garlic, anchovy, red wine vinegar, and olive oil.*

I take a bite, and it occurs to me that it's pretty unusual to see puntarelle *in the United States.*

"Where do you get this?" I ask.

"From Italy. You can also get it from California, but it's more green, and less wide."

As usual, we stop doing business as we eat. But as we approach the Silvano chapter, I feel the need to say something, because for such a loquacious guy, Pino has always been strangely stingy about the details of their relationship, which has been built up as a cold war of sorts in the press for almost three decades now. Yet whenever I've mentioned Silvano to him over the years, all Pino does is lapse into a derisive, marble-mouthed impression of the man's distinct speech pattern: "Eh, Pino. How ya' doin', eh? Eh. Eh."

I've always been intrigued by the question of exactly what transpired between these two men. In 2001, I was hired to help Silvano Marchetto rewrite his first cookbook, and I got to know him a little. One cannot observe them and fail to notice the similarities: Silvano ran an authentic Italian trattoria before Pino moved to New York City. He has a knack for showmanship and a gift for drawing celebrities. And, though charming and gregarious in the dining room, he's also a shrewd businessman with a keen eye for profit.

Silvano also interacted with his staff in a way I'd never seen anybody do before. One day we were going over some pages when his eye was drawn to something behind me and he leaped up out of his chair. I turned to see that he was stepping up to one of his waiters who had just arrived for his shift.

"No, no," Silvano chided him. "That's now how you come to work in a restaurant." I missed what had offended Silvano, but that was no problem because he pantomimed a frown and slumped shoulders to show the guy what he looked like.

"Go outside and come back in the right way."

The waiter left and did a one-eighty-degree turn under the awning as the door closed behind him. Then he walked back in with a fake but enormous smile on his face.

"There, see!" Silvano said. "Now you're ready to be a waiter."

It was exactly the same kind of thing that Pino might do, only with more good humor, and Silvano did stuff like that all the time. For years, I'd wondered exactly how much of Pino's restaurateur instincts came from his uncle and how much came from Silvano.

And so, as the puntarelle vanishes from our plates and the time approaches to discuss Silvano, I say: "Pino, you don't love the guy, but didn't you learn a lot from him?"

He takes a long pause and stares up into the ceiling. Pino clearly doesn't like to admit it, but, eventually, he does: "You know, you're right. In his own way, that guy was some kind of a genius."

FOUR

Home Away from Home

I HAD NO IDEA at the time, but I'd just landed a job at one of the hottest, most exclusive restaurants in New York City. Despite its humble dimensions and design, Da Silvano was a magnet for celebrities, a canteen for rock stars, a hangout for downtown artists, movie stars, and directors, and one of the publishing world's favorite destinations for literary lunching. It was an anything-goes, pocket-size downtown counterpart to the jacket-required uptown institution Le Cirque, where Sirio Maccioni hosted celebrities and the media elite long before they had that nickname.

I was oblivious to all of this, but I was excited by what I had stumbled upon nonetheless. I left my impromptu interview with Delfino in a state of infatuation with Da Silvano, my heart aflutter, my capacity for happiness in America suddenly increased exponentially.

The next day, I couldn't wait to start work and was almost thirty minutes early. I killed the time walking around the West Village, which wasn't far removed from its beatnik history, evident in coffee shops like the Figaro, with Italian newspapers shellacked to its walls, and the scent of sweet marijuana in the air. All of this added to the sense of rejuvenation and reawakening that I'd had since the previous night, a feeling that I was back in touch with my Italian roots and my heritage as an actor.

When the time came to report for duty at Da Silvano, I pushed through the front door, instantly spotting Delfino. We shook hands and he gave me a tour of the place, which didn't take long. I was struck that the kitchen was run entirely by South Americans with not an Italian in sight.

I took a moment to peruse the menu in greater detail. Silvano's probably had the most authentic Italian food of any restaurant in New York at the time. There were also some dishes that were decidedly *not* Italian, like oyster stew and duck with dry vermouth, but I was so excited to begin working that I didn't dwell on these incongruities.

Silvano's place was nothing like my uncle's restaurant, but the motor skills I'd developed and honed more than ten years earlier came right back and I began setting tables, making sure the place was spiffy when we opened for dinner.

As I did this, the front door was flung open and in strutted a short man with wavy salt-and-pepper hair, a round face, leather pants, and a suede vest over a pink oxford shirt. In unison, the waiters stopped what they were doing and called out, "Silvano!"

He seemed like something of a peacock to me, a bit of an exhibitionist. As he made his rounds of the waiters they each took their turn laughing at whatever he whispered to them.

Delfino led him over to me and introduced us. Silvano looked at me curiously, not making eye contact. He said something but I couldn't understand it because Silvano Marchetto speaks his own mumbled version of English that's impossible to decipher until you've spent significant time with him. Think Popeye, crossed with an Italian accent, throw in a bit of slurring, turn the speed up to about twice as fast as most people speak, and you get the idea.

After he said whatever it was that he said, I just stared at him, completely confused and unsure of how to respond or what to say. I didn't want to get fired on my first day, but I literally had no idea what he was talking about.

Throwing me a lifeline, Delfino told Silvano that, like him, I was from Tuscany.

"*Toscano, eh,*" he said.

"*Si,*" I replied, expecting that we might talk for a while. But he quickly moved on and didn't say another word to me all through dinner.

I found this rude, but as the evening wore on, I quickly developed a grudging respect for this guy's unmistakable talent as a restaurateur. Watching him work the dining room—chatting up people, personally delivering food and wine to their table, and performing eccentric bits of business—I was at once reminded of vaudeville comedians, rodeo clowns, and the mimes and other street performers of Paris. He was hyper, irrepressible, and almost pathologically eager to please, with a real passion for interacting with, and amusing, his customers.

As my first days passed, my opinion of Silvano changed like the weather. His admirable bravado on the service floor was offset by his arrogance and eccentricity; a few days later, he blew through the front door wearing a floor-length fox-fur coat that I never saw again. I also noticed that he would begin drinking before lunchtime, which seemed like a bad idea to me, but this too was balanced by the fact that he was always able to function like a pro: he'd work lunch service, then stroll over to his apartment around the corner for a nap, and then return fresh as a daisy for dinner.

Adding to my seesawing feelings toward him was the fact that Silvano continued to keep me at arm's length, but I was grateful to him for having created this restaurant that relieved my homesickness. Once again, I was part of a team—a "family" as they said in the industry—and it was like belonging to a theater troupe again, except instead of putting on plays for people, we served them meals. My happiest times were just before and after lunch and dinner when I'd stand out front under the awning and speak Italian with Delfino.

I also found comfort and familiarity in the similarities between the restaurant and theater. It occurred to me that there was little difference between what Silvano did and what I had done as an actor: he put on two one-man performances every day—a matinee and an evening show—and we were all his supporting actors and stagehands. There was another parallel to theater: working in an authentically Italian restaurant in America was an opportunity to participate in the creation of an alternate reality. I knew very quickly that this was going to be my salvation, that when I came to Da Silvano I was coming to Italy.

I could speak Italian, eat Italian food, and be surrounded by Italian furnishings.

I was also grateful for the work, and I plunged into it wholeheartedly. To compensate for the language barrier, I looked for ways to make myself as useful and indispensable as possible. Because of my experience working for my uncle, I understood how to synchronize the kitchen and dining room, and I would do everything in my power to keep meals moving along, clearing tables that were ready to be cleared and running hot food out from the kitchen while it was still giving off steam.

The cooks loved me. They saw the effort I was putting forth and would thank me with bits of food. "Hey, Pino," they'd say, and slide me a little dish of pasta on a bread-and-butter plate, just the right size for me to twirl and devour in a bite or two—a little carbo-load to get me through the next hour.

The only problem I had was that one of the American waiters, a guy named Tom—a tall, gangly college dropout with a Prince Valiant haircut and glasses—was supremely lazy and spent most of his time talking to customers. He was a master of small talk, able to stretch any topic—from the Yankees to the downtown scene to where he bought his eyeglasses—into a ten- to fifteen-minute conversation. Meanwhile, I ran around him doing my job *and* his. I came to think of him as "Mr. Finger" because he was always pointing at things, such as tables that needed clearing, and saying "Pino," treating me like his dog. It really began to piss me off, and also to threaten me. I couldn't speak English, and I didn't have a relationship with Silvano, so it was impossible for me to confront this guy directly. I lived in fear that one day Delfino would leave and Tom or the new manager would find a way to get rid of me.

Late one night while we were still serving customers, Silvano was sitting at the bar and Tom was standing there telling him stories. I walked by with a stack of dishes in my arms, sweat pouring off my face, and said to Silvano, "*Parla con te, incula a me.*" Because he talks to you, he's fucking me.

Silvano thought about this for a second, then cracked up. I could

tell it was the first time the effect of Tom's chattiness on the other employees registered for him. After that, I tried to make the point in
other ways; we had two busboys for the busiest days of the week, but I
knew that if Tom only pulled his weight, we could get by with one, and
have more room to function, so one day I told Silvano, "This is a job
for one busboy." Silvano just nodded, but he never really followed up
on it, and I began to form an opinion that he was simply one of those
people with little stomach for confrontation.

Despite my nemesis, I was so happy in my work that before long I
had no desire to be anywhere else, especially because, outside, the city remained threatening; one afternoon, while standing under the awning
out front with one of the cooks, I heard a commotion and turned to see a
shirtless and sinewy black teenager in cutoff denim shorts running for
his life from the basketball court on the corner of Houston and Sixth Avenue. Behind him, a small mob of four guys in shirtsleeves, each bran-
dishing a baseball bat, was in hot pursuit. They chased him right into the
middle of Sixth Avenue, where his escape was blocked by a moving truck
stopped at a red light. The guys went to town on him. I looked away but
I could hear the sickening sound of bat meeting bone and I remember
being struck that nobody in any of the cars was doing anything to stop
this.

Then, I heard a shriek and looked up to see another black kid, coming from the same direction, this one being chased by six or seven
guys, most of them also carrying bats, which they had at the ready like
polo mallets. They caught up to him on the sidewalk and began sav-
aging him as well. The wail of a police car caused the assailants to flee
and when I looked at the guys they'd been beating, I almost threw up:
one of them was trying to rise up off the pavement, but he literally
didn't have the strength to get to his knees. The other had been re-
duced to an inert, bloody mass, right down to his skull, which had
been split open. Cars drove past them indifferently. I was reminded of
myself, standing on that sidewalk a few weeks earlier, people rushing
by, and I thought how brutal the city could be—emotionally, physi-
cally, financially brutal.

I turned away from the circus on the street and went back into the
restaurant, back to the smells and sounds of Italy, and when the door

closed behind me, it was as if I were in another world again, safe from
the violence outside.

ALTHOUGH DA SILVANO offered me emotional refuge, it was also
challenging to be there. I was constantly surrounded by people who
were eating, drinking, and laughing, and I had no way of participating.
The sounds of a busy restaurant are happy sounds but I tried to shut
them out, or sometimes think of them as a kind of background music.
In order to survive, I also began calling even more on my theater training. I imagined that when I was at work, I was playing the part of The
Busboy. The dining room became the stage, the kitchen became the
backstage, and the patrons became the audience in what I came to think
of as a kind of experimental space where the observers were seated right
onstage with the actors. I functioned like this for several months, but
facing the loneliness every day was the biggest challenge of my life.
Eventually, though, I learned how to enjoy my own company, and my
own thoughts. I would often get into such a flow of work that I was able
to pass entire evenings meditating on aspects of my life—whether or
not I'd done the right thing leaving Italy, my conflicting feelings about
my father, how much I missed acting and my friends.

    The moments that took me out of my own head involved the
screen artists who frequented Da Silvano, many of whom, such as the
director John Cassavetes, were regulars. Ironically, by fleeing my life
in the theater I had ended up in a place that drew celebrities, including
many of my heroes, like an awards show. The irony was compounded
by the fact that I couldn't converse with them, like the first time that I
saw Robert De Niro—this icon I knew as a forty-foot-tall image flick-
ering on the screen of a Roman movie house—come in for dinner. It
was thrilling to watch him sit in the corner eating a bowl of pasta. I
can still see him there, slightly hunched over, with the lights from
passing cars dancing over him while he ate, rendering him as cinematic as ever. I would have loved to have met him, to have spoken to
him. But I couldn't, and it was hard to refrain from making eye contact, or even trying to strike up a conversation, when I would refill his
water glass or sprinkle parmesan on his pasta.

In time, De Niro came to recognize me, and he would nod to me when he sat down and unfurled his napkin. One day, I took the sign of familiarity a little too far and in my mangled English said to him, "In Italy, was an actor. I was in Italy an actor."

He smiled painfully, then put things back in their proper context by asking me: "What are the pasta specials tonight?"

BY DECEMBER, THE only two things I was concerned with, from the time I woke up in the morning to the moment I went to bed at night, were working at Da Silvano and learning English. I spent many of the service hours observing little details about the restaurant: how the tables were packed but in such a way as to grant each one just enough privacy; the level of the music and the adjustments Silvano made to the lighting during the day and evening. I'm still impressed by the way he ran the reservation book. Silvano understood, or gambled, that people were willing to wait in New York. Personally, I think he went a little far with it, because his basic attitude was, "I'm the hot shit in town, and you people will sit when I say you can." I couldn't treat customers that way, but he never suffered for his arrogance: there was a little bench outside the restaurant that got to know more famous asses than any bench in New York City because even celebrities were happy to camp out there until their tables were ready. I'll never forget the time Silvano dispatched me to take wine to a couple parked out there, and when I did they turned and I saw that it was Kelly and Calvin Klein, huddled together to stay warm, just happy to be in New York, downtown, about to dine at Da Silvano. We did three seatings, about one hundred ten dinners, in that little room between six o'clock and eleven thirty, which is impossible, but we did it most nights. That's one of the things Silvano taught me: how to do the impossible.

I'll be honest: I was stealing from him, and because he didn't pay any attention to a lowly busboy like me, he never noticed. I wasn't stealing money; I was stealing the tricks of the trade, my eyes pilfering every last detail, even little things like how to watch the door and the dining room at the same time and how to anticipate the customer's next move. It was like the New York City version of my time working for my uncle, except that the space was so small that there was an added element of physicality; when the place was fully occupied there was no room to turn or twist, so we were constantly reaching over, under, and around each other and the diners to get things done. I took to this naturally; working the floor was like dancing to me and in no time, I could clear a table, or lay down hot plates, while lifting my hip over a chair, or standing up on my tiptoes to get out of the way of a rising diner from an adjacent table.

As for learning English, I had no time for taking a course. Instead, I listened to the news every chance I got, and I conversed with anyone who would talk to me. Some of my best teachers were the delivery guys who brought food to Silvano's. "I no order veal shank," I'd say. They'd say back, "Ah, man, that's our name for *osso buco*."

I also read the papers every day, especially the *New York Post*—which I later realized uses some of the worst English imaginable, but which added a great deal of American slang to my repertoire. I also began to lean on American swear words, like *motherfucker*, *scumbag*, or *dickhead*, the way the *Peanuts* character Linus clung to his security blanket. I probably used them too much, but they were just so descriptive and created a sense of instant intimacy with whomever I was talking to, especially the guys I worked with. And I had a special place in my heart for Yiddish: *oy gevalt*, *shtup*, *schmuck*. I guess I was assimilating a little after all, going the path of Oreste and Claudio, but working at Da Silvano made me feel as if I were still living in Italy most of my waking hours so it was alright.

I was getting more and more used to life in New York, when all of a sudden another bit of violence rocked my world: During service on December 8, 1980, I learned that John Lennon had been shot. I was in shock. I had always thought of myself as a member of the Beatles generation, so it was like hearing that a relative had died. I asked one of the guys where his home, the Dakota, was and he told me. I got on the subway and rode up to West Seventy-second Street, then walked over to his building. The streets were packed with people, some of them wild with anger, others weeping, many of them kneeling down on the ground like that woman in the famous Kent State photograph.

Like many of those people I just wandered around in a daze,

eventually finding my way over to Central Park. Somebody was playing Beatles songs and John Lennon songs on his boom box, and we all
sang. We sang "Let It Be" and "The Long and Winding Road" and "Imagine," and whatever else we could think of, and we didn't stop for hours.

Nothing brings you closer to your neighbors more quickly than a
shared moment of tragedy.

That was the night I became a New Yorker.

I WENT THROUGH another rite of passage about a week later when a
huge storm hit the northeast on a Saturday afternoon. One of the waiters, Dmitri, got stranded on his way back to New York City and Tom
called in sick with claims of a high fever.

For all of his manic energy, Silvano was as cool and calm as a field
general.

"OK, Pino," he quacked as he hung up the phone with Tom. "I
guess it's you and me tonight."

We quickly drew up a simple plan for the evening: Silvano would
greet customers and take orders, and I would do *everything* else. It was
a reprisal of my role in my uncle's restaurant, although on a smaller
scale. We began welcoming diners at six thirty, and it was instant pan-
demonium. I spent the next seven hours uncorking wine bottles, shut-
tling dishes from the hot line to the tables, and then hustling the dirty
dishes from the tables to the dishwasher; I offered parmesan and black
pepper for people's pasta, made them espressos and cappuccinos, and
poured them grappa; I wrote and totaled checks for the customers
based on Silvano's scribbled tickets and collected money; I reset tables
and even mopped up spills. I was a one-man bussing, serving, coffee-
and-drink-making, maintenance, and housekeeping crew, and I loved
every second of it.

All of this allowed Silvano to do his thing, and I must say that it
was something to behold. I was most impressed at how he managed
to lavish personal attention on every party when they needed or expected it, sometimes interrupting himself mid-sentence to pull it off.
"Tonight for the specials we have . . ." he'd be saying to one table,
pausing to acknowledge a party of four who had just walked in the

door, "Good evening, give me a second," then turning back to the table and finishing up, "roasted duck with dry vermouth."

As two A.M. approached, and he ushered the last guest out into the icy streets, Silvano locked the front door, told me to have a seat, went into the kitchen, and made two orders of tagliolini. He brought them to the table and shaved a few hundred dollars' worth of white truffles over each portion, popped open a bottle of Cristal, and we toasted our triumph; then the two of us sat there eating and reminiscing until about three o'clock in the morning. It was the first time I really got to know anything much about him as a person. I learned that certain menu anomalies, like that oyster stew or specials like breaded abalone, were remnants of his time spent training in French hotels early in his career. I also began to understand that he was enjoying a relatively new level of success, fame, and disposable income, which helped explain some of his behavior: that kind of transformation can really go to your head and make you feel infallible, hence the daytime drinking.

At the end of the evening, we divvied up the tips. My half was three hundred fifty dollars, but the money was incidental. I left knowing that I had his confidence and trust and that big things were in store for me.

THERE WAS JUST one problem: in January 1981, my visa was close to its expiration date.

Patty and I solved the crisis in the only way we knew how: by getting married. We'd been together for three years, and it seemed as if it would be the answer to so many challenges. Her office was down on Broad Street, so we met at lunchtime one day and walked over to City Hall.

The City of New York's marriage office is not a romantic place, but that didn't keep the other couples there from feeling the magic of their wedding day: they were holding hands and caressing and kissing each other. Meanwhile, Patty and I were all business, there to obtain a piece of paper and move on. We looked as if we could have been waiting to see a dentist.

It was not the way I had pictured my wedding day. I had a great deal of respect for the sanctity of marriage and ours was something of a farce. But the alternative to a visit with Manhattan's justice of the peace was an appearance before a very different judge back in Italy, so I went through with it. Because my English was still lacking, we worked out a system whereby Patty would pinch me on the side of my belly whenever I was supposed to say "Yes, I do," and that's what I did, agreeing to whatever I had to in order to remain here in America.

ANOTHER HUGE DEVELOPMENT took place that month when Delfino decided to leave Da Silvano to return to Italy. Before departing, he pointed at me and said to Silvano: "He's the only one here you can trust to do my job."

Silvano promoted me to manager, and as he was often off on some vacation, that was like being crowned the king. But even though I was now able to conduct basic transactions, such as welcoming guests and getting them to the table, in English, beyond that I still got lost in the language. Because I couldn't communicate that well, no matter what a customer would say, I would crack up as if it were the funniest thing I'd ever heard, pat them on the back, and walk away laughing. This worked, but I felt like a trained seal.

Being a lieutenant did have its advantages. Fed up with Tom's laziness, and with the growing offense he took at my now outranking him, and at the real work I made him do—even universally accepted waiter tasks such as setting tables before service—I walked up to Silvano one day and said, "him or me." Silvano's response was swift: "You're the manager; you decide." Later that same afternoon, I ordered Tom to bring some wine up from the cellar. "That's it!" he exclaimed. "I'm out of here." I just waved and said, "Bye. Bye."

As time went by, my English improved, and before I knew it, I was actually conversing with those customers who had seemed unapproachable a short while earlier. I got to know John Cassavetes very well. He was a font of cinematic knowledge, even of Italian film. He loved Fellini's *Amarcord*, also a favorite of mine, and could name all the most prominent Italian cinematographers. I often forgot he was a legend himself as I got caught up in our dialogues, two film geeks just shooting the breeze.

I also became close with Steve Tzolis and Nicola Kotsoni, budding restaurateurs who were Silvano regulars. He was a Greek immigrant who had moved to America seven or eight years before me. She was a Greek raised in England. In his forties, with salt-and-pepper hair, Steve was somebody I could relate to and also something of a role model for me: he had begun his life here mopping floors in diners, all the while squirreling away enough money to buy himself a brownstone in the 1970s. He had also studied the business enough to open a restaurant, La Gauloise. Nicola was a very slim, very fashionable woman who reminded me of a porcelain doll. They were an odd couple—he was like a bull in a china shop, and she was like china—but they worked. We became friendly, and I always enjoyed talking with them: he was very charming in his forward, Greek manner, while she was more demure. It was easy for us to converse, because socially speaking, it's a small leap from Greece to Italy. I got to know Steve and Nicola's restaurant, La Gauloise, and also spent a lot of time at One Fifth, Raoul's, and John's Pizza—rarely venturing outside the Village. With the exception of my apartment, my Manhattan ended at Fourteenth Street.

Over the rest of that winter, a sort of symbiotic bond developed between me and Silvano, partly because of the long hours we shared and partly because of our common Italian heritage. In time, we could communicate a lot with just a look, or a word. We knew that when we spoke Italian to each other our customers just tuned us out, so that's how we would talk about the less favorable ones. There was one guy, this garmento who was a real cheapskate: he'd tell us he'd seen a wine for thirty dollars less *just yesterday* at another restaurant, and insist that we sell it to him for the lower price. His worst offense was that when he ordered specials featuring truffles, he'd manipulate your hand as you sliced them, forcing you to give him extra. As a result, Silvano and I omitted any truffle specials when we announced the day's offerings at his table. We longed to have some fun at his expense, and to talk about him right in front of his face. But the Italian word for cheap, *tirchio*, wasn't amusing enough, so we took the word *cheap* and

Italianized it, saying *cippone* right in front of him. Or this old dandy who used to come in with this young, flirtatious girl. We knew that there was no way, beyond the financial, that he could possibly please her, so we'd refer to him as the *cornuto*, which means "cuckold." One night, the girl heard us talking and in her perky little voice, she tugged on Silvano's vest and said, "What does *cornuto* mean?"

Silvano didn't miss a beat: he stole a quick glance at me, winked, and looked back at her, taking her hand in his. "It means you, darling," he said, resting her hand back on the table as we all laughed.

By that spring, Silvano and I were like partners, or brothers even. We did everything together. He was as obsessive about his work as I was about the restaurant. In the morning, I'd be there early, checking on the kitchen and getting the dining room ready for lunch, and he'd come in with beautiful flowers from the market. We'd go over every last detail together: what deliveries had come in and hadn't, who was going to sit at which table, and on and on.

To be honest, it wasn't just the two of us. There was a third participant in our mornings: a bottle. At first, we'd uncork a bottle of Brunello around eleven o'clock and polish off half of it by lunch, then we'd knock back some espressos for a jolt of energy. In time, we upgraded to a bottle of Delamain Pale and Dry cognac, sometimes paired with Cristal or Dom Pérignon. It was as much a part of our morning as coffee is for most people.

Silvano would go home for his customary nap after lunch service, we'd work dinner together, then we'd have dinner ourselves around eleven o'clock. By then, we could have split a bottle of wine, a bottle of cognac, and a bottle of champagne. That kind of abandon would have ruined some people, but it just made the day more entertaining for us.

As we grew closer, I learned that Silvano could actually be quite generous in his own way, mostly having to do with food. For example, if truffles were in season and he had some in the house, we'd eat them every night after service, shaving them over pasta or risotto, just as we had after our bonding moment in December. Or, in the springtime, he'd whisper in my ear during dinner service, telling me that we were going to have shad roe, and then after the last customer was gone, he'd go into the kitchen himself and sear it up with lemon, butter, and white wine. By the same token, he stimulated my taste nostalgia, and sometimes I'd say to him, "I'm going to make you something *you* never had before." After service *I'd* go into the kitchen and come out with tuna livornese with a sauce of tomatoes, capers, onions, and anchovies, or spaghetti AOP, a dish I'd been making for years; the name stands for *aglio, olio, e peperoncino* or garlic, oil, and pepper flakes. I also sometimes make it with a splash of tomato sauce, or *pomodoro*, and call it spaghetti AOPP.

I even came to love some of the less Italian, more idiosyncratic dishes he cooked, like that duck with dry vermouth, even though I still have no idea where he came up with that one.

Somehow, even after eating and drinking like this, we still had energy to burn. We'd go drinking at One Fifth, or we'd go to Heartbreak, a nightclub on Varick Street, and dance until our legs felt like they'd give out, often with customers who we'd run into there. Sometimes, we'd end up in his apartment, hanging out and drinking almost until sunrise, which sounds like compulsive socializing but was actually a well-disguised form of workaholism because for the most part we talked about the restaurant, kicking around ideas for specials, talking about how to handle certain customers, chewing over issues with the cooks, and so on. Eventually, when I began to feel my eyelids grow heavy, I'd stumble out into the street, hail a cab, and head home up Sixth Avenue.

Of course, none of this was good for my marriage. Da Silvano became my life and I wanted it to. I found myself with a place to go where I didn't have to think about my problems, my status in Italy, or earning a living. I was making lots of money, and every day I learned something new. But I was working six days a week, almost always doing double shifts, and it was perfectly normal for me to leave home at ten A.M. and not return until well after midnight, stinking of liquor and nicotine.

And there was something else, or rather *somebody* else. One night that February, a table of six was having dinner at Da Silvano and I found myself unable to take my eyes off of one of them: a slender, dark-haired woman dressed in white. I thought that she was the most gorgeous woman I'd ever seen. As their dinner wrapped up, my post-service meal was just beginning, and I asked her to sit with me. After much giggling and teasing from her friends, she came over to my table and sat down. For the longest time, I just stared at her. I think I made her uncomfortable, between my broken English and the way I was looking at her. What can I say? She brought out the man in me. I was so smitten that I blurted out the stupidest thing: "I want for you to be all mine," I said, and she stared at me for a moment and then smiled sweetly.

Her name was Jessie and she was a New Orleans native who was earning a license to work in a salon and had modeled for a while in the Garment District. I didn't wear a wedding ring, so when I asked her out, she had no reason to decline. We saw each other two times and it was going well, but when I told her I was married, she said that she didn't want to see me anymore. I told her it wasn't working out, but she still wouldn't see me again, and just like that she was gone.

IN TIME, MY other "marriage" began to fray as well.

When I first took over for Delfino it was like a gift for Silvano. He had always had to be at the restaurant all the time, but now he could get away. And he did, for two weeks, then three weeks at a time.

At first, I didn't mind. I took more and more liberties: with his blessing, I started making a mark on the menu, like introducing my mother's *pasticcio di Dante*, yellow and red peppers, sliced and wilted with olive oil and garlic, then sprinkled with capers and anchovy fillets and baked, which we served on its own as an appetizer or as a side to fish. I also came up with some original ideas: to show American diners that not all Italian sauces involved tomatoes, I made a veal ragù with bacon, red onion, celery, garlic, and carrots, but no tomato. I would almost dare diners to order it, by saying, "You ever tried a meat sauce with no tomato?"

But you know what they say: when the cat's away, the mouse will play. And I did play. Not in a devious way, but I was so in my element by then. I was speaking better English and was becoming friends with a lot of our customers, such as the art dealer Leo Castelli, and artists such as Julian Schnabel, Francesco Clemente, Jean-Michel Basquiat, and Andy Warhol.

My background in theater gave me a natural bond with other customers, such as the producer David Field or the director Michael Cimino, and with Cassevettes, with whom I was on a first-name basis by then. Cassavetes began showing up with his wife, Gena Rowlands, and actors from his films, including Peter Falk and Ben Gazzara, and I'd find myself hanging out at their table, which produced some of my favorite moments. Their conversations always began somewhat seriously, but as soon as the wine started to flow, they'd get pretty silly. One night they got so drunk that Cassavetes began challenging Gena Rowlands that she couldn't stand up. She went him one better, removing her shoes, stepping up onto the table, and performing an improvised flamenco dance to the applause of me and the few lingering customers.

Sometimes, if friends of mine came in late, I'd send the kitchen guys home and cook for them myself, treating the dining room like my own little home away from home. In 1981, Martin Scorsese was shooting his film *The King of Comedy* in New York, and David Field would often come in around closing time with the stars of the movie: Jerry Lewis, Sandra Bernhard, and Robert De Niro. I dismissed the cooks home, keeping just a dishwasher to help out. When they arrived, I'd have one table set up in the dining room with the wine already uncorked, and water boiling in the back, ready for me to make pasta. As they nibbled on chicken liver *crostini*, aged sausage, and fried sage, I finally got a chance to converse a little with De Niro, but we didn't talk movies; instead he wanted to talk about Italian food, which made sense because a few years later, he'd go on to open Tribeca Grill, Nobu, and other places.

Not that I could always have the run of the place. As Silvano took more and more leisure time away from the restaurant, he began leaving me with his father—a diminutive man, rather like my father in stature—and his mother—also short, with wavy hair, glasses, and a round face that reminded me of an owl—to look over me.

The first time he did it, he left me with them for two or three weeks. His father would come to me all the time, complaining because one employee was frequently late, or because he thought another one was stealing, not that he had any proof. It was driving me crazy and so when Silvano returned, I told him, "I don't mind you being away, but don't leave me with two owls sitting on top of me every day."

That spring, I asked him if he was going to bring them back during his summer vacation.

"Yes, why?"

"It's not going to work."

"Don't worry about it. I'll talk to them." It reminded me of my problems with the waiter, Tom. Silvano really didn't like confrontations, and he actually preferred to let problems fester.

"You should worry about it," I said, "because eventually I'm going to quit and then you're going to have to work every day."

This wasn't the only reason things were strained between us. Silvano came to resent me as customers began treating us as equals. It got so I didn't like being around when he was there. I was beginning to feel a sense of ownership, even though I wasn't the owner. When he returned from vacations, customers would ask him how his trip was, then turn to me and ask me about how things were at the restaurant, what the specials were, and so on. To reclaim his territory, he began spending more and more time on the service floor, and by the spring of 1982 we spent almost no time together in the wee hours; he'd head off into the night with his friends and I'd go my way with mine.

When he decided to expand and take over the room next door, I thought he was selling out. In the original place, there was no such thing as a bad seat. Now there were tables right next to the bathroom. It was his place and that's how he wanted it, but I thought it showed really poor taste and felt I had to say something. He didn't want to hear it from me; whenever I brought it up, he'd just walk away.

Come the summer, Silvano took off for another vacation, and I was again under the watchful eyes of the owls.

One Friday night we were packed, and Silvano's father came over to me and again told me that one of the employees was stealing. I said, "If you do not get off my back I am going to hang you on the coat rack."

He didn't know when to stop. Finally, I couldn't take it any more. I went to the cash register and took my salary and left.

It was only seven fifteen or seven thirty. Early in the night. A terrible thing to do to a restaurant, but I had had it.

I stormed up Sixth Avenue in a state of rage. Trying to calm my nerves, I stopped near Waverly Street and watched some guys playing basketball, but it was no use. I was shaking with anger. I looked around at the people enjoying the summer evening, sitting on benches or strolling along. I felt as alienated as I had on the day I arrived.

I knew that there was no way back, that I'd never hear from Silvano.

Once again, I saw myself in a movie moment, the final scene of *Three Days of the Condor*, in which Robert Redford, having crossed the CIA, has a few final words with the intelligence agent played by Cliff Robertson before walking off into a life of isolation, about to disappear into the crowd, absorbed by the city. And so I disappeared, headed back to my apartment, with no idea what I'd do next.

INTERLUDE

PINO'S DESCRIPTION *of his mastery of the English language needs a slight clarification because while Pino is fluent in English, he still, nearly thirty years after his arrival in the United States, speaks it with a thick Italian accent. It's also, perhaps because he spent so many of his formative years here with cooks, liberally seasoned with four-letter words. This is especially true when he's angry, which usually causes him to pile on the profanity, often in a nonsensical way. If discussing, say, an incompetent shoe salesman, he might say, "I don't know what his problem is, probably that he been fucked so many times he forgot what's a loafer and what's his asshole."*

I ask Pino about this.

"It used to be worse," he says. "Back at Silvano, I'd often begin sentences with shit *or* fuck. *Delfino would say, 'Pino, we're opening for dinner in five minutes,' and I'd say back, 'Fuck! OK. No problem.' I wasn't upset about anything, I just liked those words. I'd even come in in the morning and say 'What the fuck' instead of 'What's up?' but in time I toned it down."*

Pino has also maintained some idiosyncrasies that have yet to be corrected; for example, he says never *when he means* ever, *as in "that was the stupidest meal I never ate in my life."*

I ask him about this, too, and he just shrugs.

"It hasn't changed by now, it's not gonna change," he says. "Plus, I think it sounds better that way."

Perhaps this is something else Pino learned from Silvano: the inherent value and attraction of remaining a little different. In the brief time I worked with Silvano on his book, I found the man was so discombobulated that I couldn't reconcile his persona and his success. It was so incongruous that I began to entertain fantasies that it was all a brilliant put-on. I half expected him to lean in one day and whisper to me in perfect, refined English: "You know it's all just an act, right? Nobody could live here this long and still speak the way I do." Then it dawned on me that, of course, that reverse Esperanto is one reason for Silvano's celebrity: in a city where hundreds of languages are spoken, he speaks one that nobody has ever heard before.

Because of all of the animosity they display toward one another in the press, and that Pino professes for Silvano in person, it was a little jarring to me one day while we were working on this book when Pino told me that he had been walking up Sixth Avenue from SoHo and had heard a familiar quacking voice behind him.

"Pino! Pino!"

It was Silvano, and the two had engaged in a spontaneous game of catch-up, centered on injuries: Pino had been wearing a brace to protect a foot he had injured playing basketball, and Silvano loves nothing more than talking about his bum knee and all the medications he's tried for relief. Neither man is getting any younger, it seems, and their ability to kibitz on the street is as good a bit of evidence as you'll ever see that time heals all wounds; though when I comment on how much Pino learned from Silvano, he's quick to qualify.

"Don't forget about my uncle, and my mother. And remember, Silvano has a special talent for running that little place of his; you put him in some of my dining rooms, even this place . . ." Pino says, gesturing at the Centolire dining room, "and he'd be lost."

Despite their recent run-in, Pino and Silvano aren't about to start speaking with any regularity. But I've often wondered if Silvano has a grudging admiration for Pino, a paternal pride in the busboy who became a restaurant emperor, the same way his long-lost professional son secretly admires the man who taught him so much. I could pick up the phone and ask him, I suppose, but it's very much in keeping with their relationship to leave some mystery around its edges.

And, besides, Silvano is just too damn hard to understand.

FIVE

Start Spreading the News

At Silvano's, I had been treated to a preview of what life could become, *had* become for a time; but with no stage on which to play it out, it was fast becoming just a memory.

I was also alone with my thoughts again all day, thrust right back into that feeling of exile I'd had when I had first arrived here. The problem, of course, was that I was still a fugitive. Returning to Italy was not an option, at least not until my spat with the army was resolved, and so I had no choice but to call on the only trade I had learned since arriving in New York. I milked my network of downtown restaurant friends and found a job at Zinno, an Italian place on Thirteenth Street. The restaurant, entered by walking down three steps from street level, had a long bar, typical of the 1980s, that was almost like a diving board into the main dining room beyond.

Zinno was just up the street from Da Silvano, but I might as well have been on another planet. Just a few weeks earlier, as Silvano's de facto partner, I had been on the verge of a certain type of celebrity. Now I was just another waiter in a uniform—worse, it was a tuxedo. Is this it for me? I thought. Am I just going to be another immigrant working in another Italian restaurant, doomed to live in the shadows, emerging just long enough to shower snowy parmesan on people's pasta or present them with their check? Am I going to become another one of the Body Snatchers like Oreste and Claudio?

Zinno did a brisk and steady business, but it seemed too big and impersonal; to me, it couldn't make up its mind about what it wanted to be. Was it a restaurant, a lounge, or a jazz club? It was an instructive counterpoint to Da Silvano, which had such a well-defined personality. Watching hundreds of people come and go through the doors each night, an obvious conclusion occurred to me: *If this place can succeed*, I thought, *then I'm sure I could open a successful place myself.*

With that spark of inspiration, I began imagining the kind of restaurant I'd open if given the chance, and a vision began to come together in my mind. I wanted to do a very modern trattoria, which did not exist in New York City at the time, a response to that place I'd been to in Little Italy and all those other joints with red-and-white checkered tablecloths and straw-covered wine bottles that couldn't be farther from *my* Italy. I wanted it to be like the authentic Italian cousin who comes to visit his American relatives and shows them what a *real* Italian is, with his easy style—laid-back, cool, and sexy.

I also thought about the food. Most of the Italian restaurants in New York were divided into Northern Italian and Southern Italian, but nobody seemed to have heard of the *regions* and their foods—the succulent roasted lamb of Lazio, the light-as-air pesto of Liguria, the risotto with balsamic vinegar of Emilia-Romagna. Being a creature of Tuscany I wanted to celebrate Tuscan food, but in a very personal way, translating the cuisine I had grown up on and had adapted through my own experiences in Rome and New York.

I might have only built and operated this unnamed place in my mind, but one night Steve and Nicola, my old restaurateur pals from Da Silvano, showed up at Zinno looking for me. We got to talking and after a few minutes, Steve leaned in close and whispered in my ear: "So, listen, there is this guy who has a restaurant on Tenth Street. I don't know if you want to get into it, but I think that the three of us should go look at it. I think it would be a wonderful idea for us to do an Italian restaurant together."

This was a very big moment, but it also seemed somehow expected. When Steve and Nicola walked in the door that night, there was something in the air, an immediate understanding that they had come to find me. I always knew that they, like many others, thought that I was a big part of Da Silvano's success. Ironically, while it was the food that I was most interested in, I'd never cooked for Steve and Nicola; they saw me as a front-of-the-house commodity they believed could draw and maintain a following.

We made a date to meet at 32 East Tenth Street. The restaurant that currently occupied the space was some kind of nightmare of a Greek-Sicilian winter garden, an elongated space so packed with fountains and plants that it might have been mistaken for a nursery. And right in the middle of the dining room was a staircase that ran right into the ceiling. A stairway to nowhere. Talk about a metaphor.

Something most restaurateurs I know pride themselves on is that, when presented with a potential space, they can swiftly process all the necessary information: Are the shape and dimensions appealing? How's the natural light? About how many tables and chairs can be installed? How much renovation will be required? Does the bar need to be moved, or walls put up or demolished?

Sure enough, as we walked around the space, I went into an almost clairvoyant trance. I became unaware of Steve and Nicola, and the details of the restaurant faded away. I was walking in a raw space, like a black-box theater. The elements of my restaurant began to materialize, one after the other: There would be a mahogany bar where the stairway had been. I saw terra-cotta tiles underfoot and dark wooden beams running along the ceiling. The last thing I saw was the restaurant in the hours before dinner service. I visualized myself opening floor-to-ceiling mahogany doors out onto the sidewalk, where there would be cafe tables, and the whole front dining room would feel as if it were outside. For a moment I saw the cafe from across the street: I pictured a beautiful green awning stretched over the tables, the quintessential, welcoming color that you see outside so many trattorias in Tuscany.

It looked like a canteen, and a name popped into my head. *Il Cantinaro*, meaning the guy who runs the canteen. But I didn't like the sound of it—it had no poetry—and right away it became Il Cantinori, which isn't really a word, but which made a crazy kind of sense to me—the same way my mother's naming of dishes like *uova alla francesina* made sense—the sound of it, an idyllic term to describe a Tuscan in New York who would operate a canteen and offer you food.

By the time I eased out of the trance, Il Cantinori was so well de-fined for me that I could've begun building it out right then and there. I turned to Steve and said, "I got it in my head. This is going to be a great restaurant." He and Nicola smiled and we discussed how to make it happen. As the one experienced in real estate, and blessed with the checkbook, Steve would take charge of securing the space. I told him that, despite my lack of experience, I was sure I could super-vise the design and construction and bring it in for a relatively low budget. We all shook hands and decided to move forward.

That handshake was our contract. Steve was a man of his word and I stood behind mine, and though we didn't hammer out an official deal until after the restaurant opened, we never had any problems. We both assumed our roles and flourished in them: he put up $300,000 (and ended up doing more than leasing the space; he went ahead and *bought* the building), and I instantly became a general contractor. I had never GC'd anything, much less a restaurant, but my self-confidence was enough for my partners to trust me to get the job done. This was also a much different time in the restaurant business: people didn't invest millions of dollars in the kinds of gargantuan, high-concept monstrosities they build today. With the exception of Al-ice Waters and Wolfgang Puck on the West Coast, and a few people like Jonathan Waxman of Jams and Chanterelle's David Waltuck, and a few legendary French masters such as André Soltner at Lutèce, here in New York, there wasn't such a thing as a star chef. It was the quiet before the big bang that was about to take place in the restaurant busi-ness, and for a relatively low sum of money and some real passion for the work, you could break into the still-unglamorous profession, no questions asked.

NEXT THING I knew I was in the restaurant business. Or perhaps I should say that I was in the *construction* business; I had tiles in my hands and dust on my clothing and bolted out into the streets of New York every morning excited about getting downtown and realizing the dream of Il Cantinori. The first order of business was to find a way to incorporate what I had come to think of as the holy trinity of Italian style: terra-cotta, stucco, and dark wooden beams, all of which have since become common in Italian restaurants here, but at the time were unique. As I reminisced about home, these three things seemed to be everywhere: in the houses my family lived in, in local schools and restaurants, and even in the churches. The only thing that seemed more iconic to me was the omnipresent cypress trees that dot the hills and highways of Tuscany, but even if I could have afforded it, there was no way I could have gotten one of those into the tiny space.

I came to think of my new role as the director of Il Cantinori, shaping and bringing to life a vision for my customers. It was a great feeling, a feeling of working and producing, of making something from almost nothing, of taking an idea, an abstract idea in many ways, and giving it life.

The easiest effect to achieve was the terra-cotta tiles, which you could simply purchase, but the others required more creative thinking. An important ally was woodworker Bob Biondi, a real-life Geppetto in his puffy white shirts and overalls, who was a godsend to us. Bob had a gravelly voice and an unfiltered cigarette perpetually dangling from the corner of his mouth, but he was also warm and dedicated to any project he signed on to. I explained to him the wood beams I wanted to see hovering over the dining room: rough around the edges, like railroad ties; dark, almost black, like chestnuts; and with a farmhouse imperfection. Bob and I found a guy who knew how to fuse plywood together and then chop the edges to make them deliberately imperfect, and then ash and stain them.

Now I was dreaming of rough stucco walls, also with the same coarse finish you might find in a Tuscan farmhouse. But craftsmen with expertise in the application of stucco proved impossible to find in Manhattan; it wasn't just a matter of going to the local taverna and finding the guy with dried stucco on his pants. Eventually, somebody told me about the technology used for jails, where they shoot the material out of a pressurized pump; it comes out in blobs like fire extinguisher foam, but when it dries it has a rough surface. I found and enlisted a company that specialized in prison construction, and they said they could give me just what I was looking for. They also told me that because it was primarily an acoustic material it would cushion the vibrations that bounced around the room. I replied the way any sane restaurateur would: "Good!"

Having pulled off my stylistic trifecta, I decided I had to acknowledge in some fashion that Il Cantinori was a New York restaurant. I hired a talented lighting consultant named Bill Schwinghammer, who found us beautiful geometric sconces and hanging lights. They gave the room a modern smartness that said this is a New York restaurant, proud to be here—just like I was.

Working on the build-out was also a validating experience of New York, of America: I got to meet an Italian-American mason, an Italian cabinetmaker, a Greek plumber, and an Irish electrician. I loved all the different guys I'd come into contact with from all these different places. I enjoyed speaking Italian with the Italians, but my English was good enough by then that I could talk to anybody from anywhere: If I had to tell the construction guys something, I'd throw out my chest and say "fuck" a lot. If I had to say something to the Mexican workers, I'd always begin with "*mira*" (look). Instead of saying "Good morning" when I walked in at the start of each day, I began saying, in perfect New York-ese, "How ya doin'?" I probably seemed a little silly sometimes, but I was just making my best effort to fit in.

Despite the fun I was having, I was also living a bit of a double life. I had amassed a small savings, but I didn't want to deplete it. So, I was overseeing construction at Il Cantinori by day, then cleaning up, putting on a tux, and walking over to Zinno by night.

Eventually, I decided I had to say something to the guys at Zinno.

"I'm going to be opening a restaurant," I told the manager. "It's months away, and I promise you I am not going to take anyone away from here."

The manager thanked me for telling him and then, of course, a few days later called to tell me that the owners found the situation too close for comfort, and fired me.

It was the first of many lessons I'd learn in the coming years. I had tried to be straight with the guy, to operate in good faith, but I saw that this was what people meant by separating business relationships from personal relationships.

So much for honesty, I thought.

BY OCTOBER, THE gestation of Il Cantinori was nearly complete. I spent every waking moment there, conferring with craftsmen and making final design decisions.

Once the kitchen was completed, I also began planning my first menus, focusing as we did back home on seasonality and combining the food I had grown up on with influences I'd amassed in my various homes since then. For about a week I locked myself in the kitchen and cooked day and night, trying to imagine which of the dishes I'd known for years would be most welcome by New York palates tasting them for perhaps the first time. I had such a hard time whittling the list down that I decided that the offerings would change daily, so instead of a fixed menu, my goal was to define a repertoire that could be supplemented by specials. Of course, there would taken-for-granted dishes like chicken liver *crostini, ribollita,* and *pappa al pomodoro.* But there would also be Florentine-style veal tripe and *calamari in zimino* (a stewed dish intended to show people an alternative to the ubiquitous fried version). For pasta, I'd have *rigatoni alla buttera* with hot and sweet sausage, peas, and a touch of tomato and cream; penne with veal ragù; and *ravioli della fattoressa,* a Florentine derivation of a Piedmontese pasta featuring a single, large raviolo built around a nest of spinach and egg yolk. When the weather got cold, I planned to offer *stracotto* (Tuscan pot roast) and game such as venison, wild boar, hare, squab, and partridge.

To make a statement as soon as customers entered, I procured a long hutch, positioned it near the door, and devised a roster of prepared vegetable dishes that would be arranged there and served at room temperature, such as stuffed yellow and red peppers; baked tomatoes stuffed with rice and mozzarella; fried artichokes; eggplant marinated in mint, garlic, and red wine vinaigrette; and *funghetto*-style mushrooms slowly braised in tomato sauce and oregano. The idea was that the instant you entered Il Cantinori, you would leave New York behind:

you'd smell the garlic and rosemary from the vegetable display and hear opera on the sound system. By the time you sat down and were handed a menu written in Italian and your waiter came over and said "*buona sera,*" you would be transported to another place.

I wasn't the only person taken with the world that was materializing in the dining room. One day, a young Jewish New Yorker named Jack Weiss, with a broad forehead, pushed-back hair, and deep love of his motorcycle, wandered in, enticed by the Italian setting. I hired him to be our bartender and we became fast friends; he'd often come in during the final weeks of preparation to lend a hand, even though we weren't paying him yet.

Though he was one of our first employees, I considered him our first customer: if others responded with his level of enthusiasm, we had a hit on our hands.

I WAS COMPLETELY immersed in Il Cantinori, and so it was a bit jarring when I came home one night to find a note from Patty on the kitchen table: *Call Your Lawyer,* it said, meaning my attorney in Italy, the one who had been trying for years to resolve my conscription beef with the army. It was a poignant reminder of what my marriage had become; Patty was just the person asleep in the bed when I came home at night, and the ghost who had already departed when I woke up the next morning.

In addition to our incompatible work schedules, there was another reason I had drifted away from her: it wasn't her fault, but Patty was a remnant of what I was coming to think of as my old life. You'd think I'd have wanted to be put in mind of Italy, but she only reminded me of those last tormented days in Rome, the flight to the United States, and my first days here. As a result, I tried to zone her out just as I tried to shut out my homesickness. She deserved better than my resentment, but that's all I had for her.

The next day, I called the lawyer.

"Pino, we won the case!" he told me. "You can come home."

"OK." I said. "I'll call you tomorrow."

"When are you coming back?" he asked.

"I don't know. I'll call you tomorrow."

I hung up and stood there listening to the sounds of traffic through the open living room window. This was the news I had been waiting three years for. But as I heard it, I realized that it came from a world that I didn't belong in anymore. I had no idea what to do, so I did what any good New Yorker, even a relatively new one, might do at such a time: I took a walk.

I walked down Third Avenue all the way to Tenth Street. As I did, I really started to look intensely at what was going on around me. I appreciated more than ever the familiar scene you see every day in Manhattan if you live here. The dynamic, the people. It had become so close to me. I felt the past trying to pull me back, but the present, New York, was even more powerful. Details I had never really noticed seemed profound right then, like the smells of New York City in the late summer, even the hot tar of the streets and the exhaust from the cars; it all felt somehow more familiar than Italy, even though I'd only been here about three years.

I arrived at Tenth Street and started walking west along the north side. Like most streets in the city, Tenth changes character every few blocks. Right about when you arrive on the block where Il Cantinori is, it's as pretty as Greenwich Village gets: a tree-lined relic of old New York, with little boutiques and brownstones. And on a September morning like that one, there's often a gentle breeze that feels more like it's coming in off the ocean rather than from the Hudson River.

I got there and one of the guys was putting up that green awning that I had always had in my mind, stretching it tight across the storefront. The last piece was in place; Il Cantinori had come to life.

"Here I am," I said to myself in English. "I am home."

I clapped my hands together, then crossed the street and walked into Il Cantinori and got down to work for the day.

IN MID-OCTOBER, MY jubilation was briefly interrupted when two hoods—middle-aged guys in blue jeans and leather jackets—showed up at the restaurant in the middle of the morning.

"Can I help you?" I asked.

"Yeah," one of them said. "We're here to install a cigarette machine."

"I didn't order one."

"I know," said the other.

"I don't want it."

Ignoring me, they went back out to their truck and returned, hauling the machine by its base. They deposited the rogue dispenser in the corner, and one of them looked at me and said, "It'd be in your best interest to keep this." Then they left.

I might have come from Italy, but I was too naïve to know that these guys were likely low-level wise guys and made a practice of installing cigarette machines in every new restaurant in the area. So, as soon as they left, I dragged it outside and put it in the middle of Tenth Street to be battered by passing cars. It was probably a stupid thing to do, but I had worked too hard to be pushed around in my own place. It's always been a belief of mine that once you start taking your pants down for people, you never stop.

It was also, let's be honest, the Vito Corleone moment I'd always craved. Lucky for me, they never came back.

WE OPENED IL Cantinori on October 23, 1983.

It was one of the biggest nights of my life. I took one last walkthrough, stepping out to the sidewalk, then back in through the mahogany doors. All of those elements I'd visualized were right there: the stucco walls to the right, the country hutch, two massive mahogany columns in the center of the dining room, lending it a modern touch, and the triangular brass sconces on the walls. The walls were also hung with photographs of iconic Tuscan images, mostly sepia-toned portraits of turn-of-the-century farmers. Above them a long rake, a spade, a scythe, and other agricultural tools were affixed artfully to the wall. At a corner of the bar, in a huge terra-cotta planter, Nicola had designed a mammoth flower arrangement that reached all the way up to the ceiling. All of this was set to music pouring out of the overhead speakers: I played nothing but Puccini and Verdi and Bellini in our first days.

I might have been standing in Florence, or in the countryside south of the city, and for a moment I actually felt as if I could turn around and instead of looking out on East Tenth Street, I'd suddenly find the cobblestone of an ancient Italian *via* stretched out before me.

Nostalgia gave way to melancholy, but there was no time for either because there was too much work to be done: there was just me, Steve, Nicola, and two waiters on the service floor. Behind the bar was Jack Weiss, and in the kitchen was a guy named Antonio Cinardi, who I had hired away from Silvano's. (He was the only guy I took from Silvano, although somehow a rumor spread that I stole the entire kitchen crew, which I always thought was funny because that would have only been two more people.) He was a grousing, grumpy, antisocial character, but he had the most important trait in a cook: consistency. Once you showed him how to make a dish, he could produce clones, over and over, ad infinitum, which allowed me to be in the dining room as much as I wanted, or needed, to be at any given time.

There's a great divide between the opening night of a restaurant for the owner and for the people of New York City. As big as the occasion was for me, it was just one more story playing out in the universe of Manhattan, and the masses were unaware of our arrival, and so our first hours were very slow. Steve spent his time pacing in the dining room, or talking to Jack, while Nicola tended to the phones and other business. Whenever people walked by, and especially when they looked in, we all paused expectantly, hoping that they'd venture inside.

Although we had two waiters, when the first guests—a young couple from across the street—finally showed up, Steve, Nicola, and I all greeted them personally, and I served them myself. I was so eager to welcome visitors into the restaurant, into this world I had created, and to share the food with them. After my three years in New York, Il Cantinori was finally my chance to express myself, and the room and the menu were my media. I told them about the dishes, took their order, went into the kitchen and got their food ready myself, then delivered it to the table.

I lavished the same level of attention on the other guests who came in that night. We only served twelve people and took in about six hundred dollars, but I didn't care: I was in heaven.

Over the next week, there was an ebb and flow as our business was subjected to all kinds of factors over which we had no control. Sure, word of mouth delivered people to our door, and some became regulars, but much of our success from night to night was based on good, old-fashioned foot traffic, on how many people happened to walk by while hungry and take a chance on the new place in the neighborhood. And so one night we would do thirty dinners, and the next we'd do fifteen, and so on.

Even our worst night was a validation of the concept to me, but Steve—a more seasoned businessman with another restaurant in his portfolio—was focused on the bottom line. The two of us couldn't have been more different: I had about fifty dollars to my name, so any income was good news. He had sunk a few hundred thousand dollars into this place and wanted to recoup his investment, pronto. Once in a while, I would perceive that he was feeling tense, and I knew he'd be more stressed at the end of the night, when he saw the numbers. I'd see him at the corner of the bar, smoking a cigarette and talking to Nicola, and I'd decide to seduce him. I'd go in the kitchen and make three or four dishes I knew he'd like—maybe an artichoke salad, *rigatoni alla buttera*, and a piece of fish—and bring it out, pop a bottle of wine, and say, "Let's have dinner!" We'd sit there together and have a laugh and kill the bottle and bury the anguish of the present with a dream of future success.

To ramp up revenues, we decided to open for lunch, but we did less business the first day than we had for our first dinner, as just eight people showed up. For some reason lunch didn't produce the same volume or number of regulars as dinner, although there was one customer who came in quite often: an older bald man with a taste for classic, almost preppy, attire and bow ties, and a bearing and disposition that reminded me of Alfred Hitchcock. He sometimes dined alone, and he took a great interest in everything we did: he listened with perfect attention as I described the specials, and his focus on the food itself was almost religious, as if he were communing with it. I had no idea who he was, but it was reassuring to have such a devoted and appreciative customer.

Our fits and starts never got me down. I just knew we were doing something that was going to catch on. And even on our worst days, I took great pleasure in visiting the local markets—like Balducci's on Sixth Avenue, which was at the peak of its powers then—and improvising some dishes for the menu. I got to know Andy Balducci, who had been a customer at Da Silvano, and would ask him to help me find hard-to-come-by ingredients such as trevigiano, the bitter red chicory. He almost always come through, and he became a major asset to me.

As more and more people came to the restaurant, there was a growing buzz in the dining room. Many customers became regulars, returning with friends who in turn became regulars as well. We were beginning to live up to our name, becoming a little canteen for the neighborhood. After a month or so, we were taking in between twenty and thirty thousand dollars per week, which wasn't a lot, but at least it was a step in the right direction.

Even so, the fits and starts were becoming frustrating even to me. It had been more than a year since I had left Silvano, and though I heard on the grapevine that he believed I was siphoning off his clientele, I was too naïve in those days to have even been able to do such a thing. I had left Silvano's so quickly that it hadn't even occurred to me to copy down all the customers' phone numbers. And besides, I wanted to make it on my own. I can't honestly say that I would be so charitable today, but back then, I was still very idealistic.

Ironically, it was our least well-attended meal that saved us. I had developed a causal rapport with that mystery man, the one who reminded me of Alfred Hitchcock, even though we didn't talk about much more than the food itself. After he had visited several times I decided that it was time we met, so I extended my hand and introduced myself.

"I'm James Beard," he said.

Of course! James Beard, as you might know, was one of the most influential figures in food culture in the United States. His home, on West Twelfth Street, has become the headquarters of a foundation that bears his name.

He sized me up for a moment, then smiled broadly.

"We have got to help you," he said. "You have got to be *known*."

I didn't quite understand what he meant by that until one day, not long after, when he showed up for lunch with a woman I placed in her late thirties with dark hair and a friendly, if professional, demeanor. She loved the originality of the food, and she returned several times. He never introduced her by name, but I could tell that she was going to be the way in which I was helped. And when the *New York Times* called to arrange a photo, I realized that she was Marian Burros, the restaurant critic for the *Times*, and that there was a review in the offing.

A restaurant review in the *Times* in those days was a make-or-break moment in the life of a new establishment. *New York* magazine was a close second, but there was nothing like the power of the city's major daily paper to confer success or quicken doomsday for budding restaurateurs. There was no Internet, so newspapers were still in all their traditional glory. I guess it's a good thing that the *Times* has a stand-alone dining section now, but when it came along it ended one of the great traditions of New York City dining: that Friday restaurant review. It used to really stand out, on the last page of the *Living* section, a weekly event for people who cared about food and dining.

Christmas fell on a Sunday that year, and the Friday prior, December 23, was the day that our review was scheduled to run. So late Thursday night, Steve, Nicola, and I went to Zinno, the place where we had first begun talking about Il Cantinori, and had some drinks at the long bar; then we got into Steve's car and drove down to a little international newsstand at the corner of Eighth Street and Sixth Avenue, where I hopped out and bought the early edition of Friday's paper. Back in the car, we cracked open the *Times* and there, on the last inside page of the *Living* section, was our review. The first thing anybody looks at is the stars, and we had two of them, which was a big deal back then because very few restaurants had three stars, and even fewer had four.

It was a great review, a real acknowledgment of everything I was trying to do. When Marian described a "hearty soup of beautifully cooked beans with delicious chunks of crusty Tuscan bread seasoned with garlic and olive oil" as "outstanding," I thought fondly of my mother and how proud she would be of this place we had created.

The funny thing was that because of the holiday, we were going to be closed for the next three days, so we had to enjoy our euphoria in private and wait until after the weekend for the nonstop ringing of the telephone that typically followed a positive *Times* review.

THE REVIEW CHANGED everything: within weeks, all those great people I had met at Da Silvano found their way to our door and it was like the best of my old times and the best of the new. Next thing I knew, the restaurant was being frequented by all those art-world icons like Jean-Michel Basquiat, Francesco Clemente, Robert Mapplethorpe, and Leo Castelli, who lived right down the block. Andy Warhol also become a regular. People make fun of his mannerisms now, the way he dressed and the soft way he spoke, but I just found him real. And he found me interesting, too: "I love your accent," he'd whisper to me in that wonder-filled, little-boy voice of his. "Tell me the specials." And then I'd start talking and he'd close his eyes and sway his head as if he were listening to a piece of music for the first time.

Even lunch picked up, drawing the likes of Keith Richards and his wife, the model Patti Hansen. I loved Keith; he had a great sense of humor, and for such a wiry guy he loved his pasta. At night, Richard Gere became a regular, as did Tom Cruise and his then-wife Mimi Rogers. Even the mayor, Ed Koch, dropped in from time to time.

Just as at Da Silvano, many of these luminaries gave me moments to treasure forever, like the night Keith Haring arranged a Vespa as a birthday present for *Vogue* fashion editor Elizabeth Saltzman, driving it right into the restaurant to present it to her.

One of my favorite regular couples was Lauren Hutton and her boyfriend Bob Williamson. She was the great, famous beauty, the face of Revlon in those days, but Bob was the guy I fell in love with, a true intellectual who could discuss anything and everything. There were periods when he came in to the restaurant seven nights a week and dined alone, with me keeping him company as much as I could while tending to other guests. He'd linger until after hours and leave with me when I locked up for the night. Their relationship had a tragic end when Lauren discovered that Bob had embezzled millions of her dollars, and then to cap it all off he died of cancer. Despite his short-comings, I still remember him as fondly as I do any of my customers.

We also became known to many of the big-money characters of the day: Fred Pressman, the patriarch of the family who owned and operated Barneys, a notoriously expensive, cutting-edge, and attitudinal department store on Seventeenth Street, ate at Il Cantinori at least twice a week with his wife, Phyllis, and occasionally one or both of their two sons, Bob and Gene. Financier Glenn Dubin (who'd go on to marry, then divorce, Elizabeth Saltzman) came in often and introduced me to the investor Paul Tudor Jones II, who was so brilliant and focused that he was one of the few people that I mostly listened to; I'd just sit at their table in rapt fascination at his next set of goals and how he was going to attain them.

Before he went to jail, Ivan Boesky would come in quite often. I never got to know him well, but there was one enduring moment that I'll never forget: Once, while he was being investigated for insider trading, he was having lunch in the outside cafe area, and was smoking a cigar. A pregnant woman was sitting there and I watched as she endured cloud after cloud of smoke from his stogie. I couldn't hear them speak from inside, but she said something to him, clearly asking him to move, and I was able to read the one word he spat back at her: "No."

She asked her waiter for the check, and paid it. As I stepped outside, she stood up to leave and got right in his face, her protruding belly so close that her unborn baby could have kicked him, and yelled, "I hope you go to *fucking jail!*"

On another morning, my regular customer, the attorney Steve Kaufman, called me and said that a very famous client was being charged down at the courthouse and that he was going to bring her in for lunch afterward. He wanted me to arrange a table for ten in the back room where they could be inconspicuous.

He didn't tell me who it was and I didn't ask. Around noon, I was standing outside and I saw Steve leading a pack of about seven gray-suited lawyers, briefcases swinging in the wind. They were acting as a cocoon for their clients, husband-and-wife hoteliers Harry and Leona Helmsley, who were up on tax evasion charges. Leona, known to New York City as the Queen of Mean, was dressed from head to toe in red: a bright red dress and ruby red shoes. Steve might have wanted to be discreet, but clearly his client had other ideas. A blind man would have seen her coming from a mile away.

I led them into the back room and waited on them personally. Over the next hour, Leona proved herself to be worthy of her nickname, beginning with the moment she opened her menu and, seeing all the dishes listed in Italian, squinted at me and said, "What is this crap?"

I was offended, but Steve was my pal and I wanted to help him out.

"I'm sure I can find you something you'll enjoy," I said to her.

"No, no," she said, waving me off. "Just make me a cappuccino, with skim milk, and lots of foam."

I should have seen disaster coming because you can't make a lot of foam with skim milk. Nevertheless, I took the rest of the orders and gave the cappuccino order to the barista. When I was in the front dining room a few minutes later, I turned to see that two of my busboys were engaged in a heated debate with Mrs. Helmsley, whose face was nearly as red as her dress. I rushed into the back.

"Where is the foam?" she was demanding. "I asked for a lot of foam."

"Mrs. Helmsley," I said, trying to soothe her. "You can't make more foam with skim milk. It's the fat that makes the foam."

Her eyebrows shot sky high at my effrontery. "I have cappuccinos made for me all the time with skim milk and lots of foam."

I went behind the bar and did the right thing: opened a carton of whole milk and made her the most velvety, luscious, foamy cappuccino she'd ever seen in her life. I walked it out to her and she clapped her hands together. "See! How hard was that?"

On the way out, Steve thanked me profusely. I shook his hand, then went to the bar and made myself a drink.

When Leona Helmsley died in 2007, she left $12 million to her dog. I'm sure that bitch deserved every penny.

DOES THIS ALL sound addictive? Well, it was. I fell back into all my old Silvano ways—living for the work, even more so because now it was *my* place and I didn't have to deal with the ire of a jealous owner.

I was also feeling more and more confident. While it was Steve and Nicola's money that funded Il Cantinori, I believed that my vision was the crucial ingredient in its success. Maybe it was the actor in me, but I began to feel that I was entitled to some public recognition. I thought back to how we had promoted plays when I had worked with traveling troupes back in Italy. When the production rolled into a new town, we'd hire a public relations guy to create some buzz, getting the show into the papers and bringing the right people to see it. There obviously was no shortage of public relations agencies in New York, but none of them specialized in restaurants. A friend, Susan Rike, was an independent public relations agent who represented rock bands. I hired her to get the word out about Il Cantinori, but what she was really promoting was *me*, Pino Luongo, and my American success story.

But you can only make work your entire life for so long before it begins to take its strange toll. My marriage was more of a joke than ever. I was back to drinking way too much and something inside me told me that I had to find some balance. I'd take a day off here and there, but being alone at home was still terrifying. I had no thoughts outside of the restaurant. No friends outside of the restaurant. Il Cantinori had become my world, my reality, and nothing outside its walls held any joy for me.

And then, one Saturday afternoon in early May, I was standing outside the restaurant watering the plants when I looked up and saw Jessie, that dark beauty from Da Silvano who had haunted my lonely days. She was walking right at me across Tenth Street.

I had to fight to keep my composure. We began talking and I told a white lie, informing her that I was separated, when the truth was that I still lived at home. I asked her out and we had dinner at the River Café; the Hemingwayesque Charlie Palmer, who would go on to fame at Aureole, was still the chef there. I put it all on the line. I told her I was soon to be divorced, and my meaning could not have been more clear: I was ready for her to come into my life. Nevertheless, she left again, returning to her hometown of New Orleans.

I couldn't get her out of my mind. It was true love at first sight. And it was also the beginning of the real end for me and Patty. Though I never confessed it to her, she knew that my mind and heart were else-where, and she grew resentful and angry.

It all came to a head every weekend. On Friday night, her personal time was just beginning but I was in the thick of my work week, and I didn't want to be home anyway. So, she'd be left to socialize with her American friends, while I did my thing. This led to fight after pre-dictable fight and early one Sunday morning, while we were scream-ing back and forth, I made the latest in a growing series of impulsive decisions: "That's it," I said. "I'm out of here."

It was the same old story with me: sticking around was killing me, so I took off. I crammed whatever I could into two suitcases and left. I gave her everything I had in the world, all the money I'd saved up un-til then. It was like when I left Italy: my philosophy was that when you own nothing, there's nothing they can take from you. But, I have to say, of all the people I'd walked out on in my life, this was the one I felt the worst about. She deserved better.

I CALLED JESSIE down in New Orleans and told her I was getting a di-vorce. She was slow to really believe me because I'd kept my marriage a secret when we first met. But I called her every day, sometimes more than once a day, for two weeks, trying everything from charm to out-right begging to get her to come back to New York, back to me. Finally, she arranged a trip, ostensibly to visit her sister here, and we began seeing each other. Before long, she had moved back to New York and we entered into a long romance. It was life-altering to be in love, to have somebody other than myself to focus on. I was still working like a dog, but it was a different dog.

From the beginning it was a very intense relationship; for exam-ple, as soon as we got together she wanted to study Italian. We didn't want anybody else around. We were just happy to be with each other.

We dated for a couple of years, eventually living together in an apartment on Park Avenue South and Twentieth Street. It was a one-bedroom on the eighteenth floor. I wasn't kidding back in those Sil-vano days: I really did want for her to be all mine. I was very protective of my relationship with her. She had friends that she would see when I was at work but when I had free time it was just the two of us.

It was a wonderful time in my life, made all the more so by my first visit back to Tuscany. With my legal troubles put to bed, there was no reason not to return, but thanks to opening and running the restaurant and sorting out my personal life, it took a while to find the time for a proper trip. I was also a bit apprehensive: having left a fugitive, it was tough to truly believe there would be no consequences to visiting, but it was a smooth and uncontroversial trip. Seeing my hometown again put me back in touch with so much that defined me and my new career in New York, and reconnecting with my mother in person was like being given a new lease on life. Unsurprisingly, things with my father remained, if not quite cold, cordial at best.

Back in New York, as the restaurant did better and better, I had enough money to be able to partake in a great New York tradition: renting a weekend house. To find the right place, we began spending trial weekends in various towns upstate, passing the time antiquing and collecting little treasures that we planned to put in our house one day.

Before long, we gravitated to Long Island because I had come to miss the ocean. I found myself longing for Porto Santo Stefano, where I had spent those summers working for my uncle. We stayed at the creaky old American Hotel in Sag Harbor in the winter, drinking wine with the famous host, Ted Conklin. We loved the place in the off season because the quietude added to the feeling that we were hoarding each other's company. We'd stroll the empty streets of East Hampton, catch a movie and a late dinner, and then return to the hotel.

So in the fall of 1986, we decided to spend some time by the beach, in the fabled Hamptons, a weekend playground for the rich and famous about two hours east of the city (or four hours on a summer Friday when the Long Island Expressway is clogged beyond belief). The Hamptons are where everyone from Martha Stewart to Steven Spielberg goes to relax, be seen, and luxuriate in their palatial homes. The Hamptons always reminded me of *The Great Gatsby*, even though the novel really takes place in fictional towns based on Great Neck and Manhasset.

I never cared one way or another about the scene out there. What I loved was being near the ocean. It just made me feel good, so good that I didn't even care if it was summer or not; the first time we rented in the Hamptons was in the off season, from Labor Day through Memorial Day, instead of the other way around. We rented a house that wasn't winterized. It was chilly and drafty and the toilet water froze, but it was near the Napeague Bay, not far from Montauk, so I was happy to be there.

I remember driving around the Hamptons in those dark winter days and thinking to myself how few restaurants there were in the towns along Route 27, the Montauk Highway, which connects the dots on the Hamptons map from Southampton to Bridgehampton to East Hampton and on out to Montauk. With the crowds this place drew in the summer, it seemed like a huge missed opportunity for somebody (me) to really cash in on.

But it was more than the promise of business that appealed to me: the Hamptons made me almost painfully nostalgic, not only for Italy but for my youth. I remember walking with Jessie on the beach that winter, dressed in heavy coats and huddling together in the cold sunlight, and telling her about my teenage summers, painting for her a picture of those nights in the watermelon fields, those late-night drives, the sulfuric showers and falling asleep in the grass. Sometimes I would sing a few bars of "Sapore di Sale," the song about that girl by the seaside and the taste of salt on her skin.

Jessie and I got married in August 1987, on a plantation in New Orleans. We rented an apartment on Horatio Street in the West Village and before long, she wanted to start a family. Things were moving very quickly, but much to my own surprise, I found myself ready for this drastic change. I was thirty-five years old. It was the right time, and the right woman, and we began trying to have a child.

But a funny thing was going on in the back of my mind: the restaurateur in me wanted to grow his family, too. And so, even as my responsibilities at home were increasing, I began thinking about opening my second restaurant.

SIX

Dirty Dishes, and Other Things That Bring Out the Beast

Armed with emphatic opinions, a talent for shaping trends, and a volatile temper, Pino Luongo has been cutting a swath of style and controversy through New York's restaurant scene.

—*New York Times*, November 10, 1993

I T WOULD BE less than honest of me at this point not to address one of the things that made me famous early in my career, and which many people associate with me to this day: my temper.

When I was in my prime, my temper developed a celebrity all its own. As much ink was spilled describing my outbursts and obscenities as was devoted to my Midas touch and discerning palate. These things tend to get exaggerated, but I have to admit that much of what was said about me was true, particularly in the 1980s and especially when it came to my often tortured relationship with my employees.

The amazing thing is that until I opened my first restaurant, I didn't think of myself as having much of a temper. Apart from isolated incidents with my father and with the Menichettis of the world, I was basically a happy person, rarely finding occasion to get into a fight or even to raise my voice.

That all changed when I opened Il Cantinori. I poured everything I had into realizing that restaurant, every ounce of time and energy. I

gave up sleep and my personal life. I let my first marriage disinte-
grate. But I thought it was worth it. I knew enough about the downtown dining scene that I was confident that if I could make the place
run harmoniously and keep the food consistently delicious, I would
have a successful enterprise.

If only it were that easy.

You have to remember that this was 1983, when cooking and restau-
rateuring were occupations that people ended up in rather than aspired
to. So, it was difficult to find talented professionals to manage the
podium, wait on customers, or even to bus tables. The best waiters and
captains were the penguins who worked at the old-fashioned French and
Italian places uptown, and I wasn't interested in that kind of service. You
hire one guy like that and you have to staff your whole place with the
same type of professional—they don't get along well with the younger,
more causal style of American waiter—and before you know it you have
a stuffy place that nobody below Fifty-seventh Street would want to set
foot in. The dilemma was that it was next to impossible to find Americans who took pride in the art of service. And so was born one of the
great and ongoing tensions of my life: the fact that my minute-to-minute
success largely rested on the shoulders of people who had no personal
stake in that success.

I was optimistic, though, at least at the beginning. My enthusiasm
was so great that I believed that once I demonstrated how I wanted
things done, and the people who worked for me saw my passion for
hospitality, they would find it contagious and follow my lead.

Optimistic, it turns out, can be an unintended euphemism for
naïve.

Let's take busboys, for example. Bussing tables is not a difficult job,
and I have always trained busboys myself to ensure they know what I
expect. First they are supposed to remove the women's dishes. The first
dish goes on the open palm of one hand, the next dish rests on the
wrist. Then you take the silverware from the plate on your wrist and
move it to the one on your hand. Then you pick up the other plates and
line them along your arm, or stack them. A smart busboy will pick up
the plates with less food on them first so they can stack because—and
this is a cardinal rule with me—there's no scooping of food from one

plate to another, *ever*. All restaurateurs have their own pet peeves and this is one of mine. My uncle taught me never to scoop food because it's inelegant and sloppy, and it's now part of my worldview. When I train busboys I make this as idiot-proof as possible: I actually scoop some food and I say, as though talking to a baby, "This is a no-no. A no-no." To drive the point home, I shake my head from side to side and make very disapproving and severe faces. Sometimes I go so far that a trainee will laugh, and I'll say, "You think this is a fucking joke?" at which point they stop laughing and look like they might wet their pants.

I also advise all new busboys that for large parties, they must be willing to take a load of dishes into the kitchen and come back for a second one. The reason is that if they pile too many pieces of silverware on one plate, they'll do something that for me is worse than fingernails on a chalkboard: dropping silverware in the dining room. "Don't do that," I tell them. "I'd rather you stab me in the fucking leg." As with all instructions offered to the often language-challenged busboys, I act this out, too, grabbing a knife and pretending to stab myself in the leg over and over.

For all of my efforts, I've learned that there are some busboys who just can't help it. They will, no matter how many times the lesson is reinforced, no matter how many ways it's demonstrated, no matter how many times you tell them "no-no" or pantomime doing a Norman Bates on your leg, scoop food from one plate to another, drop the silverware, and screw up the table in any number of ways. I'll correct them, and they'll nod and then turn around and do the same thing again *at the very next table*. At that point, I assume that the issue isn't language or pride but an IQ deficiency. It's what I call the "involuntary fuck you in the face." They don't mean anything by it, but it's an insult just the same.

To preserve my sanity, I developed a plan B for hopeless busboys: after two corrections, I'd follow them into the kitchen and tell them, "Give me your apron, get your stuff, and get out of here." It didn't matter if it was in the middle of the busiest Saturday night of the year. I'd rather do their job myself than chase somebody around all the time. After all, I knew plenty about being a busboy; I'd been one myself just a few years earlier.

The truth of the matter is that this never-ending dissatisfaction is an inherent part of being a restaurateur, by which I mean a *real* working restaurateur, not just a dentist or celebrity who has invested some money. Each restaurant defines its own reality, and part of my job—my mission in life—is to maintain that reality at all costs. My blessing and my curse is that when I survey the dining room of one of my restaurants, waiters and customers swirling about, my senses are as attuned to the flow of food and service as they are to my own breathing, or to the beating of my heart. My eye will naturally train on the unhappy face, the uncleared table, the unfilled glass. These things offend me, because a restaurant is an illusion, a fantasy, and customers give themselves over to your vision the way audiences participate in theater or film, through the willful suspension of disbelief. A misstep on the service floor is no different from an actor forgetting his line, or celluloid catching in the projector. It takes the diner out of the experience and ruins the illusion. If you've ever heard a glass break in a restaurant, and experienced the way everything *stops* for a few seconds—then you know what I'm saying is true. As an actor, I tended to hold a grudge when a costar forgot a line, and as a restaurateur it's no different: busboys who cannot perform at a peak level are a threat to my personal and financial security, and so they are eighty-sixed. It's nothing personal. As they say in *The Godfather*, it's strictly business.

But for all the busboys I canned—and yes, the bodies did pile up pretty quickly—I was never haphazard. In fact, there were employees who I responded to in the opposite way, showering them with compliments and money, like the answer to my prayers at Il Cantinori, a young, alarmingly skinny Chinese kid named Fuzzi with alert, scanning eyes and a Ghengis Khan mustache whom I hired a few weeks after the restaurant opened. Even during his first shift, I could tell that he was going to be my hero because he exhibited all the telltale signs of a master busboy. When Fuzzi cleared a table, it was like watching a show: plates moved silently from the table to his loving arms, the silverware never clanked, and his footfalls were as undetectable as those of a cat burglar. He exhibited all the signs of a true professional, like the fact that he never emerged from a kitchen empty-handed; he would go in with dirty dishes and come out with a pitcher of ice water, then go in with another load of dirty dishes and return trailing a waiter, helping him deliver hot food to a table. He was *on it*. At the end of his first shift, he came over and stood next to me by the bar, making a big show of surveying the dining rooms. He turned to me and said, "Me alone this room. No busboy. Me bring one more. Two of us. Whole restaurant."

"OK!" I said, shaking his hand and feeling for the first time in my life that I might have just met the man of my dreams.

The next day, Fuzzi showed up with his pal, another skinny kid, who went by the name of Mr. Chow and was every inch Fuzzi's equal. I'd say that they reminded me of myself as a young man, but Fuzzi was one of the few guys whose talents exceeded my own: where I could carry a maximum of eight wine glasses in one hand (the stems go between your fingers, four glasses up and four facing down), he could manage ten, cradling two glasses between the stems of the others.

Before long, Fuzzi and Mr. Chow were permanent fixtures at the restaurant. They worked lunch and dinner seven days a week. They made good money, we cracked each other up, and they became my protégés. People knew not to fuck with them. In time, much as I had done at Da Silvano, Fuzzi became like my lieutenant, even though he was technically outranked by the waiters.

My busboy problems resolved, I was free to focus on my issues with the waiters. I could write an entire book on why I hate waiters; not the actual human beings who clock in and out, but the profession itself, which is one of the most half-assed ways in the world to make a living. Sure, there are career waiters who love what they do, but they are the exception. The majority are mercenary hourly laborers who are simply there because the flexibility allows them to pursue their acting careers, or some other artistic endeavor, at which most of them will fail. (Sorry, guys, but if you were going to make it, you'd have done it by now.) You'd think I'd relate to these thespians, but over the years I've come to resent them as liabilities. And many of them resent the jobs that restaurateurs like me provide: over the last decade or so, one of the most chic things a waiter can do is file a lawsuit with the labor department over some injustice that's been done to him or her, such as verbal abuse, unlawful termination, or unpaid wages, but in most cases, I'd bet you that the person filing the complaint is a trouble-maker, always disappearing from the service floor to make cell phone calls or smoke a cigarette and taking impressionable co-workers along for the ride. He probably got fired because he's late or his uniform is never ironed or he gets catty with difficult customers, or all of the above.

The only thing that's kept me sane is that I've become better at rec-ognizing the two biggest problems, which are laziness and attitude. A good busboy or waiter is somebody who knows that he needs to spend time on the bottom rung of the ladder before moving up, and who un-derstands that he needs to put in the time and sweat to learn and pay his dues. When I see that commitment and passion, I become a men-tor. For every waiter or busboy I ever unceremoniously dismissed, there's another who became a great American success story. Last I heard, Fuzzi was running his own chain of take-out restaurants in Long Island, and a former waiter opened his own Italian restaurant in Newburgh, New York.

Back in my formative days, I believed that I could turn any em-ployee into such a model citizen. After observing the culture of indif-ference that defined the table-waiting trade in New York at the time, I decided to do something about it, and as usual I called on my theater roots. Today, the nightly staff meeting is a given in every restaurant in New York City—a time for the manager to brief the waitstaff about the nightly specials and other orders of business so that everybody is synched up. But back then, there wasn't such a thing. I started holding a nightly meeting at Il Cantinori based on the preshow powwow we had held in my theater days in Rome, when we'd review the staging of the play. The meeting was my first performance of the evening, fol-lowed by the one I did for the customers. I'd gather all the waiters in the dining room, and my presentation always began the same way: "I've been here since nine o'clock this morning, cooking the food you are going to be serving tonight. Now let me tell you a little about it so that you can explain it to your customers." And then I'd give them a culinary lesson. If we were serving chicken livers, I'd explain that they were small, whole chicken livers, immaculately cleaned, and served medium-rare so they didn't dry out. We obtained their flavor by sautéing them in a very hot pan with white wine and sprinkling them with salt and black pepper at the last second. "If you describe it like this, you'll sell it," I'd say. "If you don't, it'll just sound like chopped liver." Same with steak Florentine: if you just say, "It's a steak, seared and sliced, with hot olive oil," you've already lost them. But if you say, "Our steak Florentine is prepared the authentic way. The chef takes a two-inch-thick prime steak, oils it, seasons it with salt and pepper, and grills it, catching the drippings, which get added to a sizzling hot herb oil that's poured over the steak just before serving," they'll be intrigued. I'd try to speak their language a little bit, asking them to describe the food as if they were auditioning for *Hamlet* and even throwing in a bit of financial incentive. "You do it right and people will tip for your passion." My nightly meetings ran about an hour, which is long even by today's standards, and when Marian Burros reviewed us in the *New York Times* and wrote that the waiters "knowledgeably and graciously explain[ed] the dishes," I felt like they were worth every minute.

But for every happy incident, there was a horror story. One night, I overheard a waiter describe *ribollita* to a customer as "overcooked vegetable soup." As soon as he turned away from the table, I ambushed him, took him by the elbow, and dragged him over to the side of the room. "Overcooked vegetable soup?" I asked incredulously. "I'll overcook your fucking mother." Then I reminded him of everything I'd said before service, recounting the long history of the dish and how we, like my mother had done, sautéed each vegetable individually. When I finished, I said, "I hear you say that again and you'll be out of here on your overcooked ass."

Just as Fuzzi and Mr. Chow won my affection in the busboy department, I also had three or four great waiters, and I had a wide-open mind about what constituted greatness. Really, all I cared about was sincerity and professionalism, and I appreciated them in whatever package they came in. For example, there was Ray, a waiter from Kansas City who was about as different from me as you could get: a nerdy, mustachioed guy who made up for his non–New York persona with his enthusiasm for food and a romantic view of the business. Ray was engaged to an Asian woman and Chinese food was his first culinary passion, but during his tenure at Il Cantinori, Italian cuisine became a close second. At every preservice meeting, he would sit forward in his chair and listen as attentively as a star pupil, then he'd take the explanation of the dishes and make them his own when he spoke to his customers.

I looked at employees like Ray as friends and allies. But the rest were a constant disappointment.

The ultimate bad-waiter story took place one night after Il Cantinori had been open for about a year. In the middle of service, I noticed that one of the waiters had been absent from the dining room for about fifteen minutes. I went searching for him, eventually opening the door to the walk-in refrigerator downstairs, where I found him, seated at the shelf of a utility rack which he had set up like his own private dining table, complete with a placemat and a glass of wine, and he was tucking into a plate of pasta. When I found him there, I cursed him out and locked him in, returning later to find him shivering in a corner, with lettuce leaves, strips of cardboard, and other meat-locker miscellany wrapped around his limbs in a desperate bid to stay warm.

That might seem severe, but actions like his had the potential to undo everything that I had worked so hard for and it pissed me off, not just because I was paying these people and they were making great tips, but because I was also a wonderful host to them. For dinner service, they showed up to work at four o'clock. By four thirty, they were sitting in my restaurant, chowing down on my food. Most restaurants in those days served mediocre staff meals, but I cooked mine as if I were serving my own family. There'd always be two courses: pasta and meat, or soup followed by fish or meat. They'd even be welcome to sit and sip an espresso afterward. Then, at five o'clock, during our nightly meeting, I shared with them the most intimate details of my life, and a little history lesson about Tuscan food. After that, they had only to perform for about five hours in order to make up to one hundred fifty dollars a night, which was great money in 1983. And so, when they failed to do their jobs, I took it very personally, as a betrayal of my friendship and hospitality.

After a few months as an owner, there was no part of the restaurant where I didn't perceive at least one or two enemies in my midst. In the kitchen, there were good cooks, but there were also people who were either incredibly stupid or just didn't care about what they were doing. My biggest vulnerability was dishes prepared *à la minute*. One of my personal favorites was calf's liver. Its success depends on attention to details: the liver must be very thinly sliced or it basically becomes a steak. The butter needs to be just browned, or else it's burned butter, not browned butter. And a little of that butter goes a long way, just enough to dress the slices. I demonstrated that dish to death in the kitchen, but once in a while, a plate would come out that was like the textbook example of how *not* to cook calf's liver, the one that should be in a red circle with a line running diagonally across it. Sometimes, I'd be on the phone taking a reservation and a calf's liver would glide by me, cut two inches thick and sitting in a pool of in burnt butter. I'd grab the runner by the shoulder, hang up the phone, take the dish off the tray, storm into the kitchen, slam it on the counter, and scream, "What the fuck is this?"

Does that make me a tyrant? From the reputation I acquired in those days, you would think that it did. But I truly felt that my own people were trying to undo me. I was so desperate to succeed every night that I just couldn't stand for less than perfection. And I have to say that I always confined my anger to the subject at hand. I never called a person a "jerk" or an "asshole." I just asked logical questions, like, "What the fuck is this?"

Am I making sense?

I'll put it another way: people believe that the restaurant business is complicated, and at moments it can be. But my philosophy is that fundamentally, it's actually quite simple. In the long run a restaurant survives on the basis of all the tedious little details—making sure water glasses are filled, bread shows up warm, food is cooked consistently, and dirty dishes are cleared when people are finished with them. You do that, and it adds up to a great performance; word of mouth will be so great that no critic will be able to destroy you. Critics, even those who like you early on, can treat you like their first fuck. When you're young and hot, they want you, but when you settle into middle age, they leave you for somebody new. If you treat your customers like marriage material, like the loves of your life, they will keep coming back. Maybe not every day, but once a week or once a month, and if you do that, they won't care about what the *New York Times* or the *Zagat Survey* has to say.

Accordingly, there was no end to my determination to maintain my high standards. Even after the busboys, waiters, and cooks were gone for the night, nodding off on the subway, I was still in the restaurant, double checking everything. And, of course, just like everybody else, the dishwashers had the power to enrage me. From my very first restaurant job, I have always loved the peace of knowing that a day has been truly *finished*, which means that the dining room has been cleared, the chairs are up on the tables, and every last dish, piece of silverware, and surface has been well and properly cleaned. After the European model, in my kitchen, the cooks were responsible for wiping down their cutting boards and the cabinets down to their knees, while the dishwashers were to finish their days scrubbing the walls and cabinets from knee-level down to the floor. Even this proved too much to ask; I'd often find a few plates and pieces of silverware in the sink, and grease trickling down the wall.

If the place wasn't cleaned properly, I'd lock the front door and wait in the dining room. When the dishwashers emerged, usually in their street clothes, I'd shake my head from side to side and make the same disapproving face I made for the busboys in my "no-no" talk. I wouldn't say a word, just point toward the kitchen, ordering them to go back and do it right.

The way I figured it, the least I could ask for was a clean start the next day.

INTERLUDE

*H*IS RANT COMPLETE, *Pino takes a deep breath.*

"You tell me: I'm right, or I'm an asshole?"

The vulnerable expression on his face would probably surprise anybody he ever chewed out, or canned. Clearly, he's given this topic some thought, and he's come to doubt whether or not he's been too severe over the years. I must say that while he usually confines himself to the offense at hand, he does sometimes get a little insulting. One day, we were meeting in his dining room between lunch and dinner when his waiters began dragging a very large and expensive country table across the floor.

"Guys, guys!" he screamed. "You need to lift it! That table is delicate, and it will break. I'm sorry if you are so weak in your arms from masturbating too much, but you need to carry it!"

As I turn that last sentence over in my mind, another moment occurs to me: "You know what this whole subject reminds me of?" I say. "That hostess at Le Madri."

"Oh, yeah," he says. "That was bad."

I'm referring to one of my earliest encounters with Pino, about ten years earlier, while we were working on the cookbook Simply Tuscan *and I lived a block away, at the corner of Eighteenth Street and Eighth Avenue. One Saturday night, half drunk on red wine and having listened to Italian opera all day for inspiration, I was craving some pasta and martinis. My girlfriend (now wife), Caitlin, and I walked over to Le Madri, which Pino* had opened in 1989, and pushed through the crush of people in the bar area, working our way up to the podium.

There was a blonde woman managing the reservation book. I asked her if they could take two walk-ins. She said to give her a few minutes. Though we were known to the restaurant's manager, and to many of the waiters, I didn't want to muscle my way into the dining room, so I kept incognito and Caitlin and I ordered some vodka martinis. Periodically I made eye contact with the hostess, and she smiled and nodded back, which I took to mean she hadn't forgotten us.

Twenty minutes ticked by. Then thirty. I figured there was a table in the offing or she would have sent us on our way. After forty-five minutes, the bar area was almost completely emptied out and we were still sitting there in limbo. I went back to the podium and asked what the status was.

"Oh, sorry," she said, throwing up her arms and speaking in a bizarrely upbeat tone, as if I'd find what she was about to say amusing. "We don't have a table!"

I was annoyed. We had wasted almost an hour sitting there, and it was well after ten P.M. at that point, too late to start over at another restaurant. If I hadn't had a personal connection to Le Madri, I never would have returned. So, the next Monday, when I met Pino in his conference room to work on the book, I felt I had to share our experience with him.

"Before we get started," I said. "I have to tell you something."

I proceeded to describe the entire saga, and as I did, a transformation took place. Pino's body tensed up and his gaze became inscrutable, but as I continued, almost imperceptibly, he began to tremble, literally simmering with anger. I was getting, I realized, my first glimpse of the famous Pino Luongo temper, and it was something to behold. I finished the story and he didn't say a word. Without looking away from me, he reached over, picked up the phone, and dialed four digits, meaning an interior extension.

"Yeah, Alan, get up here," he said gruffly, and hung up.

Pino and I sat in uncomfortable silence for a few minutes until Alan, the general manager of Le Madri, a curly-headed, swarthy, and perennially cheerful man of Moroccan descent, came up to the conference room dressed for service in a pinstripe suit.

"Hi, guys. What's up?" he said.

Pino motioned to me. "Tell him. Tell him the whole thing."

Alan's jaw dropped. He'd heard this tone before.

"Pino, I don't want to . . ."

"It's OK, I want him to hear it from you."

Pino calmly lit a cigarette as I proceeded to recount the story again, blow by blow, watching as Alan began to understand where it was going and started pulling at his collar nervously in a way that reminded me of Rodney Dangerfield.

I finished and Alan turned to Pino, bracing himself.

After a long pause, Pino said, "This is the kind of 1980s bullshit that's got no place in my restaurants." He extinguished his cigarette in an ashtray for emphasis. "I didn't want it then, and I don't want it now. This is the worst story I never heard."

"Andrew, I'm so sorry," Alan said. He clasped my hands in his and all but prostrated himself before me. "I'm so sorry. So sorry. Please, next time you come in, let me know you're coming. Please. Sorry. Please. Sorry." And continuing like that, he backed out the door and disappeared down the hallway, never showing me his back in an embarrassing show of respect and contrition.

The very next day, I was walking home and I saw Alan standing on the corner outside Le Madri smoking a cigarette.

"Alan! How you doing?" I called out.

"Hey, Andrew," he said, extending his hand.

As we shook, he pitched his cigarette butt into Seventh Avenue and said to me, sotto voce, "I took care of that thing."

I felt as if I'd been thrust into a scene in a gangster movie.

"Thing? What thing?"

"You know. The girl. You won't be seeing her no more."

"What do you mean? You fired her?"

"Don't worry about it."

"But I—"

"It's OK," he said; he shook my hand again and went into the restaurant.

I felt terrible. I thought I had just been tipping Pino off that one of his employees needed some quick remedial training, and now I found out I'd gotten her sacked. The gangster undertones of this tale might suggest The Godfather, but despite Pino's identification with Vito Corleone, a more illustrative comparison is Brian De Palma's remake of Scarface, which was released in 1983, the same year Pino opened Il Cantinori. The protagonist, Tony Montana, is Cuban rather than Italian (although he was played by Al Pacino), but he has more in common with Pino than any of the characters in The Godfather—the quick wit, the Everest-size confidence, the forwardness with women (like Tony, Pino married an American, not a paesana), even the fact that he gleaned much of his English from movies: "I learned. I watch the guys like Humphrey Bogart, James Cagney. They teach me to talk. I like those guys," Montana says to his interrogators when he arrives in the United States.

The movie's promotional tagline also served as nifty foreshadowing of Pino's budding career: "He loved the American dream, with a vengeance."

SEVEN

High Tide

I N THE FALL of 1987, on one of our unfashionable, off-season weekends in the Hamptons, I was driving along Route 27, about to round
the bend into Wainscott, when I passed what looked like a haunted
house. I had never paid much attention to this particular building,
which had been the site of Charlotte's Hidden Pond restaurant and
before that the home of a state senator. Set back from the main road
and enshrouded by shrubbery, it was fast becoming invisible to the
modern Hampton eye.

But a sign at the edge of the property caught my attention: the owners had gone into bankruptcy, it said, and the building was up for sale.

I swerved into the parking lot, got out of my car, and took a walk
around. The place was an eyesore: a hulking, Tudor-style English house
with a dark wooden frame and a sad gray tint to the stucco. It was in
merciless disrepair, with huge nicks in the walls, cracks in the wood,
and a stale stench that had no doubt been exacerbated by the damp
sea air.

The place was more ready for a wrecking ball than for a prospective
buyer, but none of that mattered, because I was having an out-of-body
experience. Inspired by the proximity to the ocean, and by the fierce
longing for summer that the Hamptons elicited in me, I began to envision a restaurant that would capture all the charm of Porto Santo
Stefano: sun, salt, sand, tanned skin, and the simple food that would
bring each seaside evening to a perfect close. In my mind, the edifice

morphed into a spot-on replica of a Mediterranean villa, with tile floors, terra-cotta accents, and generous, wide-open spaces through which the summer breeze could blow, carrying that precious scent of the sea right through the dining room.

There was nobody around, so I started singing, out loud: "*Sapore di sale. Sapore di mare . . .* " Taste of the salt. Taste of the sea.

I snapped my fingers: that was it! The perfect name for the restaurant: *Sapore di Mare.*

I knew that it would take a lot of work to turn the relic before me into the restaurant of my imagination, but after the conversion I had pulled off at Il Cantinori, I fancied myself the Bob Vila of the restaurant industry, able to turn "This Old Restaurant" into something shiny and new. I also loved the location: situated at the end of one of the splits of Georgica Pond, which flows alongside Route 27 where Wainscott and East Hampton meet, it had the distinction of being at the epicenter of the weekend scene but also offering an oasis of calm.

Back in the city, I excitedly told Steve about the space and my idea and suggested that we take the project on together. We decided to move forward, but soon after he bought the property, it became apparent that we were both making radically different assumptions. I thought that I had earned the right to be a true partner, with equity in the venture; after all, it was my efforts out in the Hamptons that would deliver the restaurant's success. He, on the other hand, wasn't looking for a partner, certainly not after shelling out his own hard-earned money for the property, and had assumed that we'd reprise our Il Cantinori arrangement.

So, although it was my concept and enthusiasm that had inspired him to buy the property, I told him that I had no interest in just running another restaurant for him and that I'd pass, essentially leaving him holding the bag. I felt bad about it because it was an honest misunderstanding, but I felt that I needed to insist on what I thought I was worth.

In the end, it all worked out: after two months, he decided that the building was a very expensive albatross and flipped it over to me. In early February, I assumed ownership and the mortgage and obtained a construction loan to finance the build-out.

My only concern was breaking the news to Jessie. Il Cantinori was a serious distraction from our time together and I knew she'd be concerned about what another restaurant would mean for us. I took her to one of the hot new restaurants in town, Da Umberto on Seventeenth Street, and told her.

"It doesn't mean I'll completely disappear," I said. "And besides, it's more money for our family. For the two of us."

"You mean for the *three* of us," she said, her sly way of letting me know she was pregnant.

"Now we *really* have something to celebrate," I said, and we clinked our wine glasses and toasted our ever-more-complicated and adventurous future together.

ONE OF THE things that appealed to me about the property I'd just bought was that it still felt like a house. There were five main rooms, and I had it in my head that I'd keep it that way, naming each one: the Bar, the Porch, the Veranda, the Fireplace, and the Terrace. I interviewed a contractor right after the closing and he suggested we convert it into one big room. A few years earlier, I might have listened to him, but I was fast developing belief in my instincts as a showman, and confidence for a restaurateur is the same as it is for an athlete: winning is a habit, and when you're on a roll, you just go with the flow and ride out the hot streak for as long as you can.

I stuck to my vision, and I didn't hire that guy. Instead, I decided to keep it a family affair. Jessie's father, John, and brother, Richard, who were in the construction business, came up from New Orleans. I bought a small house in the spring, a wooded, secluded East Hampton enclave best known as the home of the cemetery where Jackson Pollock is buried, and put them up there, along with the key craftsmen. I spent weekdays in the city running Il Cantinori while my in-laws and their team set about turning that old English Tudor into a beautiful Mediterranean villa with white stucco walls, terra-cotta tile, and rustic chairs. We also restored all the windows to full functionality so we could have them open as much as possible and let that marvelous salty smell come blowing through the rooms. Every weekend, when I got back to East

Hampton, I couldn't believe how quickly the place was being transformed from something resembling a haunted house to a cheerful white ode to the Tuscan seashore.

I think there's no surer sign that you're in the right line of work than when long days invigorate you. I was working around the clock that winter and spring, overseeing lunch and dinner at Il Cantinori Monday through Thursday, then driving out to the Hamptons and making decisions about the build-out. But I loved every minute of it and had an endless reservoir of energy to draw on.

We also revamped the landscaping, uprooting everything except for two beautiful oak trees that grew up out of a central isle in the parking lot, some junipers, a Japanese maple, and a few others. To them we added rosemary and lavender, which perfumed the garden and provided some fresh herbs to draw from in the kitchen. By the time we were finished, the landscaped areas had the look and feel of a Mediterranean garden.

The only thing that caused me any displeasure was my weekly visit to the bank officer charged with administering my construction loan. The day I would head out to the Hamptons, either Thursday or Friday, I'd drop by his office. The arrangement was that he would release funds on an as-needed basis based on requisitions as they occurred; in order to get the money, I had to bring him progress reports and a copy of my ledger tracking payments I'd made each week. This was fine in the early stages, but as we came down the homestretch that spring things were moving quickly and I needed the remaining capital, about seventy-five thousand dollars, on hand, so I asked him to release it. He told me that he thought that was too much.

We squabbled a bit, and then I lost it.

"You know what," I said. "I was approved for this loan. If you think you know better than me, *you* do it!"

I took the massive key ring I carried around in those days, with keys to everything from Cantinori to Sapore to my homes in Manhattan and East Hampton, and even my locker at the gym, slammed it down on his desk, then turned and stormed out of his office.

"Wait," he said.

I spun around and let it fly: "No. I will not wait," I said, spit spraying from my mouth. "I need the money. You can either give it to me and foreclose if I default, or you can build the fucking restaurant yourself."

"I—"

"You make me feel like you're my parole officer. What'd I do to deserve this?"

I don't know if he was intimidated or sympathetic, or if he just thought I was crazy, but he relented and released the rest of my loan.

BY MAY, SAPORE di Mare was nearly fully realized. Even before we opened for business, turning the corner into the driveway for the first time each week was a thrill, seeing how the white gravel led right up to the steps of this perfectly rendered fantasy of the Tuscan seaside.

With the construction nearly complete, I could turn my attention to kitchen concerns: the menu, the chef, and the cooks.

Because my imagination and memory were fully engaged, the menu came together almost on its own: just as we did at Il Cantinori, we would display platters of room-temperature vegetables, this time on a wooden kitchen farm table right between the reception area and the Bar Room, casting our spell on customers as soon as they walked into the room. I wanted the food to be as light and summery as possible, beginning with this display: there'd be the *pasticcio di Dante* I had introduced at Da Silvano, eggplant parmigiana, roasted zucchini with caponata sauce, and preserved tuna in oil served with roasted zucchini. My goal was for the vegetables, their marinades, and their dressings to give off the aroma of a summer garden.

As for the printed menu, I wanted it to be as simple as possible, which is the way I think about food in the summer when, as a cook, you want to get in and out of the kitchen quickly and as a diner, you want very familiar, unchallenging food. In those summers working for my uncle, I had learned that the most popular restaurants, especially during this season near the water, were the ones where people felt like they could satisfy simple cravings. The menu almost wrote itself: whole fish, *spaghetti alle vongole* (spaghetti with clams), and other basic pastas such as *spaghetti alla rustica* with caramelized red onion, stewed tomato, and Parmigiano-Reggiano, *calamari al forno* (oven-baked breaded squid), cod in white wine, filleted fish that was grilled, roasted, or served with a *livornese* sauce (tomatoes, capers, onions, and anchovies), and of course a Florentine steak. To distinguish these very simple dishes, I focused on the quality and freshness of ingredients, especially the fish and shellfish, which—true to the name of the restaurant—still tasted of the sea. I also had a theory that if the right customers showed up, the food would taste better; what doesn't seem better in the company of beautiful people?

My leading candidate for executive chef was an unlikely one: a short, portly Jewish-American kid from Queens with chubby fingers and a mile-a-minute patter named Mark Strausman. We had been introduced by a butcher we both knew and I had hired him to help at Il Cantinori. I liked Mark; he made me feel that my passion, communicated in those cooking demos and staff meetings, was contagious.

I decided to put the front of the house in the hands of a sharply dressed, smooth-tongued Latin American kid named Ariel Lacayo, who I had hired at Il Cantinori and had found to be a natural on the service floor. He was effortlessly charming and dashing, a gym rat with a flair for making preppy clothes seem stylish and a talent for never losing his cool.

"If you want to learn this business, I'll teach you," I told him when I first interviewed him, and he soaked up all the wisdom I had to offer.

From Il Cantinori, I also brought along a sprite of an Italian woman named Maria, who came to me by the strangest of routes: her son, a doctor, thought she needed to get out of the house. Because cooking was her true love, he had a friend who was in the wine business ask around after jobs in Italian kitchens. I took a chance on her and found her to be a talented home cook, more than capable of making my food. She wasn't professionally trained for the timing requirements of a restaurant kitchen, but she could make all those vegetable dishes I liked to set out every day. She also became the first in what would become a long line of maternal figures in my kitchens. Maria shared my love of the seaside and so jumped at the chance to come out to the Hamptons. I was able to communicate with her in short-hand. Because she was from Rome, near the sea, she was familiar with the kind of trattorias that inspired Sapore, places where they stuck tables right in the sand at lunchtime. All I had to do was describe those dishes to her and she knew *just* what I had in mind. Since 80 percent of our appetizers would come from the farm table, I knew this would make life much easier for me.

I decided to put myself on the pasta station: at Il Cantinori, I had discovered the hard way that of all the things I had to show cooks, making a proper pasta was the toughest, because the correct way was so different from the way they had been taught to do it. They always overcooked it and their sauces had no consistency. It took me forever to develop the right instincts in them. Meanwhile, I could make a perfect pasta in my sleep. More than that, though, I loved making pasta and decided to indulge myself until we could recruit more cooks and get them properly re-educated.

That left the position of bartender. A friend of mine from Rome asked me to interview one named Giuseppe, a flamboyant dead ringer for the actor Marcello Mastroianni. I found him charming and talented behind the bar and hired him. He didn't speak much English, but he knew enough to get by, and this only led to one small problem: Giuseppe was a proud and uncloseted homosexual, but he took great offense at the American word *gay*. If anybody referred to him as "gay," he'd insist, with indignation "I'm not gay, I'm a *pederast*." One day, I explained to him that the Italian word *pederasta* meant something else here in the States, referring to a molester of young boys.

"Well, Pino," he said, without missing a beat, "young men *are* dying for me, you know."

Because Il Cantinori had been such a success, I decided to make its opening date of the twenty-third of the month, my lucky date, and that's the day we opened Sapore di Mare, on May 23, 1988.

The restaurant exceeded my wildest expectations. Based on word of mouth, a few press mentions generated by my publicist, Susan Rike, and having a slew of Il Cantinori customers who spent a lot of time in the Hamptons, we had fifty people in the book that night. In order to maintain quality control while the waiters and kitchen fine-tuned their acts—a common practice for new restaurants—I ordered Ariel to contain the crowd at sixty people, max. But as the night wore on, we were besieged by customers who knew me from the city and to whom I simply couldn't say no. I can't say I was upset. There were little service hiccups, like too much time between courses, but it was as if I was throwing a wonderful party at my house and watching the guests arrive. Their beautiful, elegant summer attire flapping in the wind as they walked from the parking lot to our front door was reassuring. By the time the evening was over, we had served one hundred eighty dinners. And the reaction was a unanimous "wow." I knew at the end of our first weekend that we had a hit on our hands.

FLASH-FORWARD TO a few weeks later: on a weekend night (take your pick, they were all the same, starting with Thursday), the bar was three feet deep with people and the dining area was like a who's who of Hamptons royalty: it was almost absurdly star-studded, like a Hirschfeld cartoon or a *New York* magazine cover collage depicting all the people who weekended out there: Ralph Lauren at one table; Billy Joel and Christie Brinkley at another; the artist (and now film director) Julian Schnabel, a gentle grizzly bear of a man, with his wife and kids; Donna Karan; David Bowie and Iman; Alec Baldwin and Kim Basinger; music industry attorney Alan Grubman; Revlon's Ron Perelman; even Senator Alfonse D'Amato.

And me? I spent a lot of time in the kitchen. The pasta station was just inside the doors and because we were still only about half-staffed, I had plenty of room to work. I always had six pans warmed up on burners, ready to make or reheat a sauce, and behind them were huge pots where I kept salted water boiling for cooking the pasta. It was some of the hardest work I'd ever done, but also the most satisfying; I was young and strong and coordinated, and could have several dishes working at once, often putting out more than 150 pastas in a night.

I also emerged regularly to survey the service floor of my joint, checking in on the action and putting out fires when need be. It wasn't long before I began to feel like Rick Blaine, the Humphrey Bogart character in *Casablanca*, overseeing the hottest place in town.

The celebs always ate in the Bar Room up front, but one of my biggest pleasures was introducing people to the other rooms, watching as they entered the Porch for the first time and felt the intimacy of the space and took in the peaceful view of the pond.

Once in a while, I'd slip out the back door for a breather in the parking lot, and there was no more sure sign of my burgeoning success than the display of automobiles there: the lanes closest to the restaurant were occupied by the cream of the crop: Ferrari, Lamborghini, and Rolls-Royce; the next tier by Porsche, Mercedes, and collectibles; the ones beyond that with "regular" cars. I'd look over the display of wealth and think about how far I'd come in just eight years.

ONE OF MY great pleasures over those first weeks was watching Ariel grow into his job. He could handle the most irate customer with unflappable charm and grace. One night, I saw a guy so angry that spit flew from his mouth as he laid into Ariel.

"Where is my table?" he spritzed.

"Two minutes, just two minutes," Ariel said with a patient smile.

"What are you going to do for me?" the guy insisted.

"Don't worry. You're going to have the best seat in the house. I'm going to take care of you, don't worry."

Then, as soon as Ariel turned the corner out of the Bar Room, into one of the little corridors that connected the various areas to each other, he'd dab at his sweaty forehead and cheeks with a tissue and lament the interaction. "So rough, this guy," he'd say. "So rude. So bad."

It was this last bit that truly endeared Ariel to me. I saw how hard he worked on the service floor, but anybody can run around checking on tables. Maintaining your composure while being screamed at takes a special talent. It was one area in which he outshone me by a mile.

ON THURSDAY NIGHTS, I took a private car out to La Guardia Airport and boarded a prop plane to East Hampton Airport, taking to the clouds and feeling like a young tycoon as I glided out over the water and touched down on Long Island. I'd dive into Sapore's world for three days, then sneak back into the city on Sunday evening and ease into my work week there.

It was a magical summer. Jessie was getting bigger and more beautiful by the hour, and the excitement of our first child's imminent arrival only added to the sense of life beginning anew out there. The sense of family, which had been there from the start with Jessie's father and brother, was also expanded as, more than in any restaurant I'd ever been a part of, the staff became like a family. Every time I showed up for the weekend, I was treated to a new surprise, like the time Maria responded to the homey setting of the restaurant itself, turning the area behind the building into an alleyway, like a Roman quarter, where she threw up clotheslines like you see all over Rome. She'd wash the restaurant's chef jackets, shirts, aprons, and some personal clothing for Mark, hang them on ropes to dry, then iron them before service. She also set up a little coop where she kept chickens and roosters from which we'd harvest eggs, and eventually butcher and cook the birds as well.

In sharp contrast to the nightly hubbub of the restaurant was the daytime serenity. I came to think of our stretch of the pond as my own private saltwater lake. There were ducks, and sometimes I'd see a swan floating along. I rented a few canoes from a guy who had a roadside concession across the street so I and the staff could paddle around during breaks. It was everything a man could dream of.

LIKE ANY NEW restaurant, we had quirks to work out: one was that the clientele began taking the summertime theme to extremes. Many of our customers understood the spirit of Sapore and would arrive in casual but elegant attire, but others would show up looking as though they had just come from the beach, which I'm sure many of them had. Before too long, the customers wearing shorts, sandals, and bathing suits were becoming the majority.

So we made a new rule: No shorts. Just like at the Vatican.

One night, Ralph Lauren, driving home with his wife and a few friends, spontaneously decided to drop in for dinner. The friends met our dress code, but Ralph was wearing shorts.

I wasn't there at the time, and I'd guess that Ralph looked every inch his stylish self, even in shorts. But without me there to make an executive decision, Ariel was loath to make an exception to our dress policy. We didn't keep any pants in the cloakroom the way some restaurants keep jackets. So my quick-thinking maître d' ran into the kitchen and emerged with a pair of black-and-white checkered chef pants, presenting them to Ralph Lauren.

Gentleman that he is, Ralph disappeared good-naturedly into the men's room and emerged in his new outfit.

When I arrived and heard what had happened, I was mortified. But Ralph is a sport. He said it was no big deal and that he was happy to comply. And you know what? He looked good. He looked so good that I'm surprised that chef pants didn't become the next big fashion craze out there. Even in the Hamptons, I guess, absurdity has its limits.

THAT'S THE WAY it was. We were awash in celebrity and I was becoming friendly with even more people I'd heard and read about when I was still living in Rome. One of my favorite times each week was Saturday afternoon, the eye of the storm between Friday night and Saturday night. It was also when many of our celebrity customers came in for lunch, to enjoy the restaurant's patio away from the eyes of the masses.

One Saturday afternoon, we were hosting Billy Joel and Christie Brinkley, along with their little daughter Alexa Ray, and another couple that have since gone their separate ways, Alec Baldwin and Kim Basinger.

I was busy in the kitchen, getting ready for the evening service. The only management presence in the dining room was the current occupant of our revolving-door position of receptionist-hostess.

At about three o'clock, I began thinking about the dinner hour and went into the dining room to see if Ariel had shown up yet. There he was, the picture of Hamptons style, in a white linen suit with brown leather slip-on shoes.

With a list of that night's reservations in hand, we walked the floor together, determining who we'd seat where, a very political exercise at a hot spot like Sapore. We also personally greeted Alec and Kim and Billy and Christie. It was another of those perfect, lazy afternoons at Sapore, with Alexa Ray asleep in her father's lap, and him and Christie sipping wine as though they were hanging out on their own back porch at home.

As we made the rounds, I noticed, out of the corner of my eye, pedaling up to the entrance on a bicycle, a woman in her late fifties, or so I'd have guessed. It was tough to tell: she was wearing a straw hat and sunglasses, so it was hard to see her face.

But something about her seemed familiar.

We couldn't hear the exchange that followed but from the gestures—the woman spoke, the reservationist shook her head from side to side, the woman shrugged happily, hopped on her bike and left—we could tell that she had been denied a reservation.

I had a nagging suspicion that something wasn't right. I sent Ariel over to see what had happened. He returned and informed me that she was looking for a table for four for eight o'clock.

"And?" I asked.

"The girl told her that we were fully—"

I realized who it was.

"Jesus Christ, Ariel, that was Jacqueline Kennedy Onassis."

He considered that for a moment.

"Oh my God, Pino! You're right!"

I pointed to the highway: "Go after her!"

Ariel's jaw dropped, but he didn't move.

"We cannot allow this to happen. Go!"

"Pino, she's gone down the highway."

"So go chase her down the fucking highway! This cannot happen. Not here!"

With a shrug, Ariel began walking toward the road.

"You're not going to get her if you walk. Run!"

Ariel began running in his immaculate white linen suit, slipping his jacket off as he started. Our driveway was covered with gravel, so he couldn't really pick up any speed until he got to the highway.

I went out to the edge of my property and looked down the sloping highway. I could see the former First Lady about five hundred yards away, stopped at an intersection, straddling her bike, and behind her, coming up fast, my own Latin Gatsby, running down the road after her to gallantly offer her a table.

She was about to start pedaling again, but he called out to her and she stopped and turned around. They spoke. She nodded and he waved good-bye.

Ariel returned to our parking lot, drenched in sweat. He reported his success. She had accepted the reservation, and his apology.

I was so happy. I had always admired Jackie O. Not just her style, but also her strength after her husband was assassinated, and all those stories about how she had raised her children, Caroline and John Jr., to be humble and polite. She clearly lived those values herself. I mean, here she was in the Hamptons, where *everyone* wants you to know who they are, and she didn't even divulge her identity to get a table at a restaurant.

I had to compliment Ariel on his triumph: "I'm proud of you, Ariel. You did what the best maître d' in the Hamptons should do, and you should feel good about it."

Despite my good feelings toward him, the incident pointed out one of the few problems that hung over us like a cloud: because the Hamptons is basically a very fashionable, sophisticated area sequestered within a working-class region, the supply of capable front-of-the-house talent was severely limited in those days. We were the first restaurant of its size and stature out there, and so we were constantly hiring and firing hosts, hostesses, and other employees—we just couldn't have reservationists who didn't recognize Jacqueline Kennedy Onassis!—so I was presented with a challenge that would endure through the entire lifespan of Sapore di Mare: we had great difficulty finding quality support in the kitchen or the dining room. It quickly became apparent to me that no matter how many ads we ran in the paper, and no matter how many phone calls I made, we were going to have trouble filling all the positions.

As for the few employees that we *did* manage to find—locals who had worked in diners and greasy-spoon joints—they could barely handle the pressure. Most of them stopped showing up for work after a few days, never to be heard from again.

Determined to maintain my growing reputation, I told Ariel to keep the crowd to a manageable size, even turning away business if necessary. And to make sure that he didn't cave into the pressure of clamoring customers, I asked Jessie, then six months pregnant, to work the door with him.

This was a sound enough plan, but the Hamptons in the summer are populated with everyone who had ever set food in Il Cantinori, or so it seemed. So, as the hour approached eight o'clock each evening, the phone would begin to ring off the hook. Jessie would dutifully tell all comers that we were fully booked. In most towns, that would have been the end of the discussion.

But not in the Hamptons.

In fact, there was no *discussion*. A typical exchange went like this:

> *Ring. Ring.*
> JESSIE: Sapore di Mare, good evening.
> CUSTOMER: This is Ms. So-and-So. Do you have a table available at nine P.M.?
> JESSIE: No, I'm sorry, we're fully booked.
> CUSTOMER: Just tell Pino we're coming over.
> JESSIE: But . . .
> *Click. Dial tone. Sound of Jessie slamming the phone down.*

"Tell Pino we're coming over" was the most-uttered phrase in the Hamptons that summer, along with "I'm a friend of Pino's," favored by guests who didn't even bother to call and instead just showed up—their version of "Open Sesame."

About once a night, poor Jessie would come swinging through the door to the kitchen, which opened right onto the pasta station where I usually cooked. She would tell me of the latest inhuman treatment she had received, and then sulk back to the dining room.

It broke my heart to see her looking so sad and mad, but I didn't know what else to do. I needed her out there.

One night, I was going about my business at the pasta station when I had that sixth-sense intuition, unique to restaurateurs, that I had better go check on the dining room. I did: everything looked fine.

But my radar wasn't totally busted. Sitting *on* the reservation desk was Jessie, staring off into space, shell-shocked.

It was clear that this couldn't continue. All that lay ahead for me was trouble: a series of tense battles on the home front. Moments later, as I watched my dear wife withstand an earful of abuse from yet another unannounced group, I decided that I had no choice. I had to relieve her of her pain.

But I couldn't bring myself to tell her.

At the end of the night, I pulled Ariel aside and told him, "Tomorrow morning, the moment you get up, find me a new hostess. Don't go to the beach. Don't come in here. Get on the phone and find me someone and have her here by three thirty"—an hour before Jessie's scheduled arrival.

The next day, Ariel had a new hostess installed, as directed. When Jessie showed up, she jerked a thumb in the girl's direction and asked Ariel what was going on.

"Pino had to replace you," he said, trying to sound soothing on my behalf. "It was too much stress for you."

"Oh really?"

Jessie came swinging into the kitchen and stared at me with a look so cold that the pasta water stopped boiling: "You know, I really don't care about working here," she screamed. "I was trying to help you out. But *you . . . you . . .* you *coward.* You couldn't tell me yourself?"

"That's right," I said. "I couldn't do it. But what's important is I'd rather keep you as a wife than as an employee."

One of the things I've always loved about Jessie is that she can call me on my bullshit. (In my humble opinion, this is something all real men love in the women they choose to spend their lives with.) She spun around in a rage and stomped out of the kitchen. But she was home that night when I got back from work, and though she didn't admit it right away, she was happier.

The problems extended to the lower ranks as well. Late in the summer, when I was in the city running Il Cantinori during the week, I began to get frantic calls from Mark, increasingly concerned by our lack of help. Our employment problems continued unabated and we were only getting busier and busier. If I had known what an ongoing headache this would be, I probably never would have opened the restaurant.

I was desperate, so when two of my regular customers (too ridiculously affluent and influential to name) asked me to give their home-from-college kids—we'll call them Mitch and Missy—summer jobs, I thought sure, why not? And I hired them as a busboy and busgirl.

My thinking was that these kids were so well traveled and sophisticated that they'd bring an ingrained sense of good service to their work. Little did I imagine that they might be completely uninterested in the quality of that work.

But I got a quick lesson when Missy showed up for her first day in her BMW convertible and parked it in the lot next to the highway. Our innkeeper, a very serious old Dominican, instructed her to park it out back; the front lot was for customers. "Oh, Chico," she said to him without breaking stride, her blonde hair flowing behind her in the summer wind, "I *am* a customer."

Instead of showing up at five minutes to four, like the employees who needed the job, she and Mitch showed up at four thirty, fresh from the beach, unkempt and smelling of the sea and sand.

"You, boy," I said to the young man. "Do you have a watch?"

"Yes, Mr. Luongo."

"What time are you supposed to be here?"

"Four o'clock."

"And what time is it?"

He looked down at his Rolex. "Four thirty."

"So?"

"I'm sorry, Mr. Luongo. I fell asleep at the beach."

I looked at his unshaven face, his salt-caked hair. "What are you going to do about a shower?"

"Oh, I don't need a shower, Mr. Luongo. I'm just a busboy."

"Just a busboy? Look at these other people who are 'just busboys,'" I said, gesturing at the well-groomed crew in freshly cleaned black slacks and white shirts: my proud, hard-working team.

"How many times have you come to my restaurant? Do the busboys look like this?" I pointed at him, to make sure he understood what *this* meant.

"You're right, Mr. Luongo. I'm sorry. It'll never happen again."

Once they got to work, things weren't much better. Missy had an aversion to dirty dishes, an unfortunate trait in a busgirl. When she approached an abandoned table, with its half-eaten pastas, napkins dropped in sauce, and lipstick on the wine glasses, she would scrunch up her face and hold her breath. Then, to avoid breaking a nail, she would only pick up one or two dishes at a time, scurry to the kitchen with them, and come back for the next puny load.

On a scale of one to ten, I'd say she was a minus ten.

As if I didn't have enough problems to deal with, every time I left the kitchen, I'd find these kids doing something unbelievable. Like the time I discovered them in the middle of Saturday night service, passing a cigarette back and forth in the parking lot out behind the kitchen. Or when they took a break that same night to sit at the bar and have a cocktail.

When I saw *that*, I pulled them aside.

"People, listen. In Italy, we have an expression that if you look the other way three times, you are stupid. And I'm starting to feel like an idiot."

I presented them with a choice: "I'll give you one more chance. Be here at four o'clock tomorrow. *Or else*."

Mitch—he's probably a lawyer today—jumped right in. "Yes, Mr. Luongo. That's perfect. I feel like the past few days, we've just been breaking the ice."

"Listen," I said. "We're not breaking the ice. You're breaking my balls. Now get out of here."

The next day, with a fool's optimism, I pushed myself all morning and into the afternoon. I got *my* work done early so I could spend some time with Mitch and Missy when they arrived, show them how I expected them to work, turn them into the kind of proud workers I respected.

I had been a busboy in my life. I had done everything you could do in a restaurant, and that's part of why I resented them so much. I didn't care who their parents were; the fact that they thought they could disrespect my beautiful Sapore di Mare, the place I had built with my own sweat and hard work—that was the most offensive thing of all.

You already know what happened next. They didn't show up at four o'clock. They didn't even show up by four fifteen. When they finally did show up, at four thirty, I was sitting in the balcony overlooking the dining room. I watched them prance in through the front door, even though Chico—hard-working, proud Chico—told them not to every day. As always, they were fresh from the beach, with messy hair and that salty smell.

My already famous temper was engaged. It didn't matter that these two were the spawn of rich and famous power brokers; they threatened to undo my success.

"You two," I said as I stood up and charged down the stairs. They looked terrified, like they were about to be gored by a bull.

"You know what? That's it. You better get out of here. In fact, you better get out of here right now. Actually, you know what, GET THE FUCK OUT OF HERE. NOW!"

They didn't move.

"NOW!"

"But, Mr. Luongo," Mitch said. "What about our tips from last night?"

"*Tips?*" I actually laughed. "You want your tips? I'll give you a tip: you go home and tell your fathers that you are *fired*. You incompetent, spoiled, rich brats." They stood there for a second, in shock.

Mitch jerked his head in the direction of the bar, suggesting to Missy that they have a drink before leaving.

"Now!" I bellowed. "Get the fuck out of here, you little brats. Out, out, out," and I chased them right out the door.

Both Mitch's and Missy's fathers called me, outraged, vowing that they'd never come back to Sapore di Mare again.

But they did. They had to. They were friends of Pino's.

EIGHT

Why Pasta Matters

I F THERE'S ONE accomplishment I'd like to be remembered for, it's popularizing Tuscan food in America. If there's a second, it would be improving the quality of the pasta served in American restaurants.

I love pasta. For me, it summarizes and epitomizes much of what I've always responded to about Tuscan food, specifically its intersection of history, economy, and flavor. As with most deeply felt food connections, though, my affection for pasta exists somewhere beyond my ability to fully explain it. I can't put words to why I fell in love with Jessie when I first saw her, and I can't exactly put words to why I have had a love affair with pasta that's gone on for more than half a century.

But I'll try. With all of Italy's regions and all of their differences, pasta is the thing that they all have in common, which is what led Giuseppe Garibaldi to say, in 1860, "It will be maccheroni, I swear to you, that will unite Italy." Pasta is, in my opinion, the most complete food ever invented by mankind. Just as Americans have endless varieties of sandwiches (the original, burgers, wraps, and so on) that put meat, vegetables, and starch in a neat, pick-up-able package, we Italians have pasta, which often combines the same elements into something moist, substantial, and delicious.

I know that I'm not alone in my adoration. I've seen it in my restaurants every day for more than two decades: the look on customers' faces when a plate of piping-hot pasta is set down before them is more anticipatory, more gleeful, than it is for any other type of dish;

and when they take that first bite, I can see that something deeper than mere appetite has been satisfied.

The amazing thing is that for all the passion they inspire, the majority of pastas, including the most beloved ones, are intrinsically simple. Like pasta carbonara: to my mind, it's a perfect dish and one that I never tire of. I also never tire of making it: the fact that the egg and cheese are cooked by the heat of the pasta itself amazes and delights me every time.

When I arrived in New York, if I wanted a well-made pasta I had to make it myself. Most of what I saw in restaurants was limp noodles in a soupy sauce. Recipes had been misinterpreted and reinvented so many times they had become like the story in a game of telephone that, by the time you get to the last person, bears little resemblance to the original. For example, to many Americans, even some wonderful chefs, Bolognese means a meat sauce to be served over pasta. But a true Bolognese isn't really a sauce: it's ground meat that's cooked with tomato and wine, then enriched with milk and cream, but only enough to facilitate its coating the pasta.

Part of the beauty of a Bolognese, and of many pasta recipes, is that once you know how to cook, you don't need a scientific formula, just the gist of the steps. Don't believe me? Try this: Procure some ground pork, ground veal or mortadella, and ground beef. (Don't worry if you make too much because you can refrigerate or freeze it.) Heat some olive oil in a wide, deep, heavy pan and add some minced onions, carrots, and celery. (This mixture is called a *soffritto*.) Add the meats to the pan, season them with salt, pepper, and ground nutmeg, and brown them really well, breaking them up with a wooden kitchen spoon or, even better, with a fork. Sprinkle the meat with some red wine, just enough to moisten it. Then add some crushed canned tomatoes and tomato paste, but only enough to coat the meat. Stir the meat and tomato products together until they are indistinguishable. If the meat seems dry, you can add a little chicken stock or veal stock. Next add equal amounts of cream and milk, cook just enough for them to thicken, then cover the pan and braise the meat in the oven until smooth, dark, and creamy. After about an hour, toss the meat with cooked pasta and, if it seems a little dry, add some of the pasta's cooking liquid (we'll talk about this in a moment) to bind the sauce and make it just wet enough to coat the pasta.

The Bolognese that these steps produce is rich and meaty, and when I serve it to customers, many of them think it's my interpretation of a Bolognese. But the truth is that this is as classic as you can get; the other sauces that Americans have been eating for years, those crimson-red, creamless sauces, are something else entirely, an Americanized version that seems like a crumbled-up burger stirred into a tomato sauce, with no seasoning or intensity.

This is why I ended up cooking the pasta myself when we first opened Sapore di Mare, because there was so much *unteaching* to be done, so much wrong knowledge to remove from cooks before I could impart the right way.

So, if you can try to free your mind for a moment, to forget all you think you know about pasta making, if you are willing to reboot your pasta hard drive, then allow me to share some thoughts about how to cook and think about pasta.

The first thing you need to understand about pasta is that it's a dish of uniformity; it's not the application of a liquid or a semiliquid to a solid. To some degree, the pasta and its sauce are supposed to be indistinguishable from one another; it should be impossible to tell where one ends and the other begins. This sounds like a simple concept, but it's not. As with any seemingly simple cooking—any dish that involves only a few ingredients and a straightforward technique—the success or failure rests in the cook's keen eye, a sense of smell that's canine in its sensitivity, and hands that think for themselves. In other words, the only way to be a good pasta cook is by cooking and eating a lot of pasta.

Things are better than they used to be when it comes to pasta in the United States, but there's still much that isn't understood, even by some of the best chefs. The most important phrase in pasta cooking, when it comes to dried pasta anyway, is surely *al dente*, which means "to the tooth." We say that properly cooked pasta is still toothsome; not chewy, but offering some resistance to the teeth. But even pasta that's properly al dente often fails the crucial test of being fused with its sauce. The reason is that pasta should only be partially cooked when it's drained of its cooking liquid; it's supposed to finish cooking *in its sauce*, soaking it up as it reaches doneness, and attaining that crucial uniformity.

So, when I teach somebody how to make pasta, the first thing we focus on is how to cook the pasta itself. It's, of course, important to select a good brand; my favorites are De Cecco and, for short pasta, Setaro. If you can't find those, Barilla is widely available and perfectly respectable. You need to begin with a lot of water, enough that the pasta will tumble when it boils so that it cooks evenly; you want each piece or strand to move about freely. The water should also be well salted because you want to actually taste the pasta, both its flavor and some of the salt.

Pasta that's cooked al dente will have a pinpoint of chalk-white rawness at the center, and there's nothing wrong with removing a strand from the boiling water and biting or cutting into it to check for this. Before draining the pasta in a colander, it's a good idea to scoop up some of its cooking liquid in case the dish needs correcting at the last second; that liquid can thin a thick sauce, and the starch it's taken on helps bind the dish. Once the pasta is drained, it should be added to the pan in which the sauce has been prepared or reheated. The pan should be wide and deep enough to allow you to toss them together, over and over, until the pasta has taken on some sauce and the remaining sauce generously coats the pasta.

There are two marks of a perfect pasta: one is that it should stand up on the plate. What I mean by that is that when you take your tongs and transfer a serving from the pan to a dish, the pasta shouldn't collapse into a stringy puddle; instead, the mound should maintain its shape and height, even when one starts to eat it. The other mark of a well-made pasta is that when the pasta is gone, the plate is empty, save for perhaps a thin coating of sauce—just enough to be mopped up with a piece of bread (called *scarpetta*, which means "heel" because the hunk of bread resembles the heel of a shoe).

(These two defining tests, by the way, led to many arguments between me and my customers in the early days of Il Cantinori and Sapore di Mare. There were innumerable times when diners would send their pasta back to the kitchen because they deemed it "raw," or because it didn't have enough "sauce." Sometimes, in the heat of service, I'd get pretty angry and sarcastic about it, like the time a waiter brought a *spaghetti alla rustica* into the kitchen and told me the customer had said that it wasn't *"saltati"* enough, *saltati* being the word for "jump" or "sauté." I put the plate on the floor, hopped back and forth over it three times, then picked it up and handed it back to the waiter: "Now it's *saltati* enough," I said. "Take it back." But I usually took the plate back to the table myself and did my best to explain the situation, namely that this was the right way to make pasta and that I wasn't able to make it any other way. Some people were curious and grateful; others not so much. But I simply wasn't willing to serve pasta the wrong way in my own restaurant.)

Those are the basics of pasta making, but there are many decisions that go into any pasta. The one that must be answered every time is what type of pasta goes with what sauce, which is of course a very complicated question because there's often no single correct answer. I look at it in a rather abstract way: it's like choosing a suit. The right suit will show off the beauty of a man's body and also the elegance of the suit. By the same token, there's a conversation that goes on between pasta and sauce. They should complement each other in a way that, in hindsight, makes their coupling seem inevitable.

Once again, examples are the only way to illustrate this. One of my signature dishes since the days of Il Cantinori has been *rigatoni alla buttera*, made with hot and sweet sausage, peas, and a touch of cream and tomato. The rigatoni offsets its intensity with the size of the pasta and also with that big, gaping tube of space in its center. Pasta carbonara only works with thick strands or tubular pasta like spaghetti, bucatini, or fettuccine. I usually opt for fettuccine because it's both long and flat, so there's more surface area to accept the sauce. The caramelized onion and pureed tomato in *spaghetti alla rustica* might be overwhelming with short, thick pasta; instead, a long noodle is required to ensure balance.

Another age-old debate is when to use fresh pasta and when to use dried. In many ways, it hasn't been resolved, but many American food critics have a predisposition against dried pasta. They believe that true fine dining, if it includes pasta at all, means fresh pasta because to them dried connotes a bulk item. Years ago, a prominent food writer had dinner at my restaurant Coco Pazzo, then went to a supermarket and figured out how much the individual ingredients cost. He then wrote an article about the huge gap between what we charged and what you could make the dish for at home. I took great offense at this because I wasn't in the food preparation business; I was in the fine-dining business and I put enormous value on the ability of me and my cooks to make some of the most authentic pasta in New York City. It wasn't just the ingredients people were paying for: it was the know-how that went into the dish and the setting in which they ate it.

That debate aside, my general feeling is that fresh pasta is best for rich, creamy, smooth sauces, and for tomato-based and seafood sauces dried is the way to go. The one pasta that should be avoided at all costs is capellini, also called angel hair pasta. Though it's used in many seafood dishes here in the United States, in Italy it's only called for in one dish, *capellini in brodo*, or capellini in broth. That's what it was created for and that's the only way we use it.

But all of this information is only somewhat useful. You can only be told so much about making pasta. If you want to understand and master it, you need to immerse yourself in it until you've absorbed it and it's become a part of you, like that perfect, elusive coming together of pasta and sauce.

NINE

Mothers and Sons

I N AUGUST 1988, as Sapore di Mare was going full tilt in the Hamptons, back in the city Il Cantinori had settled into a very pleasant, half-speed respite. It was that laid-back time when the Village undergoes its annual transformation into a ghost town, so quiet that you can hear your own shoes clicking and clacking on the sidewalk as you stroll the breezy tree-lined streets on your way to work each morning.

I didn't mind the calm at all: a lot of the restaurants back home would have been closed during August, so I looked at whatever business we did as gravy, especially since I had seen the way it picked up again every fall—the reanimation of the city that starts with Labor Day and ends with the Jewish High Holy days. It was also a welcome counterbalance to the action at Sapore, which was bursting at the seams on the weekends, beginning with Thursday night, when our customers migrated from the city to the country. I actually had come to love the end of summer because the break from our normal pace afforded me all sorts of indulgences, like spending more time chitchatting with customers, or checking out new restaurants. The dining scene in New York was mutating, expanding, evolving a little bit every six months. Within a few years of when I threw my hat in the ring with Il Cantinori, a number of American chefs and restaurateurs had begun to change the face of the dining scene in New York. Down in Tribeca, Drew Nieporent had opened his first restaurant, Montrachet, with the chef David Bouley. Just a few blocks away, Danny Meyer had opened

Union Square Cafe; and a few blocks the other way, Jerry Kretchmer and his partners had opened Gotham Bar and Grill, which after a dodgy first year had found new life with a young chef named Alfred Portale. It was true what they said about rising tides lifting all boats. New restaurants were popping up left and right and chefs were becoming celebrities, garnering more and more coverage in newspapers and magazines—and not just in the food pages. New Yorkers were becoming passionately interested in food, and I'm sure that it was one of the things that kept Il Cantinori going so strong for its first five years.

That August, one of my regular customers, Fred Pressman, the owner of Barneys department store, pulled me aside and told me he had a piece of possible business to discuss with me. I had always considered Fred something of a kindred spirit, a fellow merchant and man of good taste, so I was curious to know what it was that he had in mind.

"Would you be interested in opening a restaurant with us in Chelsea?" was the question.

Today, Chelsea is perhaps the hottest neighborhood in New York City, but in the late 1980s is was a semi-industrial wasteland, a spillover area just north of the West Village and one of the city's curious no-man's-lands, long past one heyday and awaiting the moment when the cyclical nature of New York life would make it fashionable once again. I had never expected that I might help bring that eventuality about, but that's what was about to happen.

The Pressmans owned a four-story building a block north of Barneys where they had planned to open a restaurant in partnership with Roberto Ruggeri, owner of Bice restaurant in Milan. But something had gone down with Roberto. Fred declined to say what it was, but he gave the impression that a major catastrophe had been averted, and that he didn't want to be associated with Roberto any longer and had pulled the plug on the deal.

I already had partners, and I didn't really need another restaurant, but I couldn't resist the attention, and I was intrigued. To me, the Pressmans had more money than God: with partners like them, who knew what kind of access—to people, to money, to prestige—I might end up with? For all of my success, there were still times, like those moments when I'd stand out behind Sapore and gaze over the collection of cars in the parking lot, when it didn't seem real, when I still expected that it might all go down the tubes or be taken away from me. There were still times when I felt like that mute in the airport when I first arrived in 1980, with that sensation of being stared at like King Kong, like a curiosity, a side show. Part of my success was based on my "otherness," but that same quality made me always feel like an outsider, a permanent foreigner. So the Pressmans didn't just represent advancement to me; they represented the security and acceptance of people with access to the power brokers of New York.

In addition to all of that, there was that feeling of easy camaraderie with Fred, the sense of a soul mate, of somebody who "got" me.

The only thing was that I was just getting my financial legs under me: Jessie and I had a child on the way, and I had taken on a lot of debt when I assumed ownership of Sapore.

So I told Fred that the only way I'd want to pursue anything was if the Pressmans bankrolled the project; my contribution would be my know-how, my taste, and my time. He said they were fine with that and we made an appointment to look at the space together. I walked over from Il Cantinori one midweek afternoon and was struck that Chelsea was almost without character: it had neither the skyscrapers of Midtown nor the old New York charm of the Village. It was a sprawling neighborhood of housing projects and 1960s-era apartment buildings with a smattering of delis and diners. Eighteenth Street itself wasn't any more promising: there was an electrical substation across the street from the restaurant space, and next to that was a plumbing supply store—not exactly the view New Yorkers liked to be presented with when they entered and exited a restaurant.

But when we stepped inside, I could see right away why the Pressmans thought a restaurant would be the thing to put there: the room was high-ceilinged, with western exposures, meaning that it would be light, but not blindingly so, at lunchtime. There were enormous arched windows and exposed brick walls. In the only-in-New York department, the space had once been a storage facility for floats and such from the annual Macy's Thanksgiving Day Parade, but it had been cleared out and so was empty except for some industrial kitchen equipment that had been delivered when they were getting ready to open it with the Bice team. There was also an emergency exit that led to the enormous Barneys parking lot, and it occurred to me right away that we could build a patio there for outdoor seating, which in my opinion was a must, if only because I myself loved dining outside in the summer and had become addicted to it on the Porch at Sapore.

It was the perfect union of functionality and theatricality, and I began what was fast becoming a familiar exercise for me as I imagined the new restaurant we might build there: I saw an airy dining room with long white tablecloths, dark wood at the edges, and flowing drapes over the windows. I had been thinking that my next restaurant should have a pizza oven, and I imagined it along the western wall. I could smell the smoke and I began to smell the food: garlic and herbs and that winey, beefy aroma that made me think of my mother's kitchen, which naturally led to one of the biggest ideas I'd ever had: home cooking was the root of all Italian cooking, so why not go to the source and bring together a team of Italian mothers and grandmothers to consult on a new restaurant? In a matter of seconds, I could see the public relations potential: food journalists hungry for the next big concept would eat up the idea that the restaurant's recipes came from actual, bona fide Italian mothers whom I would import from Italy and parade in front of them. My only immediate concern was finding home cooks who also knew how to function in a professional kitchen, but I didn't see why I couldn't simply hire an American chef to pull it all together.

The name popped into my head: *Le Madri*. The mothers. There was no question about it: a home run.

FRED RESPONDED TO the idea and we decided to try to make it work.

There was just one problem: I might have had two successful restaurants, but when it came to doing business—real business, big business—I was an idiot, or at least an innocent. Steve, Nicola, and I had done everything ourselves, with just a handshake between us. We had even handled the acquisition and transfer of the Sapore space

with a breathtaking lack of legal intervention; though we had our differences from time to time, there was an unspoken bond between us,
three immigrants and small-business owners who understood that we'd
each make our share of mistakes along the way and would never take
advantage of each other.

But with the Pressmans it was different. They were natural-born
Americans with an innate grasp of how to do business here. They understood contracts the way I understood pasta: it was in their blood.
Besides all of that, they could buy and sell me and had high-powered
attorneys at their beck and call. So as the time approached to meet
with them and hammer out a working agreement, I grew increasingly
fearful of making a bad business deal, of promising more than I could
deliver or of being taken advantage of. Fortunately, I've always known
what I don't know, and so I went into the process with a great deal of
humility and with my eyes wide open.

One sunny August afternoon, I showed up at Barneys' corporate
offices, across the street from the department store, for the Big Meeting. It was an unassuming building and the executive offices were on
an upper floor, tastefully and humbly decorated. I hadn't put on a suit
and tie, because I didn't know how to stand on ceremony back then.
Instead I arrived in slacks and a sport coat, perfectly in keeping with
my relationship with Fred. The only problem was that Fred had magically disappeared. In his stead, waiting for me in the rather cramped
conference room, were Irv and Mark, respectively the company CFO
and in-house legal counsel, slender men with pale complexions and
power ties who, it was clear from their cool reception, were going to
treat me as an adversary.

To make matters worse, we couldn't get right down to business because we were waiting for Fred's son Bob, to whom he had turned
over the handling of our negotiations. It was tense in the room. I
maintained my composure, but the fact that Fred had thrown me to
the legal dogs only heightened my anxiety. My opinion of lawyers and
accountants was that they are there to make better deals for their
clients than their clients would be able, or willing, to make for themselves, and not only because their clients don't know the intricacies of
the law: the American attitude, it seemed to me, was that your lawyer

could royally screw somebody on your behalf, but as long as you didn't do it yourself, your hands and your conscience were clean.

I didn't know how exactly to protect myself, but I had never forgotten the cost of being too direct, too honest, back when my forthrightness with the GM of Zinno had cost me my job there. This time, I'd keep my cards close to my vest.

The two suits and I sat around making painful small talk for about thirty minutes.

At one point, Fred appeared in the door way of the conference room, rapped on the open door, and said, "Don't beat Pino up too much. He's my partner," then disappeared laughing down the hallway.

I remember thinking it was a power play disguised as a joke, and I steeled myself for the worst. As the minutes ticked by, it became increasingly apparent that these men considered me beneath their master's reputation and family, a smooth-talking immigrant charmer who had somehow wooed the old man and convinced him to invest money in him. Did they ever say this to me directly? No. But when you know how to read people, instinctively, the way animals read each other, such sentiments are as apparent as the color of their eyes.

Finally, Fred's son Bob, the co-CEO of Barneys, showed up. I disliked him from the moment I laid eyes on him: he looked like a pasty, corpulent member of the Lucky Sperm Club if ever there was one. He came bounding into the room and began talking right over us.

"Pino!" he said grandly, as though we were best of friends when in fact I don't think we'd ever said more than two words to each other in all the times I'd visited his father's table in my restaurant.

I shook his hand, tried not to laugh in his face.

"We love your restaurant. Been there many times. And now we're going to do a restaurant together."

He was a study in insincerity, which, as a former actor, I found doubly insulting.

"You know we were going to do a restaurant with Roberto, right? Had to pull out. We have a name to protect."

"Sure," I said.

He sat down, gathered himself up, and took a deep breath.

The room came to a hush as we got down to business.

"OK, Pino. What is the most important thing for you?"

He was so transparent that all my inhibitions went right out the window and I spoke my mind freely: "Three things," I said. "I'm in charge, I'm in charge, I'm in charge."

Bob looked at his people and grinned, then looked back at me.

"I guess you're in charge."

I let it go.

"Yes," I said. "I'm in charge of the design, the menu, and how we manage the business. I don't want anybody to talk to me about what the menu should or should not have on it, who can cook, or how I run things."

He held up a hand.

"Wait a minute," he said. "We have to be involved in the design."

Of all the things on the table, this I could live with because I trusted the family's taste, even Bob's.

"OK, as long as you understand we're doing an Italian restaurant. This isn't going to be a French establishment," I said.

I thought it was important to say this because despite the rise of all those young American restaurateurs and chefs, French food still ruled in New York City. When it came to cuisine, Americans had a serious inferiority complex: they saw, and continue to see, themselves as lesser talents. All you need to do is examine the list of four-star ratings, still owned by French and French-leaning restaurants, to know that this is true. And, despite the financial success of people like me and Silvano, noses still turned up at Italian food, so I wanted to be clear that Le Madri was going to be unmistakably Italian in every aspect, regardless of whether or not it cost us a star.

"We're fine with that," he said.

We all nodded.

"OK," Bob said. "Now. How much money are you going to put down?"

That's when I realized how dysfunctional this scenario was. Either Fred hadn't fully briefed Bob, or Bob hadn't paid attention to his old man—or maybe he was trying to see if I'd budge. If I had to guess, I'd go with the last one: Bob and his sidekicks were going to protect Fred from himself.

"Excuse me?" I said.

"Your investment? What's your investment going to be?"

"My investment?" I said, wiping imaginary perspiration from my forehead with my index finger. "*Sudore,*" meaning "sweat." "That's what I'm here for. If that's not the deal, then we're having the wrong meeting."

Before he could respond, Bob's secretary knocked and came in, leaning over to him and whispering in his ear.

"Listen, guys," he said. "I have to go. Let's move on. Let's make this happen."

And he left.

Irv and Mark took over the meeting and we began trying to hammer out a working budget for the construction phase of Le Madri. Their position was that because I was going to function as general contractor and wanted autonomy in calling the shots, I was going to be the one responsible for its accuracy, a guarantor. Financial words and terms began to fly around the room, some of which I was familiar with; others were new to me. My acting skills really came in handy because I just pretended to understand what they were referring to, nodding and taking notes in my yellow legal pad. I also settled on a strategy: no matter what they said, I just listened, made more notes, smiled, and said "I'll get back to you." I could tell that this began to frustrate them, but I simply refused to agree to anything, not even the date when I'd get back to them.

When I got off on my own, with the help of my attorney, I assembled a team of lawyers specializing in liquor licenses, permits, and construction. This opened up a new world of hourly rates to me and I found it shocking. Some of the guys charged two hundred or two hundred fifty dollars per hour, and this was in the eighties. Whenever I called one of these lawyers to go over my notes from my meetings with the Pressmans' attorney, I would look at my watch right before dialing the phone and make a note of the time so I could track it. This became an obsession of mine and I started to convert my legal bills into restaurant food: for example, to pay for a thirty-minute call I had to sell four main courses. I'd see a tray loaded with pastas float by on a runner's open palm and think, *That only pays for about twenty minutes of counsel.* In time I realized that this was self-defeating. Attorneys are just a part of doing business here. They are criminals without guns, but you can't do anything about it, and the sooner you accept that, the better. You know who told me that? A lawyer, and he charged me for the ten seconds it took him to make the suggestion.

Part of me felt that I was making a huge mistake, but the rest of me knew that unless I wanted to scrape and claw for every advancement in my career, I would need partners with pockets as deep as the Pressmans'. If being in business with them meant a crash course in law and finance, then so be it. Once I came to terms with that fact of life, I embraced the challenge and took a new view of it: I knew how to open and operate a restaurant. I'd done it twice already and done it successfully. As I thought about it, my confidence grew, and I realized that I actually knew more about the nuts and bolts of the job than these guys Fred had caged me up with. All I had to do was figure out how to translate my experience into their lingo. A friend of mine gave me some important advice: "Don't promise them the world because you will get nothing for it," he said. "Don't give them the optimistic scenario. They are already in bed with you, so be conservative."

I was adjusting. Slowly but surely, I was learning how to be a businessman, but it was a difficult metamorphosis: with Steve and Nicola, and on my own in East Hampton, there was an understanding that we were engaged in a human enterprise, that there would be mistakes and that we would learn from them, but that everybody had his or her heart in the right place. This was different: I was putting myself on the line. And the number we ultimately came up with to finance the build-out and opening expenses was enormous: $1.25 million, which to a guy who had shown up in the United States with empty pockets eight years earlier was a terrifying sum. When I eventually got around to signing the contracts we'd drawn up, I was a coguarantor, not responsible for the same amount as the Pressmans, but still responsible for

enough that any creditors would be well within their rights to come after me for some of their money. There'd be no room for learning experiences this time, no margin for error.

AS OUR NEGOTIATIONS progressed, Fred introduced the one and
only contingency to our moving forward: he wanted me to sever my
ties with Il Cantinori, which was only a few blocks away and, as he saw
it, a conflict of interest. Fortunately for him, Steve was quickly developing the opinion that Sapore di Mare was taking me away from Il
Cantinori too much of the time.

As I became increasingly scarce around Il Cantinori, the tension
between me and Steve built. When I was there, and we sat down for
our dinner at the end of the night, he'd turn his chair away and talk to
me over his shoulder.

Finally, one evening, as we were sitting like that, Steve turned to
me and said, "We got to talk."

"I agree," I said, and we slowly began having the conversation that
had been so long coming. I knew that it was going to end with Steve
buying me out, but he was such a shrewd businessman that I felt I
had to at least bluff that I might purchase his and Nicola's shares of Il
Cantinori.

"You can buy me out," I said. "Or maybe I buy you out."

Steve smiled at my chutzpah. "Pino," he said, as though schooling
a little boy. "I own this building. You going to buy me out? I'm going
to become your landlord? I think you'll go." It reminded me of Moe
Greene in *The Godfather* telling Michael Corleone: "You buy me out?
No, no! I buy *you* out."

I agreed and after that awkward evening we swiftly put whatever
tensions there had been behind us and hammered out a deal in record
time. Before I knew it, I was out of Il Cantinori.

This plunged me into a period of bereavement. Il Cantinori was
like my soul. It was my first restaurant, the spring from which all my
confidence flowed. This was the early fall, the low season of Sapore, so
I was in the city most of the time. There were some mornings when
I'd get in my car and begin daydreaming and suddenly realize that I

was parking on Tenth Street instead of in Chelsea, having driven my-self to Il Cantinori on autopilot. And with no restaurant at which to spend my evenings, I'd sometimes walk over to Tenth Street around six thirty and sneak a peek into Il Cantinori. It looked the same, except that I wasn't there; instead I was a ghost discovering to his horror that the world could function just fine without him in it.

The pain was eased by new arrivals in my life: Jessie gave birth to our first son, Marco, in September 1988, and I myself was birthing Le Madri. I poured all of my energy into the development of the restaurant.

It was the most extensive overhaul I'd yet been involved in. Some-where along the way I decided that I wanted to have a vaulted ceiling, found the right craftsmen to do the work, and watched every day as they painstakingly constructed it, first fashioning a wire lathing, then applying the stucco. There was also green river hemlock wood floor-ing to be installed and a beautiful wood-burning pizza oven.

While all this was going on, I was also consumed with finding the mothers. The first would be Maria, my cook from the Hamptons, whom I was starting to think of as a sort of good-luck charm. For the others, I reached out to a network of friends, including a Piedmontese winemaker named Bruno Cerreto, to identify some talented female Italian chefs. (I also phoned my own mother and asked her to be a part of the restaurant. "That's the respect you have for me," she scolded me. "You want me to become an employee.") Bruno meanwhile found me Bruna Alessandria, a classic Italian beauty in her early forties from the farmland of Piedmont with a taste for colorful hand-knit clothing, and two other Piedmontese cooks, Margherita Aloi, just eighteen at the time, and Silvana, just nineteen, neither of whom—to be honest—was an actual mother, but both of whom could cook as if they'd raised a dozen happy kids. The mothers all arrived together; it was as if we'd placed an order, only instead of two pounds of white truffles we'd or-dered three women.

Neither Bruna nor Margherita had been to the United States be-fore, or had spent much time in any big city, so they were a bit over-whelmed. I set them up in an apartment in the Flatiron District, at Twenty-second Street and Broadway. To serve as funnel for all their combined ideas, I enlisted a young American chef named Alan Tardi, a modest, professional, and soft-spoken guy who had worked at Chanterelle and Lafayette.

Alan or I would meet them downstairs and escort these women— dressed in their earth-toned country threads—all over town. My first priority wasn't to get them into the kitchen; it was to treat them to a few weeks of the tourist life, to give them a sense of American culture and get them excited about being here. I wanted them to soak up New York City, so we took them to Central Park, the Statue of Liberty, Rockefeller Center, and other landmark locations. At a time when I was becoming more and more Americanized, these women reminded me who I was and where I came from; maybe that's why I came up with the concept when I did, to help myself preserve my essential identity. I loved taking them around Manhattan. I so related to what it was like to feel like a fish out of water here that I was highly protective of them. Whenever they were in my presence, I was their human force field, acting as bodyguard, interpreter, and sugar daddy. No matter where we went, they stuck out like a handful of sore thumbs thanks to their country attire and the fact that we all spoke Italian. It wasn't long until, like me before them, they were drawn to the Village, which felt the most like home, and that's where they'd often gravitate in their personal time.

We also wanted to introduce them to the Italian restaurants here and took them everywhere from Italian-American joints to hot restaurants, with the notable exceptions of Da Silvano and Il Cantinori. They were definitely *not* impressed by what they saw and tasted, usually pushing their plates away with a smirk after a few bites. Bruna was especially severe in her appraisal of the food, saying things like, "I don't even feed the pigs with this."

Our first "official" meeting was a few weeks later in the restaurant's unfinished dining room. As construction workers hammered, drilled, and sawed all around us, we sat and talked about food.

"I want you to give me lists of your favorite dishes," I told them, speaking in Italian, of course. Since they all hailed from Piedmont, the dishes they named were distinctly Piedmontese: those little ravioli called *plin*, tagliatelle with porcini mushroom ragù and white truffles, and a whole roster of risottos, including ones made with asparagus, chicken liver, and a red risotto made with Barolo wine. They also expressed a reverence for *vitello tonnato*, or sliced cooked veal served with a tuna mayonnaise. Clearly, Le Madri wasn't going to specialize in Tuscan cuisine, which was fine with me because all I really cared about was that the food be authentic and have that unmistakable feeling of home cooking about it.

After we kicked around these and other dishes, I said, "Now, I want to take the essence of *our* cooking, the unwritten flavor of Italy, the way we all eat at home, and communicate it to New Yorkers."

They all nodded. None of us had the words to express what we were talking about—but the food itself spoke volumes, and after we had discussed our favorite dishes at length, the women took to the kitchen. The first order of business was to acquaint them with the ingredients available here, almost all of which were different than what they were used to back in Piedmont. This was well before the upgrade in regional American farming took place, so vegetables didn't have the same big flavor they had at home. The women also had to learn to adjust to different cuts of meat, substituting, say, brisket for an eye round in *stracotto* because an eye round wasn't as fatty here, and that fat was essential to a successful pot roast. Even the water and flour were different, as I discovered when they complained about the lack of elasticity of the pasta dough the first time they made it.

Once this orientation was complete, we slowly began to start planning the menu. Cut loose to do their own thing, these country mice became as ferocious as tigers, turning the place into a flurry of flour and wine, knives and rolling pins. With those women in the kitchen, filling that enormous space with the scents of authentic Italian cooking, Le Madri became, more than my first two restaurants, a portal to my own past. When I left our apartment downtown, I felt like I was going to another home, populated by not one but four mothers. I think it was the same for them. They had only been in New York for a few weeks, but they were feeling homesick as well. Their food had a heightened intensity and I knew why: they poured all of their nostagia into their cooking.

As the women acclimated to life in New York, I had constant

reminders of my own evolution as when, like me years before, Margherita ended up doing an imitation of the construction workers she spent her days with, peppering her conversation gratuitously with "fuck." She also took a liking to American slang and loved spitting out phrases like "Don't piss me off."

It was also great fun to watch the women interact with the construction workers, most of whom were originally from Southern Italy. One night, as the smell of food wafted out into the dining room, one of the guys, I guess feeling teased by the delicious aroma of home cooking, called down from the scaffolding, "I guess we are not Michelangelo." It was a funny reference to the legend that Michelangelo, when he was painting the Sistine Chapel, had had meals served to him while he was lying on his back. This became a running joke in the restaurant, and eventually the women took the bait and began taking lunch and dinner out to the men, letting them taste the dishes we were testing.

To me as a fellow transplanted Italian, it was a joyous scene, but as a businessman I had a concern: the application of the stucco was slowing down. I pulled the general contractor aside and told him, "Look, I don't care if your guys eat here. We're cooks, and we like to share. But our price isn't going to change, no matter how long it takes."

Things didn't speed up, and so I brought the hammer down, telling the women to stop feeding the men. They were upset: Bruna was just plain pissed off, and Maria scolded me, telling me that it wasn't as though she were making any extra food to serve the men; she was just sharing what had to be cooked to test it.

One day, I realized that although I saw the women cooking and there was a glorious and garlicky aroma in the air, I hadn't seen a plate of food in more than twenty-four hours. I went looking through the kitchen, the office, and even out on the back patio. There wasn't a trace of food to be found.

On my way to check the refrigerator, I passed by the scaffolding, and on a hunch, I climbed up to the top. Sure enough, piled there were a few small stacks of dirty dishes. I should have been upset at this minor mutiny, but I wasn't. All these Italians were having a ball, and maybe I was being a little bit too hard on them; I didn't want to stifle the spirit that would lead to our success.

Besides, spending time at the restaurant site, and with these women, was heaven for me, but when I wasn't there I had to keep some anxiety at bay: with nowhere to go in the evenings, I was suddenly coming home to an apartment populated by my family. Sometimes at night, I'd watch as Jessie held Marco in her arms, nursing him, and think about how much I'd put at stake to pursue Le Madri. Though Jessie never showed anything but support and belief, there was no money coming in, and I was accountable for a good chunk of the million-plus dollars the Pressmans had poured into our joint enterprise.

But it wasn't really the money that worried me. The Il Cantinori buyout had left me flush for the time being, and I knew that at the end of the day I'd be able to bring the project in on time. No, what really weighed on me was the fact that Le Madri was a more ambitious restaurant than my first two. I had acquired a reputation as a talented restaurateur. My name meant something in New York, and I wanted it to go on meaning something for a good, long while.

AGAIN MY PUBLICIST, Susan Rike, stepped up to the plate, interesting *New York* magazine's Richard Story enough that he came to the restaurant to see it and taste some food before we opened. The result was a five-page spread in the magazine, an unprecedented promotional score. It made me feel like the king of the city, but I also heard rumblings about resentment from other restaurateurs; I could feel anger rolling down Seventh Avenue like hot lava. Nobody had ever had a spread like that and here I was dancing on their stage. It pissed a lot of them off, but I didn't care.

The article was a revelation to me: at the time, there was no shortage of concept restaurants in New York City. Some succeeded and some failed, but I realized that what made my restaurants work was that they were all founded on a true and deeply personal inspiration: it could be a song, as it was for Sapore di Mare, or a longing for country dining as it was at Il Cantinori, or the memory of home cooking as it was at Le Madri. They were my attempt to stay connected to my own past, to re-create a little of it right here in New York City, and what people responded to was their authenticity and their sincerity.

As I watched restaurants come and go around me, I realized that this was one of the things that set me apart: my places sprang from my own deep well of nostalgia and there wasn't an insincere detail anywhere in any of them, from the wooden beams and stucco walls to the displays of vegetable dishes at the door to the historically accurate recipes. The reason I was succeeding was the same reason I sometimes went off on waiters or cooks and the reason I had told Bob Pressman, "I'm in charge, I'm in charge, I'm in charge": *I simply refused to compromise.*

I ALSO REFUSED to compromise in my first cookbook, which was published in October 1988.

Just as I had a knack for naming restaurants, I thought I had one for naming books. My title for my first book was *A Tuscan in the Kitchen*. My idea was to try to capture between two covers what it was that people responded to about me in my restaurants: the food and the stories behind the food, both my personal anecdotes and the legends of such places as Maremma and Siena.

I also wanted to teach people how to cook the way Italians cook, which isn't by following exact recipes to the letter. It was the same reason I brought those women in to be a guiding force at Le Madri: in Tuscany, virtually any recipe you can think of is interpreted and personalized by the individual cook, so there are as many versions of, say, *pappa al pomodoro* as there are homes.

To capture this spirit and with hopes of inspiring the readers, part of my vision for the book was that recipes would be presented with no quantities or cooking times. So, I'd begin, say, a recipe for risotto, fisherman's style, by writing "Make sure you have enough liquid for making the risotto. Otherwise use white wine." Or I'd end a recipe for pasta-and-bean soup by advising, "when everything smells right, serve the soup with a little olive oil on top."

It would be impossible to sell a book with that kind of instructions today, but my agent had no problem setting it up with one of the top cookbook publishers, Clarkson Potter. Working with coauthors Barbara Raives and Angela Hederman, I spent hours describing the most famous dishes in Tuscany, along with the legends behind them and personal associations I made with them. In a way, it was an autobiography, though it had the structure of a cookbook.

By the end of the process, we had put together a handsome and modestly proportioned book that I was very proud of. It had a charming photograph of a view through a window of the old town of Montalcino on the cover and both color and black-and-white photographs throughout.

The book debuted and, to my dismay, we were savaged by critics who were shocked that I had left out the quantities and cooking times. The consensus was that the average American home cook was not able to relate to, let alone use, *A Tuscan in the Kitchen*. Never mind that many of the great cookbooks of all time, like those by Auguste Escoffier and, in Italy, Pellegrino Artusi, didn't specify quantities or cooking times.

In the midst of such explosive times for me, the cool reception the book received was a major disappointment, a reminder that although things were changing in America, I was still, in many ways, standing in that supermarket in Ozone Park, holding that anemic, cellophane-wrapped tomato in my hand.

The only silver lining was that the book developed an enormous cult following over the years; I still hear from people who tell me it's their favorite cookbook. And I was able to go on to do several others. But it remains a heartbreak for me.

I HAD REALIZED by this time that you put together a restaurant the way you assemble lasagna: layer by layer. The top layer was the front-of-the-house team, and I pulled together an improbably complementary band of Italians: Gianfranco, a Florentine with aristocratic features set off by a shaggy mane of black hair with a taste for tweedy sport coats and short, thin ties; Ariel, whose pretty-boy charm and flashiness translated effortlessly from East Hampton to Chelsea; and Cesare, a Roman who had been a bartender at the ancient Gino's restaurant on Lexington and then at Cipriani before tiring of uptown customers and spending his working hours in a tux. Cesare understood what pushovers many American women were for a foreign accent, and so made an art of shameless flirting. His trademark was the drawing out of the word "darling" until it seethed with the promise of sex: "Dahling, have a martini." "Daahhling, what's on your mind tonight?" "Daaa-hhhling, you look lovely."

These men could not have been more different, but they each reminded me of a very specific personality type from back home. My understanding of what I wanted to do in my restaurants was being sharpened with each new venture: I was no longer looking to simply serve Italian food and wine; I was building grander and grander sets and populating them with real Italians. Part of the reason for this was selfish: the more complete the experience was in my restaurants, the more I had the feeling of being back home. But I also believed that the range of characters would help ensure an element of spontaneity when a customer walked into Le Madri because the trip from podium to table would vary depending on the host with whom it was made.

Of course, I picked May 23 for the opening. How could I not, after all the luck that date had brought me? To be sure that Le Madri lived up to the expectations created by all of our preliminary press, I did five days of "friends and family" tastings—practice sessions at which friends of the owners eat for free in exchange for patiently enduring any lapses in service or misfires from the kitchen. (Some restaurateurs even go so far as to distribute comment cards or questionnaires at the end of these experiments, but that was never my style.) Between the food and the payroll, we spent about twenty thousand dollars on these dress rehearsals, but it was worthwhile because we worked out a lot of kinks. One night, as the grill was maxed out with Cornish game hens and steaks, all of them throwing copious amounts of smoke up into the air, the exhaust system shut down. I kept hitting the reset button, but it wouldn't come back on. I starting barking to the cooks to get everything off the grill as soon as possible because I knew what was coming next: a blast of cool fire-extinguishing foam from the hose that dangled over the cooking surfaces. We got the food out of the way just in time, but no sooner did the foam spurt out than the smoke began drifting out into the dining room. With images of the sprinkler system's sensors trigging the nozzles and showering our diners, I grabbed a construction ladder, ran out of the kitchen, set it up, and climbed up into an access panel hidden in the vaulted ceiling.

Though I succeeded in shutting off the sprinklers before they triggered, I was too late to prevent a team of firemen dressed as if they were headed for Three Mile Island from showing up and marching into the dining room.

"Hey, Pino," somebody yelled out. "Are they friends or family?"

Everybody had a good laugh, but I was pissed off. Still, I'd much rather it happened during our dry run than when we had paying customers in the house.

THE FOOD AT Le Madri was the best I'd opened with so far. Usually a restaurant's menu has to be tweaked to synch it up with the demands of the customers, but all the dishes we began with, firmly rooted in home cooking, sold well. Many of the dishes that debuted at Le Madri are still with me today, such as a beef and artichoke stew; blind baby eel cakes (fritters); and a *fritto misto* (mixed fried seafood) primarily comprising white bait. And, of course, there was that marvelous wood-burning oven where I collaborated on a number of original creations with a sweet young Italian-American pizza maker named Ciro. We introduced a pizza that's become something of a legend: the *focaccia robiola*, a thin wheel of rosemary bread, split in half horizontally, spread with creamy robiola cheese, baked, drizzled with white truffle oil, and cut into small triangles. It was an almost obscenely fragrant, melt-in-your-mouth signature dish that had people moaning with pleasure, and it fast became something that customers ordered along with their cocktails the moment they sat down.

The only bittersweet aspect for me was accepting that part of the price of operating more than one restaurant was the need to turn the orchestration of the kitchen over to other chefs, but the truth was that having an experienced restaurant toque like Alan Tardi was invaluable. Under his guidance, the women of Le Madri were transformed from individual home cooks into a well-organized kitchen brigade, though some things didn't change: Maria still prepared the antipasti offerings, an even bigger assortment than we served at Il Cantinori or

Sapore—fifteen or more dishes set out every night along the ledge that fronted the pizza oven.

As was the case with Sapore di Mare before it, and Il Cantinori before that, Le Madri became a magnet for celebrities and the bold-face names from publishing and finance. Loyal customers followed me wherever I went, from Tenth Street out to East Hampton and back to the city and Chelsea. Because of our location, convenient to many boutique literary agencies, we became a popular lunch destination for agents, publishers, and editors, as well as their high-profile writer clients. We drew some of the biggest names in fashion such as Ralph Lauren, Calvin Klein, Giorgio Armani, Donna Karan, Nicole Miller, Vera Wang, and Betsey Johnson; business tycoons like Steve Forbes; art-world figures like photographer Patrick Demarchelier and my by-then regular customer Julian Schnabel, who always turned heads in the summertime when he showed up in his preferred ensemble of elegant pajama pants, ornate pajama top, and slippers. And, of course, a great many seats were occupied by the high-rolling customers of Barneys, who made a full day of shopping and lunch, or shopping and dinner, taking full advantage of the parking lot we shared with the department store, which was a real coup in Manhattan.

Everybody who succeeds in New York has a few times in his life when he feels like the king of Manhattan, as though he's been embraced by the city, and this was such a time for me. When I traveled from my apartment to Chelsea each morning, I felt like everybody, from deli countermen to cab drivers, had a smile and a kind word for me.

Our success was so immediate and well reported that it wasn't long before I received phone calls from friends tipping me off to imitators—unaffiliated restaurateurs who had announced plans to open restaurants called Le Madri—as close as New Jersey and as far away as Colorado. I guess a part of me was still pretty innocent because this shocked me. Over the previous summer, in the trade magazine *Nation's Restaurant News*, I had noticed that restaurants featuring the word *Sapore* (which was unusual enough as a restaurant name that only a native of Italy would think to use it) had begun turning up in the South and Midwest, but nobody had had the gumption to actually lift

the full name Sapore di Mare, so I let it go. But now, the fact that people thought they could appropriate the name, and—who knew?—
maybe even the concept, that I had come up with offended me. I know
that many believe that imitation is the sincerest form of flattery, but to
me plagiarism is plagiarism and my response to it was "fuck you," delivered across state lines in the form of a cease-and-desist letter from
my attorney. As usual, my learning curve was steep but swift; to protect
myself against any future would-be thieves, I trademarked the name Le
Madri and resolved to do the same with any other names I devised in
the future.

I NEVER KNEW where my presence would be most required, where
the next fire would need to be put out. One summer day, I was working in the city when Mark called me from Sapore in a state of panic. A
group of INS agents had marched into the dining room unannounced
and had begun interrogating everybody on the staff. They hadn't checked
for proof of citizenship or asked to see green cards; instead, they had
simply corralled and carted off anyone who didn't speak English, leaving
Mark with a fraction of his staff heading into the final prep and evening
dinner service.

"Thank God I can still manage a Queens accent or they might have
taken *me*," he said, forcing a chuckle.

I hung up the phone and looked into the kitchen. The cooks were
finishing their prep for that night's dinner at Le Madri. The *mise en
place* containers—the little stainless-steel vessels in which prepared
ingredients are held along the line—were full and, having been there
since the early morning, the prep crew was winding down and thinking about going home for the day.

"Guys, listen up." I told them what had happened at Sapore, and
that I needed them to go out to my car. I was going to drive them to the
Hamptons, they would work a shift out there, and I'd have them back
by morning.

I hated to do it to them, but I had no choice. We had to be ready for
dinner at the beach. So we piled into the car and drove out to the
Hamptons, and I assigned each of them to a station. They were real

troupers, prepping and then cooking all night, only to pile back into my car at eleven forty-five for the return trip to Manhattan.

It was an exhausting day. But here's the sick thing, and the reason I believe I was born to be a restaurateur: I loved moments like those. Loved the rush of adrenaline. Loved opening the doors at five thirty and welcoming customers into a dining experience that bore no sign of the crisis that had preceded it. What was that old line from "New York, New York"? "If you can make it here, you'll make it anywhere." Damn straight.

Though I enjoyed the constant pressure, sometimes it did get the better of me, and my temper periodically erupted, even occasionally at a customer.

One night at Le Madri, a couple had barged past the maître d' podium into the dining room and were standing there yelling at Gianfranco.

"What's the problem?" I asked.

Gianfanco explained that they wanted a table and we didn't have one for them.

"Well, if Gianfranco says we don't have one, we don't have one," I replied.

The man protested, uttering my least favorite phrase in the world: "You don't know who I am."

My temper went from zero to sixty in no time. I climbed up on a chair, told all the customers in the surrounding area to be quiet, then turned to the guy and said: "OK, go ahead, tell us *all* who you are. Please, tell us who the fuck you are."

He thought about it for a second, looked around at the people staring at him, then gave me the finger and stormed out.

I never learned who he was, and I never saw him again.

THAT FALL, THE *New York Times* finally got around to reviewing us and gave us two stars, thanks to the open-mindedness of critic Bryan Miller. *New York* magazine's Gael Greene, francophile that she is, never warmed to me, but it didn't matter. We were hot, and we were buoyed again the following spring when Andy Birsh reviewed us in *Gourmet* magazine. In the 1980s, a review in the pages of *Gourmet* would drive people to your restaurant for months; they'd actually show up with the magazine in hand and scan the review to decide what to order.

Because things were going so swimmingly, when Alan decided to leave Le Madri the following year I was determined to replace him with a bona fide Italian mother, making the restaurant as true to its name as possible. A friend of mine from back home told me about a wildly talented woman named Marta Pulini, who had worked at Bice in Paris before returning to her hometown of Modena. We spoke by phone and clicked via long distance; she talked about food exactly the way I did: with a reverence for seasonality, immediacy, and simplicity. She flew to New York to meet with me and I found that we had something else in common: we had both led full lives before getting into the restaurant business. She had been a semiprofessional tennis player, raised a family, and then decided to take up cooking as a career, attending Le Cordon Bleu to supplement her innate palate and talent with professional kitchen training. She preferred lighter food than I did, but we were still very compatible and we decided that she would come work for me as executive chef of Le Madri, becoming the latest in a long line of women culinary figures in my life.

With that hire, things felt very stable. I had Marta in the city and Mark in Long Island, and everything was firing on all cylinders.

And so, it was a bit jarring when I came home one day to find Jessie waiting for me, on the verge of tears.

"Pino, I can't take it anymore."

I was oblivious. What was the problem?

"I can't go anywhere with Marco. Everywhere I go it's dirty. Even the parks. There are syringes everywhere. I want out of here." It was hard to argue her point: by that point in time, the crime in New York was truly out of control; there were horrific violent acts described in the tabloids and local news broadcasts every morning, and friends of ours had actually taken to walking in the middle of the street late at night for fear of being pulled into doorways and robbed, or worse.

I played the strongman for my wife. "Sure, baby, whatever you want."

She was right: for Marco and for her, the thing to do was to get out of the city. Personally, I had no desire to leave. I had left my home twice in my life: left the country for Rome and left Rome for New York. Somehow, I had ended up in the right place, and I didn't want to let go. But I wasn't really letting go; I was about to enter that Jekyll-and-Hyde existence called "commuting," in which I would act the role of the suburban dad on weekends but maintain my life in the city from Monday to Friday.

Another challenge to be met, more energy to be expended. It was all right.

And so, shortly after our daughter, Jacobella, was born in 1990, we found a very beautiful, though also very old, Tudor-style home in Rye, in leafy Westchester County, New York. It was well maintained but would need a little T.L.C. to bring it up to modern standards. Despite my busy schedule, I was excited to take it on, and I had a vision for how to make it perfect. Just like a restaurateur to choose a place that needed fixing: I guess I have to make my mark everywhere I go.

TEN

Critical Condition: The Problem with Restaurant Reviewers, Blogs, and Surveys

WHEN I GOT into the restaurant business, it was a last resort—an unglamorous business of good craftsmen who weren't stars, even in their hometown. Now, the cooking industry has become a media darling. There's more interest than ever in restaurants, and more people than ever are offering their assessments in print and online. In addition to the food critics who have always been a fact of my life, and the annual *Zagat Survey*, we now have a community of bloggers tasting food and snapping digital photos for their mostly self-financed, self-produced Web sites.

There's just one small problem with all of this. For the most part, restaurant criticism is a sham.

Before I explain why, I want to be clear that I don't have anything against the critics. Some of them have been very kind to me over the years, some have barely acknowledged me, and others have gone after me with a vengeance. I don't begrudge them their opinions and I don't blame them for any of my problems.

But there are some things that must be said, and since I have a reputation for speaking my mind, it might as well be me who says them. First of all, most newspaper and magazine restaurant critics' credibility begins with the assumption that the critic a) dines anonymously, and b) is a stand-in for the person reading the review. Both of these premises are often false, beginning with the notion that restaurant critics travel incognito. This is one of the great myths of the profession, at

least in New York City, and especially when it comes to the critic for
the *New York Times*. In many cases the reviewer *attempts* to be anonymous, but members of the industry, even sworn enemies, unite to be
sure that he or she is almost always recognized. If there's ever been a
photograph of the *Times* critic published, you may rest assured that the
photo is tacked to the wall like a wanted poster in some employees-only
area of the restaurant, so that they can all have their eyes perpetually
peeled and on the lookout. (In many cases, the critic is also known to
the chef, restaurateur, and managers from his or her previous stint as a
reporter.) Restaurants share lists of aliases that major critics use to
make reservations, the names that appear on their credit cards, and the
phone numbers they give out for confirming reservations.

As a result, despite their best efforts to travel under the radar, these
men and women are routinely granted one of the best seats in the
house. They are tended to by the best waiter or waitress, and the chef
personally fusses over their dish to ensure perfection—or as close to it
as he or she is capable of. Restaurant staff are on especially high alert
during the opening weeks of a new restaurant, when the chefs never
leave and the entire staff functions like a team of air marshals, scanning the faces in the crowd for anybody on the watch list. The experience critics have during these important, make-or-break weeks can be
doubly inapplicable to the average diner, because not only is the critic
getting the best possible treatment and food, but there are many famous chefs around town who work every night until the *Times* review
breaks, then bolt the scene and return to their usual golf schedule.

I empathize with the critics themselves, who have a near-impossible
job to do, dining out on a daily basis, often returning to places they de-
test and putting food they don't care for into their bodies in order to
complete their research. I can't help but think that it doesn't take long
before critics lose the ability to relate to what it's like to be a normal
diner. And I know that many critics get bored with their work, because
I've watched more than one of them go from being an enthusiastic
chronicler of cuisine to an anthropologist more concerned with incidental details like what the people at the next table are wearing or doing, or the décor of the bathrooms. When you start seeing comments
about that kind of thing, it's time to find a new critic to read.

Where I don't pity the critics is in their feeling of superiority. There's no question that critics have the right to pen a review of a restaurant, but over the years, whenever I've written them letters or phoned them up to complain that they didn't understand Italian food, or that they had been too harsh in taking away a star, which former *New York Times* critic Bryan Miller did to Il Cantinori and which I wrote him about, or *whatever*, they have taken offense at the mere fact of my daring to confront them—not writing me back, but subsequently taking potshots in articles and reviews. But where is it written that freedom of the press is a one-way street? What's wrong with criticizing the critics? If they have the right to assess—in public—how I do my job, why can't I offer an opinion on how they do theirs? These people have had their asses kissed for so long by restaurateurs, chefs, and publicists that when somebody has the balls to disagree with them to their face, they take it as an affront. But I don't kiss asses. You do it long enough and it destroys your palate.

Now, blogging is a relatively new profession, but the problems have already revealed themselves. First of all, blogs are for the most part an unregulated industry, a Wild West of pseudo-journalism where anybody with a few hundred dollars and an opinion can have a stage equal to that of major publications that have been around for generations. Unlike most critics, many bloggers make no effort at anonymity whatsoever. It's not at all uncommon to see food bloggers hanging out at a restaurant's bar, gabbing with the chef, or his publicist, or at industry parties, chowing down on free food. Then they slouch back to their homes and, sitting there in their underwear, bang out posts that have more and more power over consumers' restaurant-going decisions. I don't want to sound like Jerry Seinfeld, but "who are these people?"

And then there's one of the most powerful publications in the world of New York City restaurants: the *Zagat Survey*. I happen to like this publication; it's light, compact, and updated every year. It saves you a call to directory assistance or a visit to the Internet.

But as a *survey* . . . well, there are a number of problems. In principle, I have nothing against the concept of a survey. In fact, I love the spirit of it. The idea that a random sampling of diners would be given a vehicle to share their opinions with fellow food enthusiasts is very democratic. But in reality, the *Zagat Survey* is anything but random.

I wonder, for example, how many of the people who purchase the survey understand that many chefs and restaurateurs, as the annual deadline for survey forms approaches, send out e-mails to their customers, encouraging them to fill out the survey, electronically stuffing the ballot box. Another obvious question I have to ask is how many restaurateurs pay people to fill out surveys. I know that Tim Zagat is a lawyer, so I want to be very clear about this: I don't know of anybody who actually does this, but I also know that I could pay some young kid a few bucks an hour to fill out a number of surveys on my behalf, and nobody would be the wiser. Am I the only person who's ever had this idea?

Then, of course, there's the logic-defying curiosity that has been an industry joke for more than a decade: the dominance of Union Square Cafe as the most popular restaurant in New York for more than five years, until it was unseated by Gramercy Tavern in 2003. Since then, the two have reigned as the number-one and number-two most popular restaurants in town in the survey, and there's barely a chef or restaurateur in town who hasn't shared a good and hearty laugh over this fact. We don't laugh out of disrespect to restaurateur Danny Meyer, who owns them both, or to the restaurants themselves, but rather because it strikes us as curious that a random survey would result in these restaurants' seemingly infinite dominance. More than that, what value exactly is "most popular" supposed to have for people looking for a place to eat? The most popular restaurant in the United States is probably McDonald's. A more accurate title for that page at the front of the survey might be "Best Marketed Restaurants" or "Best Restaurants at Getting Their Customers to Fill Out the *Zagat Survey*."

There are other things I could point out, such as how tired the style of the survey is. I mean, how "clever" is it to "encapsulate" the most "obvious" of comments by putting "every" other "word" in "quotation marks"? After "a while," it begins to get "annoying."

So what's a restaurant-goer to do? Where are you supposed to turn for advice and direction?

It's easy to imagine the perfect critic: somebody knowledgeable in the cuisines of various countries, with a finely honed palate that can distinguish not just good from bad, but also excellent from exceptional—distinctions that aren't always obvious, especially in today's anything-goes dining scene. Someone possessed of a grasp of the classics, with a mind open to new things but not susceptible to being seduced by originality for originality's sake. A person as happy to enjoy a good meal in a greasy-spoon neighborhood hangout as in a four-star restaurant. And somebody who doesn't play favorites and whose reviews aren't affected by the goings-on in his or her own life.

Easy to imagine, but such a person does not exist.

Would it be hopelessly old-fashioned of me to suggest you ask your friends? To me, there's no better recommendation than one from somebody you know personally, who loves the same kind of food and experience that you do (or knows your likes and dislikes). As a restaurateur, most of my business ultimately comes from the word of mouth of my customers either bringing people in or sending them with their blessing. There's something pure about people finding restaurants this way, and unlike some of the patrons who come (or worse, stay away) because of the critics, they always seem to get just what they expect.

ELEVEN

Strange Bedfellows

HISTORY HAS A funny way of repeating itself. I had a customer named George Kaufman who came to see me every Monday night at Le Madri, and one Monday he pulled me aside and told me that he had a space on the Upper East Side that he wanted to show me. He described it in less-than-flattering terms: with the exception of the south-side entrance, it was an almost windowless room located on East Seventy-fourth Street that had been operating as a restaurant called Metro where Patrick Clark (now deceased) was the chef. The place had failed and was recently shuttered.

"You come take a look, and if you like it I'll make it work for us."

There was a lot that didn't make sense about that location for me: it was uptown, where I had once lived but where I'd never worked. Yet something about the notion intrigued me and it wasn't hard to figure out what it was: once again, it was the proximity to money and influence, climbing to the top of that ladder. This was the land of Cipriani and Le Cirque, where if you opened the right kind of restaurant, you'd be hosting business leaders, movie stars, and politicians every night of the week.

I went to have a look at the space and found myself immediately drawn to it. For the neighborhood, it actually seemed right that it be a bit sequestered, so all those power brokers could have their privacy. I thought about fashioning the space after the style of a 1940s villa in Tuscany or Umbria, with wood paneling and murals inspired by the still-life paintings of one of my favorite artists, Giorgio Morandi. My interest was based in part on the fact that Mark, stranded out on Long Island, had expressed a desire to return to Manhattan, and I thought this restaurant would be a way to keep him in the family.

The only thing missing was a concept. I told George that I'd get back to him and gave myself a few days to let the idea develop, setting it aside to simmer. A few thoughts began to come together in my mind. One of my favorite pastimes back then was opening the windows at Le Madri and letting the breeze blow through the dining room, causing the tablecloths and draperies to flap in the wind. One night I was sitting there having dinner with my friend Bob Krasnow, chairman of Elektra Records. He was thinking about moving to the Upper East Side and I told him that I might be opening a restaurant up there.

"What are you going to call it?" he asked.

"I'm not sure," I said. "But I've been thinking about the food, and I think what I want to do is break the rules. Just put Mark in the kitchen and let him go crazy. It's like *coco pazzo*," which is an Italian expression meaning "crazy chef."

He laughed: "I don't know what you just said, Pino, but that is a great name."

Encouraged, I trademarked the name, because I knew that even if the restaurant didn't work out, I was going to use it for something.

But things did work out. I took the concept to the Pressmans, with whom I had a two-way first-refusal arrangement: neither of us could commit to a new restaurant without first inviting the other to be a part of it. "It's a no-brainer," I told them. "The landlord is a gentleman who just wants to see the place rented, and I've got the perfect concept."

After our success with Le Madri, they jumped right in and I convinced Irv to not rock the boat in the lease negotiation. The deal we were being offered was a great one; there was no need to get cute and potentially blow it.

Everybody followed my lead and next thing I knew we had secured the space and I was once again developing a new restaurant. To earn the Coco Pazzo name, I decided that we would fly in the face of convention: we'd do very simple, casual food in a part of Manhattan where the prevailing wisdom was that you couldn't do casual dining. There was a small private nook on the north side of the restaurant and we stuck a communal table in there, so single diners and walk-ins would sit side by side—another radical idea. And we decided to borrow a page from the Italian tradition and serve family-style dinner on Sunday night, something that had never been seen in this neighborhood of the city, though in time it would become the hallmark of restaurants like Carmine's in the Theater District.

To serve the high and mighty, I installed a trio of shamelessly sycophantic and highly competitive dining room personalities. The maître d' was John Fanning, a bespectacled preppy blond. The floor captains were Tom Piscitello, a stocky, fast talker from Philly with a firm grasp of food and wine, and Carlos Carmona, a lovable South American with a smooth, soft manner and great style, evidenced by his collection of reading glasses that allowed him to match them to his pocket square or tie. These guys spent their days and nights trying to outdo each other—see who could dress the most dashingly in the well-to-do style of the Upper East Side, lavish the most attention on the customers, use the most extravagant language to describe the food and wine. The casting at Coco Pazzo was inspired, if I do say so myself, even if the bottom line was that they were trying to get the most tips. You know the Pirandello play, *Six Characters in Search of an Author?* This was *Six People in Search of Tips.* In fact, Mark and I had a private joke: to imitate the maître d's escorting guests to a table, we'd say "follow me" and whip one arm over our head so that our hand landed, palm-up, behind us, coaxing a gratuity.

Because the space had been a functioning restaurant when we took it over, the redesign was quick and easy. I once again adhered to my lucky number when we opened a few months later, on November 23, 1990.

On day one, we were flooded with all those bold-face names from downtown, plus senators and superstars like Mick Jagger and Rod Stewart. David Geffen came in every day, and Revlon chairman Ron Perelman loved the restaurant so much that he asked me to hold the same table for him every night. I told him I'd have to charge him whether he came in or not and he said that was no problem.

As if things couldn't get any better, the *New York Times* wrote a love letter of a review, laying three stars on Coco Pazzo and calling us "the best restaurant to open in New York since last fall." Suddenly, we weren't just a place for the neighborhood; we were a destination restaurant for everybody in New York, the must-try hot spot of the moment.

There was a downside to all of this, although it was a good problem to have: the restaurant almost became *too* inside, too clubby. Everybody in attendance wanted, and deserved, a face table. I had never intended to do it, but we had out–Le Cirqued Le Cirque because we had the fabulously wealthy uptown crowd but also the downtown cache of rock and rollers and artists.

I began a new nightly ritual: making the rounds, beginning at Le Madri then hopping into a car around eight o'clock and climbing uptown to Coco Pazzo. There was an in joke at the company in those days, if a customer asked "Where's Pino?" The answer was "Everywhere." It wasn't far from the truth. My challenge was different at each restaurant: at Le Madri, where we did most of our business early, I wanted to be sure that we were ready for the night ahead, drawing on all the mistakes I'd seen made at the places I'd worked and doing what I could to head them off. It sounds like a small concern, but one of the most important things I'd learned to check on over the years was the supply of folded napkins and tablecloths. I can't tell you how many times I'd seen restaurants grind to a halt because they ran out midservice and couldn't get tables set for the next round of customers, and so I'd check on that personally and if we were low, I'd get busboys in the kitchen folding napkins.

At Coco Pazzo, the focus was on keeping all waiting customers happy. When I arrived, I'd walk into the bar and if it was packed with people, I knew that some of them had to be getting impatient. I'd spot a customer with a cocktail in hand and say, "How are you doing?"

"How do you *think* I'm doing?" was the reply I most dreaded, usually followed by, "Do you know how long I've been waiting? Where is *my* table?" I'd do what I could to make them happy, send them an appetizer, or pick up their drinks, and 99 percent of the time they left happy, not just because of my efforts but also because of something they'd never admit: they *liked* waiting because it meant that they were part of the action at one of New York's of-the-moment hot spots. They might have been annoyed that Ron Perelman's table was sitting there empty while they waited for theirs to open up, but they were excited to be dining among the Masters of the Universe.

I have to be honest: as intoxicating as it was—and there were times when I had to make a conscious effort not to let it go to my head—there were moments when hosting so many celebrities was less than glamorous. Like when Sylvester Stallone came in to dinner with Ron Perelman and Ron treated him to a bottle of Gaja reserve wine, one of the most revered wines in the world. A few days later, Stallone returned to the restaurant with his family and told the maître d' he wanted the same wine Ron had been drinking when they had been in together. The waiter promptly took him a bottle of Gaja. By the time Stallone was finished with dinner, he'd had two bottles. I wasn't at the restaurant at the time, but one of the managers informed me that when he was presented with the bill, Stallone was shocked to see that he had an eight-hundred-dollar wine tab. Nobody had thought to mention the price to him, and I agreed with my team; he hadn't asked to see the wine list, and besides, if Rocky couldn't afford Gaja, then surely Rambo could.

A few days later, I was out in East Hampton, golfing in a charity event, when my cell phone rang. It was Maggie, my assistant, telling me that she had Sylvester Stallone's assistant on the other line. I instructed her to patch him in. It turned out that he was calling to complain about the wine incident.

"Listen," I said. "He asked for the same wine that Mr. Perelman had had. What were we supposed to do?"

The assistant covered the phone and I heard him relaying what I said to a third party, presumably Stallone.

"Well," he said a few moments later, "Mr. Stallone thinks that somebody should have told him how much the wine cost."

"Listen," I said, my anger almost impossible to hide. "If he can't afford, or doesn't want to spend, a lot of money on wine, then he shouldn't order things without *asking* how much they cost."

We quibbled a little more and then both testily hung up.

And that was that. But it wasn't the last time I'd hear, indirectly, from Mr. Stallone. Just as in *Rocky II*, there *would* be a rematch.

PART OF THE reason I responded so intensely to the Stallone incident was that, even if they can afford it, it's always been a pet peeve of mine when people buy something without asking what it costs. This is especially true when the person works for me and is spending my money. The worst offenders are chefs, who will tell their food vendors, "Give me the best, no matter what the expense," which is no way to turn a profit. Everything has a price and that price has to be weighed against other factors, such as the value of the good or service to your business.

Once I had Le Madri and Coco Pazzo, I began to take advantage of owning more than one restaurant. For example, to help keep tabs on everything, I promoted Jack Weiss, my old Il Cantinori bartender, to director of operations. I also hired a friend of Alan Tardi, a bulldog named Chester Howell, who had trained as a chef but had more passion for numbers than for food. A lanky kid with light blond hair, Chester delighted in extracting the best possible deal from each vendor. He was the nastiest, most stingy negotiator I ever met in my life. And I mean that as a compliment.

Chester's first job with me was to set up a centralized purchasing department for the company. We were making about $7 million in food revenue each year and were spending between $1.6 and $1.8 million on the raw product, about 24 or 25 percent. At that level, it was worth creating a salaried position to get the number down even just a few percentage points. I told him that if he could get our food costs down to 22 or 23 percent, I'd give him a bonus. He did, and I rewarded him accordingly.

Chester also helped me set up my own private laundry service. We were spending so much money on linen companies—which provide rented napkins and tablecloths, as well as a cleaning service, to restaurants—that I had a theory we could have the very best linen if we set up our own laundry and delivery system. Chester leased a van, rented space on Sullivan Street, put in washing machines and dryers, and hired three guys and a driver to do all the work. Because of the way the math worked out, this saved us enough to buy the very best linens, which to my mind was Frette, adding another layer of elegance to our dining rooms.

That might not sound like an earth-shattering development, but to me, it signaled the next stage in my maturation as a restaurateur, able to improvise new ways of doing things that saved me money *and* improved the customer's experience.

My uncle would have been proud.

BY 1991, I was starting to get that itch again, the need to try something new, to push myself. My exposure to corporate America was beginning to rub off on me and I decided that the logical next step in my evolution would be to open in another market, to see if I could *expand*. Most people faced with that impulse would begin thinking about Los Angeles or, today, Las Vegas, but I never had the interest in opening there. Instead, I had a long and abiding attraction to Chicago that dated back to a drive through the Midwest that Patty and I had taken in 1981, when we had visited her family in Sheboygan Falls. The theatricality of the city had stayed with me, especially the architecture which, for my money, is the most American of any of its big cities.

After a bit of networking, I found a space in the heart of Chicago; there was a chocolate factory nearby so you could step outside and smell cocoa in the air, like in *Willy Wonka and the Chocolate Factory*. After a few years of dealing with New York City landlords, working things out with the one in Chicago seemed as easy as renting a one-bedroom apartment back in Manhattan. Before I knew it, I was off and running on Coco Pazzo Chicago. I wanted somebody I knew and who I could trust long-distance to manage it for me, so I offered Jack Weiss the opportunity to become the general manager of Coco Pazzo Chicago and he jumped at it.

As much as I enjoyed developing new concepts, there was something very satisfying and comforting in re-creating an existing one in a new locale. There wasn't the same high that came with starting from scratch, but there was something almost as good: the sense that we were putting together a restaurant the way you assembled a children's toy from a box: insert part A into part B, screw on part C, snap into part D, open the door, and start making money!

I'm not saying it was *easy*—that's a word I would never apply to the opening of a restaurant—but there was a natural flow to the work from the moment we began. Unlike most projects, when you continue to hone the concept with each decision almost until you seat your first customers, with Coco Pazzo Chicago, we had a working template, the original place in New York, to guide us along the way. It took almost all the stress out of the process and whetted my appetite for more potentially expandable concepts.

I already had one. For a while, I had been thinking that I'd like to combine everything that I loved about food and wine in one place: a restaurant, take-away shop, wine bar, pastry counter, wood-burning oven, and espresso bar all in one. I wanted to have customers sitting in the middle, like you might find in a public square in Venice or Rome. While visiting Chicago, it occurred to me that perhaps such a place might dispense Tuscan kitchenware and housewares as well. The more I thought about it the more drawn I was to the concept: I saw it as the ultimate expression of my nostalgia and romanticism, a way to actually create a little patch of Tuscany right here in the United States.

At the end of 1991, Fred and Gene Pressman approached me and asked if I'd like to open a restaurant in the new Barneys they were planning on Madison Avenue in Midtown. I pitched them my still-sketchy notion of a food piazza and retail hybrid. They loved the idea of a piazza, but they weren't interested in the retail component for fear that it would cannibalize sales from Barneys. It was still well worth doing, and so I gave it some thought and came back with a name. Given the location—the restaurant would have an entrance at Madison Avenue and Sixty-first Street—I threw out something that echoed the "crazy" element of Coco Pazzo that so many had responded to: Mad. 61.

They loved it and we decided to move forward, only this arrangement would be a little different because I wasn't going to be a partner with them; instead, I'd be contracted as the operator of *their* restaurant within *their* department store. This was fine with me; in fact, it would simplify my life because they'd be dealing with such day-to-day concerns as payroll and paying vendors, leaving me to focus on the stuff I loved most about being a restaurateur.

But there were headaches to come. The store wasn't scheduled to open until the fall of 1993, but because the Pressmans kept having second thoughts about design elements, the overall construction of the new Barneys was on an insanely tight schedule. When they took stock of the situation in early July 1993, they realized that in order to meet the desired opening date of Labor Day, they'd have to have the construction crews begin working 24-7 in shifts, and that's just what happened: for the rest of the summer it was the Babel of construction—you could enter the building at any time, day or night, and find lights on and the buzz of power tools filling the air. (The workers were obviously delighted with all their overtime pay: one day I took the elevator to the construction manager's office on the ninth floor and saw a sign for LMB, the initials of the construction company Lehrer McGovern Bovis, tacked to a plywood wall. Under the initials, one of the guys had given a new meaning to the initials by scrawling "Let's Milk Barneys.")

It wasn't until about this time, just two months before Labor Day, that the contractors finally began dealing with the restaurant build-out, which was important to me but was a minor concern to everybody else relative to the overall project. They took a down-and-dirty approach, triaging the situation in order to turn something functional over to me by opening day. I had no power over them because they weren't my hires, so there was nothing I could do to push them

Every time it seemed things were finished, we'd bump up against another obstacle. Mad. 61 was in the basement level, and the ground floor was cut away to offer shoppers an aerial view of the restaurant. So that they wouldn't just be looking down at the tops of diners' heads, the designers had the idea to put a shallow pool in the center of the dining room with tile work that would produce a reflecting effect. But when they filled the pool with water for the first time, just a few days before we were scheduled to open, it leaked into the floor below, which housed, among other things, the telephone control station. This was obviously unacceptable, so a decision was made to scrap the pool. I asked the construction guys to level it off into a raised platform and called on a designer friend to devise something we could install there to fill up the space.

"I want something crazy," I told him. "Maybe a sculpture."

He mulled it over and said, "What about using potatoes?"

I thought it was a little out there, but I trusted his instincts and he brought in countless bags of Idaho potatoes and fashioned a massive and compelling pyramid, which we decorated with orchids.

When we finally opened, Mad. 61 was only about 75 percent completed: the Madison Avenue entrance wasn't yet functional (making the name a bit of a misnomer, at least temporarily), the flooring needed grouting, the paint job was a few layers short in places, and the kitchen equipment was only about three-quarters installed. To add to the drama, our gas wasn't turned on by the city until the day before we opened. Despite all of this, we made our debut on time, and it was like Coco Pazzo all over again. There were hordes of people clamoring to experience Mad. 61; the effect of a happening was heightened by the fact that there were different lines for each division: one for the restaurant, one for the cheese counter, one for the wine bar, and so on.

Of all the restaurants I ever opened, I still think Mad. 61 was the best, most complete expression of my love for food, and of food as theater. The team I assembled was like my own group of all-stars, some company veterans, and some new talent: Paula Oland, who would go on to run the bakery at Balthazar, did a brilliant job running our bakery, as did my cheese buyer Steve Jenkins, whom I adored, despite his sarcasm-first, work-second disposition. Marta, working with chef de cuisine John Schenk, an intense and twitchy guy with a frantic Quentin Tarantino speech pattern; the delightfully opinionated pastry chef Patti Jackson; and Ciro, my pizza maker from Le Madri, kept the kitchen running full-bore. On top of all that, we had a long espresso bar with all the requisite Italian pastries and baked goods, and a wine bar offering twenty-five wines by the glass. It just went on and on. The sheer ambitiousness of the place would be noteworthy even today;

there were a handful of concepts under one umbrella, each with its own unique demands, and they all functioned with the efficiency of a Swiss watch.

I **WAS STILL** readying Mad. 61 for its long-anticipated opening when I got an inside track on a prime space on East Fifty-ninth Street, with corporate offices available right upstairs. Again partnering with the Pressmans, I grabbed up both spaces. I didn't have a big concept at the time, but I had been thinking of the Emilia-Romagna region, mostly because Marta was from Modena, and we'd had a long and ongoing dialogue about how underrepresented the food of that region was in the United States. This was, we felt, a shame because many Italians believe it's the best cuisine in all of Italy; it's certainly the most complex with dishes like *bollito misto* with *salsa verde* (assorted boiled meats with green sauce), *piadina* (a flatbread blanketed with melted cheese), and *tortellini in brodo* (filled pasta in stock). The idea gained extra steam because one of the chefs at Mad. 61, Giancarlo, was from that region and was itching to make the concept a reality. I thought of myself as a director making a more minor, intimate film, and so took the name of a movie that I associated with my own childhood, Fellini's *Amarcord*, which means, "I Remember."

The restaurant opened at the end of 1993, but by 1995 it was failing. I realized that American customers just didn't have the stomach for the unfamiliar dishes of the region. I revamped the concept to a more casual, less expensive Tuscan place called Il Toscanaccio, which means "The Naughty Tuscan."

Despite the slight turbulence of Amarcord/Toscanaccio, it was a fantastic couple of years, during which I also opened a smaller, more casual Coco Pazzo Cafe in Chicago. My relationship with the Pressmans was smooth and I had even become closer with Gene, spending time with his family in Larchmont, just up the road from us in Rye.

But things were about to change, and they did so suddenly. On January 12, 1996, I was sitting at my kitchen table at home in Westchester, when I opened the *New York Times* and read that Barneys had just filed for bankruptcy. I turned on the television and there it was on the local news. I knew that there had been tension between the Pressmans and their Japanese investors, and that the project had to have gone over budget during the summer of overtime in 1993, but this was something of a shock, as was learning about it in the newspaper. I guess, despite all the history we had together, I was still an outsider to them after all.

I was also, of course, worried about what this meant for Mad. 61, but another concern quickly superseded it: though I'd been operating Mad. 61 for three years, my contract had never been signed. This isn't terribly unusual in business relationships, especially between partners with multiple past projects together, but now that the company was in bankruptcy, I had no idea how to protect myself.

Though the restaurant continued to operate, I really wanted this detail nailed down, and I tried repeatedly to get in touch with Irv. His secretary kept putting me off, telling me, "Oh, Pino, this is a crazy time for them."

Despite the instability, Mad. 61 was still packed at lunch; you'd never have known we were doing business on a sinking ship. One day, I was talking with some customers when an executive from the National Restaurant Association introduced himself to me.

"Did you hear that the Sfuzzi chain just filed for bankruptcy?" he asked.

"No," I said. I had heard of Sfuzzi, but I didn't really know anything about it.

"You should take a look at it, think about taking it over."

"I'm not interested," I said. "I have enough going on."

It was a conversation I'd have cause to remember again before too long.

DESPITE AN INCREASINGLY strained relationship with the Pressmans, I was about to enter into another partnership with another unlikely collaborator: Ian Schrager, one half of the legendary duo responsible for the symbol of New York City in the 1970s, Studio 54. In the late 1980s, Ian created a second act for himself as a hotelier with the revolutionarily affordable and stylish Morgans Hotel in the Murray

Hill neighborhood of New York and the Paramount Hotel in the Theater District, and yet another hotel, Mondrian, was about to follow in
Los Angeles. Like the Paramount, it would be designed by Philippe
Starck, who I thought was a genius for his minimalist modern style.
Ian and his former partner, Steve Rubell, who had died in 1989, had
been customers of mine for years. Both were regulars at Il Cantinori,
and Ian and his wife, Rita, also frequented Sapore di Mare and Coco
Pazzo. I liked Ian. Like me, he had come from modest roots and made
it big on his own, and we had an easy rapport and an ability to communicate in industry shorthand.

One night, while visiting at his table at Coco Pazzo, I asked him
about the restaurant at the Paramount. When the hotel opened, there
had been a French bistro on the ground floor, but I had heard through
the grapevine that it had closed. One thing led to another and next
thing I knew I was once again having a conversation in one of my
restaurants about opening another place.

I went to meet with Ian at his office in the Paramount. Though I
had known him for years, I realized that I had no inkling of his business persona, which I soon discovered was as intense as any I'd ever
seen. This was apparent from his office alone, which held several tables covered with overlapping piles of spreadsheets, architectural
drawings, and other papers. He was constantly taking calls from his
secretary, then turning to me and saying, "Give me a second," so he
could pick up the phone and dispense with a furniture-design issue or
a crisis at one of his hotels. In our very short meeting, it became clear
to me that he was a control freak of the highest order, making me look
laid back by comparison. He was also superhumanly connected; there
were three Ferris-wheel-size Rolodexes lined up on his desk, and in
the course of our ninety-minute meeting, he referred to them three or
four times. I realized there wasn't a person in New York, Los Angeles,
or London whom he didn't know. Calvin Klein, Mick Jagger, Paul
McCartney—you name them, and they were there. He was on a first-
name basis with all these people, and they seemed to be real friends of
his, not just casual acquaintances from his club and hotels.

Watching all of this only deepened my respect and affection for Ian,
but it also made me *not* want to be his partner in a new restaurant, nor

even to be a hired gun. It seemed inevitable that if we set up a Siamese dynamic, eventually we'd drive each other crazy. I told him I'd do a place in the Paramount if he'd lease me the space and let me operate autonomously. He agreed, and I decided to further expand the Coco Pazzo brand and launch a restaurant inspired by the proximity to Broadway: Coco Pazzo Teatro.

I'd be operating on my own this time. The Pressmans were unable to come along due to their current financial constraints. It was an awkward relationship that was getting more uncomfortable by the day.

WHILE WE WERE preparing to open Coco Teatro (as I called it), I interviewed one of the cooks from Le Madri for the job of executive chef. He came to my office above Il Toscanaccio, and I was immediately struck that the guy was as skinny as a string bean, with a shaggy head of hair and a face anchored by droopy, expressive eyes and framed by a chiseled chin.

In our first interview, he ran down the places he'd worked previously. His experience in Italian food was thin, to say the least, and he seemed to perk up only when discussing French cuisine.

"Jesus," I said, "How are you going to cook Italian?"

I lit up a cigarette, and he took it as license to smoke himself. Once he started, he didn't stop for the rest of the meeting. We filled the room with smoke and once we got comfortable, we began talking about everything *but* business, which is a real weakness of mine with people whose company I enjoy. Waving the cigarette around like a prop, he told me all sorts of stories about the places he'd worked, painting effortless sketches of former employers and his line-cook colleagues, all of it soaked in a uniquely sour, cynical sense of humor. I found him quietly confident and effortlessly charismatic. I had the feeling that he didn't take very much very seriously, least of all himself.

"You should be a writer," I said to him.

"Actually, I'm working on a novel," he said, matter-of-factly. "I don't know if it'll ever be published, but I'm working on it."

The guy's name was Tony Bourdain.

Tony devoted a chapter to me in the best-seller he wrote years later, *Kitchen Confidential*, so I think it's only fair that I share my impressions of him from back in the day, long before he was a world-renowned author, or even a known cook. The job for which I was interviewing him would be his first position as executive chef.

After our interview, I invited Tony to cook an audition menu at Mad. 61 for me and Marta, who by then had been promoted to corporate chef, helping me oversee all my restaurant kitchens and menus. He came to Mad. 61 and put out a number of small plates for us. One was a *raviolini of brandade*, the Provençal staple of pureed salt cod, potatoes, and olive oil. It's one of my favorite French dishes, and his was a knockout. He also served bluefish, which, he went on to say in *Kitchen Confidential*, he thought I took as a sign that he had a "pair of balls" on him, but in reality was about the safest thing you could serve somebody with my culinary upbringing, since it was one of the things my mother was raised on.

I loved Tony's food. In a time when every young chef seemed concerned with reinventing the wheel, he was happy to be a steward of the classics; it's no wonder that he ended up as the executive chef of the bistro Les Halles, because he was born to cook that kind of stuff.

I hired him a day or two later. We had about two months to get Coco Teatro ready and we spent the time furthering his education in all things Italian. He spent his days and nights with Marta at Mad. 61 and with the gang down at Le Madri. He seemed particularly enthused about perfecting his pasta know-how; even though he himself wouldn't be cooking the pasta, we wanted him to know what great pasta was, and before long, he *got* it. Watching him cook and eat it, I had the feeling he was discovering it for the first time, or really thinking about it the first time. I felt like a matchmaker, introducing somebody to his true love.

I broke a number of my rules for Tony. One was that by that point in my career, I really tried to avoid spending too much time with chefs. I have a lot of respect for anybody who can cook well and manage a kitchen, but so many chefs, especially young American ones, seemed more focused on advancing their own celebrity than on improving their own talent in the kitchen. As a consequence, I would usually take a minimalist approach to dealing with them, sticking my head in the door and asking, "Did you take care of this? Did you order that? Can I get an expense report and a sheet of numbers and hours?" and then leaving.

But Tony was so entertaining that not only didn't I mind spending more time with him, I actually went to Coco Teatro just to hang out. Tony was real. Maybe he wasn't the best chef in the world, the best expediter, but he had a frank honesty that I found refreshing. Spending as much time as I was in the company of financiers and would-be celebrity chefs, I felt that Tony was just Tony, and he was the funniest guy I ever knew in the kitchen. That voice you hear in his books, dripping with world-weariness and irony, is the way he actually talks; he did a nightly routine about how the grease traps overflowed that was worthy of George Carlin. But I have to spill the beans and say that Tony isn't as much of a badass as he makes himself out to be. Oh, I'm sure he's partied plenty hard, but the guy is, when you get right down to it, a sweetheart. How else to explain the only chef I ever met who had a distaste for firing people? Most chefs have been screwed over so many times by so many prep and line cooks that they have developed emotional calluses and are able to fire them with a gunslinger's nonchalance. But Tony once told me flat out that he didn't have the stomach for it.

We were something of an odd couple, but I think that Tony and I related because we both truly loved food, and didn't really love business, and because we were bullshitters who spotted in each other a reluctance to bullshit in our own relationship. I don't know why we had that special dynamic, but if I had to guess, I'd say it was the *brandade*. We also shared a sick passion for Marlboro Reds and an appreciation for great French cigarettes like Gauloises and Gitanes.

And so, because of Tony, I enjoyed visiting Teatro.

Once it opened, Coco Teatro, true to its name, did a huge pretheater business, which is one of the true circles of restaurant hell. To work in a kitchen that experiences such a rush is one of the most thankless jobs of all time. Every afternoon anxiety builds as five forty-five approaches. Between then and seven thirty, it's the same drill every day: customers arrive, sometimes later than their reservation;

they sit down, order a drink, and chat with each other as if they have all the time in the world; and then, when there's about an hour and fifteen minutes to work with, they ask their waiters, and by extension the kitchen, to do the impossible: prepare them a three-course meal, often with special orders and substitutions, and get them out the door in time for their curtain, but without rushing them. And all of this takes place absent the usual staggering of tables that permits a restaurant kitchen to function when all of its seats are occupied at the same time.

Ironically, the fact that I enjoyed hanging out at Coco Teatro with some regularity hastened Tony's departure because I often ended up eating dinner there and couldn't help but notice the signs of stress in the dining room. My eyes, so well trained to discern discontent, perceived it everywhere: when you see three quarters of the tables without food on them at seven o'clock and waiters muttering to themselves every time they push out through the swinging kitchen doors, there's a problem. There was never an issue with Tony's food—in fact the *New York Times* bestowed a generous two stars on us; it was the timing.

After one particularly stressful service, I excused myself from the table and asked Tony to step outside for a cigarette with me. I thought of it as a last cigarette for a condemned man about to face the firing squad. My plan was to say, "My friend, you're through." Unlike him, I never had any problem firing people. But I was so fond of Tony personally, and so sympathetic to the absurd demands of pretheater chefdom, that I couldn't bring myself to do it.

And so, I took the coward's way out and had the general manager do it for me. We offered Tony the chance to stay on as sous chef, but he declined and I don't blame him. We didn't see each other again until years later, after his flattering portrait of me in *Kitchen Confidential*. We've had dinner a few times since then and picked up right where we left off, as though no time had passed at all, the way true friends are able to do.

WHEN MONDRIAN WAS finally set to open in Los Angeles, I persuaded Ian to lease me the restaurant space so I could open a Coco Pazzo there as well.

We did well, and I was thrilled to have a restaurant designed by Philippe Starck, a relaxing motif of whites and beiges with an outdoor dining room separated from the Alice in Wonderland courtyard by playful, seven-foot-tall flower pots. While I always was drawn to the idea of spending time out west, after a few months of regular visits, I came to dislike the scene, especially all the effort made to sequester celebrities and ensure their easy passage in and out of hotels and restaurants. The extra security measures at Mondrian made it an adventure for people to get from the carport to our restaurant. Meanwhile, at Coco Pazzo, hostesses would lead diners to a table only to discover that Whiskey Bar patrons had stepped between the flower pots to take it. This became a nightly struggle as people in bathing suits would have pushed all the silverware and plates out of the way and were sitting there with their drinks sweating into the tablecloths. And they didn't want to give up those tables. One night, while I was trying to evict a trespasser, a bronzed blonde in a denim skirt and bikini top, she said to me, "Why do you need a restaurant in LA? We don't eat. We *drink*!"

After that, I began stationing busboys between the flower pots every afternoon until the first wave of diners were in their seats and the tables were firmly in our hands for the night.

The final straw between me and Los Angeles was the sequel to an earlier incident: I was on vacation with my family in Forte dei Marmi, on the seaside of Tuscany, to the west of Lucca, when my satellite phone rang. It was Ian Schrager.

"Pino, what the hell did you ever do to Sylvester Stallone?" he asked.

I told him the story of the wine and the golf course phone call, then asked, "Why?"

"He was going to have a private event with us. A lot of people. But when he found out you were the restaurateur here, he canceled it."

I had to laugh. I guess I didn't have the same talent for maintaining those celebrity relationships that Ian had. But our business arrangement would last for a few years, if only because I had the foresight to not become his partner. He might have been upset with me, but at the end of the day, it was me, not him, who was losing the private party.

Was it worth missing out on a profitable function over the cost of a few bottles of wine and the right to stick to my guns and do what *I* thought was fair?

You bet.

AS 1996 PLODDED along, I decided that it was time to move on from the Pressmans. Not only couldn't I get them on the phone, but I just couldn't shake that concept I'd originally pitched them for Mad. 61, of a place that combined restaurant and retail under one roof. Over time, the idea had grown into a full-fledged vision for a complete, self-contained Tuscan experience where we'd serve food and sell everything from tablewares and housewares to soaps and fragrances to clothing, draperies, and bedding, and anything else that represented the artisan tradition and style of Tuscany. I wanted to secure a gargantuan indoor space and re-create the experience of a Tuscan city square, along the lines of the Piazza della Repubblica in Florence, right in the middle of New York City—the Manhattan equivalent of a Florentine marketplace populated by merchants selling goods from their carts, with dining available nearby. I wanted there to be a fine-dining room, a bar, a takeout shop, and an event venue, with marble columns, a chestnut-wood bar, and a huge open kitchen. I even had a name for the project: Tuscan Square.

I finally got Irv on the phone and told him I wanted to move on to other projects, and he understood. With the help of a broker, that winter I met a gentleman named Bill Nimmo, a tall, mild-mannered investor from Prudential Equity Partners, a private investment group, and we explored the possibility of their investing in my company by funding my buyout of the Pressmans and possible future projects. It wasn't long before the Prudential Equity team was on board and was even prepared to finance the leasing of three contiguous spaces in Rockefeller Center for me, and to raise the financing to make Tuscan Square a reality. Our venture, by the way, not just Tuscan Square, but the umbrella corporation that would own all the restaurants, needed a name as well, and I fused *Toscana* and *corporation* and came up with

Toscorp. It sounds a little scary to me now, like a villainous corporation in a bad science-fiction movie; but at the time, it was a perfect reflection of what was going on: I had affixed my Tuscan dreams to a
corporate machine.

We approached my partners and, after much haggling, came up
with a proposal that worked for everybody. The only remaining relationship would be my (still unsigned) operating contract at Mad. 61.

SADLY, FRED PRESSMAN died of pancreatic cancer that summer, but
his passing made it easier, even appropriate, for me to sever my ties to
the family. He was the only one with whom I ever really felt a kinship.
I finally signed the papers that would put control of the restaurants in
my hands that July.

In mid-August, I was sitting in my office above Il Toscanaccio,
smoking one my favorite cigars, Hoyo de Monterrey Number Two,
when the phone rang. It was one of the maître d's of Mad. 61, and he
was hysterical.

"Pino, they're shutting down the restaurant!" he exclaimed.

I sat forward in my chair. "Who?"

"Barneys."

I snuffed out my cigar and hurried around the corner to Mad. 61.
There were just a few customers polishing off their dinner, while
Barneys' chief operating officer, a real can-do hard-ass who had been
brought in to help steer the corporate ship through bankruptcy—and
who dressed like he was the forgotten Blues Brother—prowled the dining room accompanied by four or five Barneys' security guards in their
gray flannel slacks and blue blazers.

The COO and I went right for each other, like a baseball manager
and an umpire engaging in a dustup on the field. We met up in a corner near the bakery and began a chest-out confrontation.

"What's the problem?" I demanded.

"We're closing the restaurant," he said.

"Why?"

"The family wants you out," he said. I guess there was resentment that I, the little restaurateur who had needed their money eight years earlier, was now buying *them* out. "They're in bankruptcy and it's for the benefit of the estate. I'm just following orders."

"It's not going to work that way. I have rights. I have a contract," I bluffed. "You're going to have to make me go."

"No problem," he said, his face going purple with hostility. "We're going to lock you out."

"You know what," I said, as one of the security guards stuck his arms between us to keep us from coming to blows. "I have no idea what my remedy is, but I'm not going to sleep tonight. I'm going to spend the next twelve hours figuring out how to *fuck* you and the family."

I stormed out, then spent the weekend calling my employees, telling them not to show up for work until further notice. My concern was that because the company was in bankruptcy, we wouldn't be able to pay them. And, sure enough, 110 payroll checks cut around this time bounced. I organized the staff and they began striking on Madison Avenue, picketing for their money.

(It took three years, but eventually all the employees and vendors got paid. The only person who didn't, as far as I know, was me, because the judge decided not to honor my unsigned management contract.)

In September, Barneys announced plans to reopen Mad. 61, but I had a surprise for them: unbeknownst to anyone, I had—following my own advice—trademarked the name Mad. 61, just as I had trademarked everything since Le Madri. So when I read about their plans in the paper, I filed a trademark infringement suit in federal court and had my lawyer send them a cease-and-desist letter.

By this time, the COO had been replaced with a more reasonable, collaborative executive, who called me up and asked me how much I wanted for the name.

"Two million dollars," I said.

He told me to keep it and I said, "You bet I will." That October, they ended up opening a makeshift restaurant called Fred's in the space that had been the site of my biggest accomplishment as a restaurateur.

I could never have expected that my real education in big business, begun in that conference room at Barneys in 1988, would end up coming full circle and applying to my final transaction with the Pressmans, but there you have it.

And so, one of my partnerships ended, and a new one began. It was supposed to be the one that freed me, but it ended up being the beginning of the end, or something very close to the end.

INTERLUDE

WE STOP INTERVIEWING *as a waiter puts a plate down before each of us: lamb stew, but not a particularly stewy one, no vegetables, just a pile of meat, looking not unlike pulled barbecued beef, with a mound of arugula stacked alongside it.*

"Taste that."

I spear a piece of lamb with my fork, put it in my mouth. The first thing that strikes me is pungent, hot black pepper. The second thing, as I chew it, is how meltingly tender it is.

"How do you make this?"

"I don't sear the meat," he says. I nod and think about this. I've never seen or cooked a stew recipe that doesn't begin with searing the meat. Browning it leaves behind a fond *in the pan, a coating of crusty bits imbued with flavor. His technique sacrifices that intensity in exchange for such soft lamb.*

"My mother taught me to cook it this way," Pino says. "You put the lamb, the stock, the spices, the wine, in the pot at the same time and bring it up . . ." (He pauses here, hitting the brakes on his voice, lowering to a delicate whisper.) ". . . very, very slowly. Very gently." He sounds not unlike a man instructing a younger man in the finer points of love-making.

I'm struck, as I am most times we eat together, that Pino still feels food very intensely and treats it, talks about it, very sensually, even after all these years. I watch him plow through the lamb, eating with real gusto, a fork in one hand, in the other a hunk of bread with which he dabs at the sauce. I think of what food means to Pino, of how to this day it still seems to carry him away. For a moment, I feel as if I'm watching something private and personal, as though I've wandered in on somebody deep in prayer.

Thinking about his story as he's told it so far, a thought occurs to me. It's probably too psychoanalytical for Pino's taste, but I feel I have to voice it.

"Pino?"

Almost startled, as though he'd forgotten I was there, he looks up from his food and stops midchew. "Yeah?"

"Did it ever occur to you how many times you've walked out on fathers in your life?"

He puts down the fork and the bread and folds his hands on the table. I think that maybe I've offended or even angered him. His eyes reveal absolutely nothing, making it impossible to gauge what exactly I've embarked on.

"Go on."

"You left your biological father in Italy, and then all of your professional fathers: you left Silvano and his father, you left Steve, and you left Fred Pressman."

He considers this for a moment, then averts his eyes and shakes his head from side to side, but it's not a gesture of denial. Rather, it's a kind of weary resolution.

"You're right," he says. "Jesus. I never thought of it in this way."

"Why do you think it is?"

He keeps shaking his head. "I don't know. What do you think?"

"I don't think you like anybody else to have authority over you. Not your father, not your employer, not your partners."

The side-to-side shaking becomes an up-and-down nod. "That's true," he says. "But they all had something in common; they all wanted to control me. I was a good son to my father. I was a great employee to Silvano. I made money for my partners. But at some point they all felt like they owned me. None of them wanted me to move on, to be myself."

"What does that mean, 'to be myself'?"

"I'm a leader, Andrew. I'm not a follower."

"So you were meant to be on your own all along?"

"When it comes to business, probably so."

He picks up his fork and that bread and gets back eating. I do the same.

We polish off the stew, then the salad, which is a perfect, cleansing chaser. Pino orders us two more glasses of wine and continues.

TWELVE

The Hidden Table: Running a Reservation Book

I F YOU DINE regularly at popular restaurants in New York, or in any major city, then you've probably experienced something like this: the restaurant opens its reservation book one month before a given date. With this in mind, you call exactly thirty days prior to your spouse's birthday, or your anniversary, or just a date you've set aside to finally eat at this hard-to-crack bastion of fine dining, and are told that they only have tables available at six o'clock or nine thirty. You wonder how it's possible that they're already down to those two times. The phone was only busy on your first attempt; how many tables could they have given out in three minutes?

Your confusion turns to anger on the night you show up for dinner. Standing at the bar, waiting for the lingerers at your table to vacate it, you see a handsome young couple walk up to the podium and get all lovey-dovey with the maître d'. He casts an eye over the dining room, then over his reservation book, discreetly summons one of his hostesses, and has her escort them to a table. From the look of the transaction, you're 100 percent certain that they just walked in and scored a table with thirty seconds' notice, compared to your thirty *days* of advance planning. And you're still waiting at the bar!

If you're wondering how such a moment is possible, you're not alone. There's perhaps no aspect of the restaurant industry less understood by the dining public than the way tables are doled out, booked, and managed. There's a science to running the book in a restaurant, and one of the reasons civilians don't know much about it is that most restaurateurs do it their own way. It's like the work of an artisan: different techniques are passed down through the generations, so how you do it is a blend of the ways of your mentors combined with your own inventiveness, ingenuity, and personal style. The notable exception to this is the relatively new development of Open Table, a Web-based business through which reservations can be booked for restaurants all over the world, and of other software and Web sites that turn the procurement of a table into a transaction no different than the purchase of a ticket to a Justin Timberlake concert.

Call me old school, but when it comes to The Book, I could never, for a second, consider using a humanless system. The reservation book at my restaurant is a physical tome that would have been at home in a restaurant of the 1950s or '60s: a fat registry, held closed by an elastic strap, with a list of tables available for each time slot. The first thing we do on each page is list the times and the tables by hand, then they get filled in as people call for reservations.

Each day, the reservations are reviewed, a seating chart is created, and we determine who to seat where.

But here's another reason I could never use Open Table: when I wake up each morning, I know that a devoted customer or a friend is going to call looking to come in to dinner. These people feel they have the right to be able to call at five thirty or six P.M. and tell me they're coming over.

And I'll tell you something. I agree with them. Being a regular, or a friend of the owner, should come with certain benefits.

So that's the situation: Open Table versus "I Want the Table."

And what's the solution? Very simple. I *hide* the table.

I learned my lesson early. Way back at Il Cantinori, I began teaching maître d's to never promise anything out of the ordinary. The reason is that they always have the option of saying to a customer, "Let me check," but when a customer reaches me, I don't have the luxury of saying, "I don't have the table." Nobody believes that an owner doesn't have a table in his pocket, even when it's the truth.

That's when I began hiding tables: at Centolire, there are four tables that don't appear in our reservation book or on the seating chart:

one deuce, two four tops, and one six. Those are my secret tables, and they've given me peace of mind for years now, both here and at other restaurants, like the night Prince Rainier of Monaco showed up spontaneously at Coco Pazzo, completely unannounced. What was I going to do? Turn him out into the street?

Their owners and managers may not admit it, but any hot restaurant has some version of this system. Many restaurateurs actually list "hold" tables in their reservation book or software, but I learned over the years that certain maître d's with a taste for extortion couldn't resist selling those tables themselves. To a person, they all do it the same way: make a promise to a customer, then come to me with their tail between their legs. "Oh, Pino," they say. "I'm so sorry, but I overbooked at eight thirty."

"No problem," I say, as I release one of *my* tables. "But if you ever do it again, you're going to be overbooked on your ass and you're not going to have a job."

They never argue. Because we both know the truth. And at some level I almost pity them, because the temptation is overwhelming, not just to make the tips, but to please—which ought to be part of the psychological makeup of any restaurant professional. Back in the heyday of Sapore and Coco Pazzo, as evening approached, I could feel the devil waiting at the door, an invisible presence ready to tempt my staff, to rob John, Tom, Ariel, and the great Carlos of their virginity, to turn them into front-door whores willing to keep a reservation-holder cooling his heels at the bar for an hour in exchange for a quick hundred from a walk-in. Sometimes, I'd hover over my hosts all night to help them resist the desire.

As if all of this weren't enough to contend with, at some of my restaurants it wasn't enough to score a table; customers also wanted to be seated in the best *location*.

The ultimate example was Sapore di Mare, which had two hundred twenty seats spread out among five rooms. The way I explained the seating philosophy of Sapore to my maître d's was that Sapore was a show: live theater powered by *spaghetti alla rustica*. Our celebrity clientele were the stars of the show; the unfamous-but-glamorous guests were the nonspeaking supporting cast who got to share the stage with the stars. The rest of the customers were there to *watch* the show.

The coveted seats were the forty-five in the Bar Room. This was where you might see Billy Joel and Christie Brinkley, Calvin Klein, Ralph Lauren, Chevy Chase, Alec Baldwin and Kim Basinger, and Steven Spielberg—not just having dinner but table hopping as if they were in a high school cafeteria.

There was nowhere in the restaurant where I would have sat those people other than the Bar Room. It's just the nature of the business. The French have a great expression, *physique du rôle*. And that was the prerequisite for a table in the Bar Room—to have the physique for the role. If that offends you, then I'm sorry.

The other enormous ongoing challenge was Coco Pazzo, which only had 110 seats to play with, and only three marquee tables—19, 32, and 40, the only ones that I could keep an eye on while also manning the podium—with the supporting characters populating the seats right around them. The challenge was that on many nights we were attended almost exclusively by media and entertainment royalty, but we only had those three thrones to assign. So, we'd put the crème de la crème there and make the others happy with personal attention and little treats from the kitchen when I felt it was in order.

There were nights when the challenge required a different solution, and I look back on these the way I imagine athletes look back on their most hard-won victories. On one evening, we were expecting Frank Sinatra and Julio Iglesias at one table and the Rolling Stones and Rod Stewart at another. My instincts were finely honed enough that I knew that these guests would be celebrities even to the other celebrities, so rather than seating them in the "face tables," I sat one party in the back right corner and the other in the back left corner, affording them some privacy. It was a total reversal of the usual way of doing things. The only hiccup came when Sinatra got up to go to the men's room. At his advanced age, he had a bit of a tough time making his way around tables, which often resulted in adjacent seatbacks forming roadblocks, turning the room into a maze. He was stranded there, having a senior moment, and I noticed as more and more customers took note of him and began staring.

I quickly navigated the room. "Are you looking for the men's room, Mr. Sinatra?" I asked.

"Yeah, actually I am," he replied.

I offered him my elbow and escorted him to the front of the restaurant where the restrooms were, then waited for him to emerge and escorted him back to his table.

Now, New York City has some of the savviest diners in the world, so as people were leaving, they'd notice where Ron Perelman was seated, or the hot model du jour, and they'd whisper to me, asking for the table number. Like a young beauty subject to frequent, unwanted requests for her phone number, I quickly learned that the path of least resistance was best: I gave them the number, but I also did as those girls do and changed one of the digits.

Some customers didn't know when to say when, and this was one of the few times when my desire to please would give way to my desire to teach somebody a lesson.

The ultimate example took place one Saturday night during the heyday of Sapore, when a guy showed up at the podium wearing baggy, pleated linen pants and a tropical shirt, flanked by two blondes as least ten inches taller than he was.

"Can I help you?" I asked.

"Table for three," he said.

I looked over my shoulder. There wasn't a square foot of unoccupied space anywhere in the restaurant, just a great sea of the prettiest, wealthiest people on the East Coast.

"I'm sorry, we're fully booked."

The guy took my hand in his and slipped me what I later realized was five hundred dollars. It was the least subtle payoff in the history of hospitality. It wasn't a single bill, and it wasn't neatly folded: it was a spool of cash roughly the diameter of a rolled-up magazine.

OK, I thought, if you want a table so bad, I'll give you a table.

"Give me a minute," I said.

I stepped away and out the back of the room, into a little corridor that connected the Fireplace Room and the Patio. Along one wall was our bread table, where the waiters and busboys came to fill baskets.

I stopped a busboy as he breezed past and instructed him to

remove all the bread to the kitchen and set this table up with a table-cloth, silverware, and wine glasses.

He looked at me like I was crazy, but I just told him to do as I asked.

It was a short, dark, corridor, with no action except the passing of restaurant staff. If they were lucky, maybe they'd see Chevy Chase on his way to take a piss.

I took the guy in and I could see the disappointment in his face, but the deal was done.

I divided the money up among the three dishwashers in the back; those guys worked their asses off and if anybody deserved some extra appreciation, it was them.

"This is from Mr. Schmuck," I said, a private joke for my own amusement because they had no idea what *schmuck* meant. In the months and years to come, whenever I sold the bread table to a pushy customer, I repeated the routine until I decided it was poor form for a restaurateur to treat any guest that way, and began turning them away. One day, a dishwasher, I guess missing the occasional bonus, asked me, "What happened to Mr. Schmuck?"

"I'm sorry, he doesn't come in anymore," I said.

In any event, the moral of the story is there are some things money can't buy. And in my restaurants, the hidden table is definitely among them.

THIRTEEN

The Restaurant Junkie

FREE OF THE Pressmans, the first order of business was to begin bringing Tuscan Square to life, but just as I was getting rolling on the massive construction phase, Bill Nimmo came to me with a proposition: the Sfuzzi chain—a nationwide group of Italian eateries, sort of an upscale Olive Garden with a Pompeii motif and Americanized food—had recently filed for bankruptcy and was on the auction block. Prudential Equity wanted to purchase Sfuzzi—fourteen restaurants including two each in New York City and the Dallas area, plus other units in Baltimore, Scottsdale, Philly, Atlanta, Las Vegas, Cleveland, Atlanta, Austin, San Diego, and Costa Mesa, California—and have me work my magic on them, converting each one into a Coco Pazzo with a less casual setting and more sophisticated food.

Their logic was sound, at least when explained in broad strokes: though the company was in dire financial straits, many of the individual restaurants did a respectable *gross* business—several million dollars a year in some cases—but their food costs were too high, so at the end of the day, they lost money. Food costs are one of the great barometers of a chef's or restaurateur's grasp of bottom-line reality and one of the things that seasoned industry professionals pride themselves on being able to control—not unlike the way chauvinists boast of controlling their wives. This was more true than ever in the mid- to late 1990s, when the growing legions of celebrity chefs managed to convince restaurant owners that the toques' work in the kitchen was an

191

important artistic endeavor and that the owners should consider themselves patrons of the arts, with a near-moral obligation to spend whatever it cost, not only for the best, most expensive ingredients, but also for the number of people it took to execute the very elaborate plating of them, with no regard to what they could reasonably expect to charge for the final product. The ultimate example of this is one of contemporary chefs' favorite indulgences, foie gras (duck or goose liver), which you can charge a lot for, but which is expensive to begin with and doesn't keep for an especially long time. (Fortunately, I'm Italian and we cook with one of the *least* expensive alternatives, chicken liver.) Other luxury ingredients such as caviar, truffles, sturgeon, shad roe, and soft-shell crabs create a similar quandary: they're highly perishable and unless you charge an exorbitant price for them, opening yourself up to charges of larceny and the possibility of customer resistance, you risk making little or no money on them.

This was never an issue in my restaurants. From all the way back when I worked for my uncle, I understood how to manage a restaurant's budget, and the food I served was straightforward enough that it would simply be unthinkable for food costs to become a problem. The key is using at least 90 percent of what you buy, and for me that was second nature because my mother never wasted anything in her kitchen; it all got used, even leftovers, which were repurposed into something new the next day, like cooking the remains of a pasta with scrambled eggs in a *frittata*. I've adapted and expanded this approach in my kitchens, milling *stracotto* into a sauce and offering it as *rigatoni allo stracotto*, for example, and almost never purchasing cuts of meat or poultry. Instead, I buy a saddle or a leg, butcher it myself, and use all the pieces. From one leg you can harvest several pounds of ground meat and stew meat, three osso bucos, two small loins, fifteen to twenty paillards, and enough top loin for a few servings of *vitello tonnato*. As if that weren't economical enough, you can also use the bones to make stock.

Thanks to this philosophy, and to my secret weapon, Chester, among my peers I was known as one of the most ruthlessly efficient food-cost wranglers, bringing mine in as low as 22 or 23 percent of food revenue versus anywhere from 30 to 38 percent for most mid- to high-end places.

The other problem with Sfuzzi, it seemed, was that there was enormous corporate overhead. The infrastructure in place to run the company was overstaffed and inefficient, with no centralized purchasing or other economies of scale to balance the expense of having a corporation in the first place. This seemed simple enough to fix: just employ the kind of systems I had in New York, like my own private linen company, which had by then moved to a larger facility in Long Island City, just across the Fifty-ninth-Street Bridge.

Nevertheless, from the moment the Sfuzzi idea was first presented to me, I knew it was a bad one. In my opinion, food costs and overhead alone couldn't explain the situation. It seemed to me that the parent company simply wasn't earning enough to service the debt they had incurred to get the business off the ground. Plus, even if these didn't seem like difficult problems to solve, just thinking about them turned me off. I was a restaurateur and a chef, and I had no interest in becoming a corporate leader. I liked to handle areas such as human resources myself, or turn them over to my most trusted lieutenants, such as Marta in the kitchens or Jack Weiss and a new guy, Joe Essa, who had come on board in the final days of Mad. 61 and stayed on to help me run my New York places. Beyond that, there was a reason that I had never opened restaurants in most of the cities where we'd be taking over Sfuzzis: the understanding of true Italian food took years to flow westward from New York and eastward from California. In many ways, outside of the major metropolises of America, Italian food is still misunderstood today, and there's almost no awareness whatsoever of the different regions. People know that there are lots of sunflowers in Tuscany and that you get around Venice in a gondola, and that's about it. In this way, Sfuzzi, with its Pompeii murals on the wall, was more user-friendly to many markets than a Coco Pazzo might ever be.

But more than that, Sfuzzi represented everything that was anathema to me: it was an artificial representation of Italy, right down to its silly name. Accordingly, many of the Sfuzzis did a huge bar business and were lapsing into something closer to lounges than restaurants. I had made my bones by committing to being 100 percent sincere in every detail of my places. Even though I owned a number of restaurants,

I took great pains to keep tabs on all of them, and I was proud that I still signed off on everything, right down to the selection of silverware and napkins.

As if all those weren't enough reasons to say no, the proposed means of financing the acquisition of Sfuzzi was to borrow six million dollars from the Tuscan Square funding, putting the project of my dreams in jeopardy. I was told that the money would be replaced by an anticipated influx of cash, but it felt like an awfully huge stack of chips to be moving around the table.

And yet, I have to be honest: despite all of these almost life-threatening misgivings, I was strangely attracted to the idea.

Why?

That is a question that I still wrestle with today, because at that moment, my life was just about perfect. I was being bankrolled by a company that put total trust and faith in me. I was the impresario behind two of the hottest restaurants in New York City, plus Sapore di Mare in East Hampton, and other places in New York and Chicago that were performing well. I was making a good living, and Jessie and I had three kids now, having welcomed our second son, Lorenzo, in 1995.

If you had told me when I arrived here in 1980, with little more to my name than a pocketful of confidence and a few pairs of creased blue jeans in my suitcase, nursing a broken heart and wanting nothing more than to get on the next plane back to Rome, if you had told me then that I would have attained this level of success in America, I . . . well, I won't say that I would have told you that you were crazy, but I would have said that it would be a great deal. I would have signed up for that right then and there.

But I wasn't happy, or perhaps I should say that I wasn't content. I had moments of exhilaration, many of them. I had a driver in those days and at night I'd get into the back of my 500 Mercedes and make cell phone calls while he shuttled me from Il Toscanaccio down to Le Madri and then uptown to Coco Pazzo. I felt like a mogul sitting in the shadows of my chauffer-driven ride, and every time I made my entrance at one of the restaurants, I had that old Rick Blaine rush, the natural high of a restaurateur.

But the truth of the matter was that there was an even bigger rush for me, and that was the irreplaceable intensity of opening a new and preferably bigger restaurant. Nothing made me feel more alive—and by alive, I mean like I was on the high wire—than shepherding a new restaurant into reality.

Slowly but surely, I had become a junkie, but it was a socially acceptable, even socially *celebrated* type of junkie. In addition to the money, I was addicted to business deals, to expansion, and perhaps even to codependent relationships and drama. I'm not alone: the restaurant world is rife with ill-fated partnerships. But you'd think that after Silvano and the Pressmans and even Ian Schrager—with whom things were ongoing but less than perfect—I'd have known enough to be happy with what I had, to be content to have even just Le Madri, Coco Pazzo, and Sapore di Mare. Most restaurateurs would kill for those three restaurants. Hell, most would kill for *one* of them.

But not me: slowly but surely, I had developed an almost vampiric thirst for the Next Big Thing. And that thing had to be more outsized and outlandish than any that had gone before it. Tuscan Square was far from complete, and once open, it would be difficult to imagine anything bigger, so the Sfuzzi chain and its promise of adding fourteen new restaurants and scattering the Coco Pazzo name all over the nation in one fell swoop was attractive.

Nevertheless, I said no to Bill. He asked a second time, and again I said, no, and I did the same on his third pass.

The fourth time, he offered me an economic incentive that I couldn't refuse . . . and I didn't. I finally relented, and against all of my instincts, I said yes.

There's a moment at the end of *The Graduate*: Benjamin (played by Dustin Hoffman) has just run off with Elaine Robinson. They escape from her angry family and jilted fiancé by getting on a yellow city bus and deposit themselves on a seat in the back. Her wedding dress is tattered and his face is smeared with grease. They smile at each other, but in the coming seconds, their faces go blank, empty. They don't really know what they've gotten themselves into. Or maybe they do, but don't want to admit it.

That's the image that comes up for me when I remember agreeing to take on Sfuzzi. Because I knew way down deep that I was making a mistake. The truth was that I'd almost been too successful. I'd come to believe in my own great good luck, and if that failed, in the ability to talk or hustle my way out of anything. I had an intoxicating sense of business immortality. And so, despite my grave misgivings, I thought, "Hey, I'll deal with the problems when they come; that always seems to work."

There's nothing more dangerous than a bullshitter believing his own bullshit. Despite what came out of my mouth, and what I allowed myself to believe, there was no doubt that Sfuzzi would be my undoing, that when I affixed my name to the paperwork in early 1997, I'd be signing something akin to my own death sentence.

NEXT THING I knew I was in Dallas, Texas, standing in the gallery of a courtroom with Bill and one of his associates. We weren't there to watch a trial; we were there to bid in the auction of Sfuzzi. If I hadn't been so preoccupied by my own growing sense of dread, I'd have found the scene funny: from the bench, the judge accepted one offer at a time. Before another group could raise the stakes, they'd huddle and confer in whispers, or ask for a recess to step outside and make cell phone calls to financial partners and attorneys.

The only thing that cheered me up was, of all people, our chief rival in the bidding: Al Copeland, also known as the Chicken King of New Orleans because he had founded the Popeyes chain. A middle-aged hillbilly playboy in shiny black boots and a huge Stetson-type hat, he exuded enough energy to power a small city, speaking his mind freely and loudly enough for everybody to hear. During a recess, I was milling around in the corridor outside the courtroom with Bill and his associate when Copeland came up to us.

"Hey, y'all," he said. "I'm really only interested in four of these locations; why don't we hook up and stop driving the price so high?"

I thought it sounded like a great idea, but my partners were doing the talking, and they brushed him off. It made me sad. It would have been great to get out of there and go celebrate over a few beers with the Chicken King of New Orleans.

At the end of the day, my team won, mostly because we came up

with the most cash up front. But I took no pleasure in the victory, and back in New York, my apprehension was validated: once the ownership was transferred, I began receiving profit and loss reports. When you've been in my line of work long enough, you can read a spreadsheet the way a doctor reads a bedside chart, and as soon as those reports came rolling in through my fax machine, my eye went right to the danger signs. For example, the Vegas unit would show $300,000 gross sales for the month, but when I scanned the itemized breakdown, it became clear that about 20 percent of that was in redeemed coupons, which are not the same as cash, because the cash had been taken in months earlier, and by the *corporation*, not by the individual unit. The more I studied the charts, the more I gathered that Sfuzzi wasn't a restaurant chain; it was a patient in the throes of a disease, and it was up to me to determine if the condition was fatal.

Follow-up tests were in order. I administered the first of them by visiting the two New York City locations, one in the World Financial Center, a huge downtown waterfront mall of shops and restaurants, home of the Winter Garden (a giant solarium) and, of course, neighbor to the Twin Towers of the World Trade Center; the other in the West Sixties, near Lincoln Center. My first excursion was to the one in the World Financial Center. The profits for that restaurant were actually very encouraging, so I thought it would be a way of easing myself into things.

By that time, we had moved out of the offices above Il Toscanaccio and were leasing the three floors above Le Madri to accommodate Toscorp's growing needs: the second floor was to be Tuscan Square's showroom, the third floor was for the accounting staff, and the top floor housed executive offices and a conference room. There was a subway station right downstairs, and I walked down and took the number 1 train to the World Financial Center, walked through the mall, and showed up anonymously for lunch at Sfuzzi.

When I set foot inside I was immediately reminded how tacky the concept was, with frescoes on the wall and chalky white pillars strewn about in a poor imitation of the architecture of Rome or Pompeii. Sfuzzi had originated in the Dallas–Fort Worth area of Texas and the food was like a bizarre cross between Wolfgang Puck and Yosemite

Sam—anything-goes pizzas, salads topped with barbecue-seasoned chicken, and so on—the exact opposite of everything I had been trying to teach people about Italian food for more than a decade. There was even one of my pet peeves, angel hair pasta with seafood sauce.

But the thing that bothered me the most was that no manager was present. The busboys and waiters were doing the best they could and I watched with something approaching pity, both for them and for what I was inheriting, as they tried to get through a service with no coordination between the front of the house and the back. The time between courses was interminable, and I noticed that at tables with more than one diner, very often one person would be served his lunch while the other was kept waiting for his, which is one of the cardinal sins you can commit in any dining room. But my growing temper wasn't trained on the poor souls doing the work; it was focused on the absentee managers. It wasn't the orchestra's fault that they had no conductor.

Toward the end of my meal, a swift-walking young guy with soap-opera good looks, wearing a dark suit with pointy lapels, walked up to the podium, spun the reservation book around, and, while reviewing it, found about three reasons to lay his hands on the hostess, a frizzy-headed young thing who didn't seem to mind in the least. He was the prototypical low-rent general manager: all strut, no stuff. The fact that he was clearly either sleeping with or on his way to sleeping with the hostess only solidified the cliché. And his obliviousness to the disarray on the service floor spoke volumes to me; a man like this would not be hired by anyone who knew how to run a restaurant. It's not uncommon for restaurants to treat lunch as a there-for-the-taking enterprise, figuring expectations are lower than at dinner and many diners are simply looking to fuel up for an afternoon at their offices. This might sustain a business for years, but it doesn't engender loyalty; customers who know you this way will abandon you the moment a better option presents itself. To me a paying customer was a paying customer and lunch should be treated with the same respect as dinner.

I wiped my mouth, calmly and methodically folded my napkin, and walked across the dining room as the manager and the hostess stood giggling away. As I got closer and closer, I felt like the shark in *Jaws*, about to devour two unsuspecting and frolicking young lovers.

"Excuse me. You're the general manager, right?" I asked.

He turned around. They suppressed their giggles and he addressed me, "Yes, sir. How can I help you?"

"I'm Pino Luongo, the new owner of this restaurant."

The laughter stopped. He shushed the hostess.

"Oh, Mr. Luongo, of course. Great to meet you." Then, as the realization dawned on him, he squinted: "Were you . . . were you in for lunch?"

"Yeah, I was," I said. "Let me ask you something: you always show up to work at two thirty in the afternoon?"

"No," he said. "I had an emergency to take care of."

Cupping her hand over her mouth to stifle a laugh, the hostess walked away quickly. He shot her a cross look, as though he'd have been putting one over on me if she hadn't blown his cover. It was then that I realized that I actually needed a human resources department after all, if only as a buffer, because my instinct was to wrap my hands around this guy's neck and strangle him. And I don't mean that in a figurative way: I actually wanted to kill him.

The guy gave me a quick tour of the dining room and then excused himself to go to his office. I had the distinct impression that he had hurried off to circulate an internal e-mail, warning his fellow employees: "Caesar has arrived in Pompeii!"

I spent the next several hours sitting at the bar and watching the afternoon unfold. It was some of the most shameless thievery I had ever witnessed in my life. The workers from the lunch shift stuck around while those from the evening shift showed up at three o'clock, a good hour or two earlier than was common, and clocked in, then all these people stood around talking and working at a snail's pace, milking the company for thousands of dollars during the restaurant's dead time between meals. By the time I left, my blood was boiling. I'd usually have taken the subway back to my office at that hour, but I needed to get above ground for some fresh air.

My experience at the Sfuzzi near Lincoln Center was almost identical, from the décor to the service to the food and the late-arriving GM.

All I really wanted to do was focus on Tuscan Square, but these two units alone forced me to devote a lot of attention to starting the Sfuzzi conversions. Because the World Financial Center location was making money despite the manager's best efforts to the contrary, I made the Lincoln Center spot a priority. I actually loved the location and saw a huge potential for pre- and post-theater and opera dining. I decided that it would be renamed Coco Pazzo Opera. I was so bullish on its promise that I thought perhaps we'd spend some money and really rebuild the design from scratch. Before doing that, though, I wanted to be sure we could remain there for a good, long while to recoup the investment, so I approached the landlord to see if we could extend the lease. He came back and revealed that it actually included a demolition clause, meaning that he could kick us out with six months' notice if he wanted to demolish the building for any reason. In a shocking move by New York City standards, he actually gave me a piece of friendly advice—"Don't do it"—the implication being that he was planning to bring in the wrecking ball at some point.

I was trying to muster some enthusiasm, but at every turn I was met by an impediment. Finally, I came up with a very simple plan for recasting these places as scaled-down, moderately priced Coco Pazzos, something between the original one on the Upper East Side and the Coco Pazzo Cafe in Chicago. Working with my team, I devised a basic design philosophy that could be transmitted across all the units, along with a mandate of seasonal cuisine that could be adapted by the chefs at the individual locations, some of whom we'd keep and some of whom we'd have to replace. We also made a calculated business decision to *not* overhaul all the restaurants. In hopes of ditching a few of them, I phoned up Al Copeland, the Chicken King of New Orleans, the one who had brought a smile to my face back in Dallas, and asked if he wanted to buy the units he had originally wanted.

He cut me off quickly: "Don't even tell me the price. I know what you paid for them and you're not going to sell them to me for less." Then, after a pause, he shamelessly and charmingly added, *"Are you?"*

I wasn't prepared to do that, but as none of the promised replacement funds had materialized for Tuscan Square, we would end up selling off the restaurant in Atlanta, even though we'd spent the money to turn it into a Coco Pazzo, for a quick and necessary infusion of cash.

That's the problem with being a restaurant junkie: you end up like any other kind of junkie, doing whatever you have to in order to survive from one day to the next.

I TRIED NOT to let these gathering clouds overshadow my excitement and enthusiasm for Tuscan Square. As I had come to see it, this new project would be the ultimate expression of my nostalgia for home, a nostalgia that had sifted out the ordinary and unpleasant: every summer's day in Tuscany was sunny, but not too hot; every autumn afternoon was cold enough to let you see your breath, but not enough to produce a shiver; every meal was an occasion, something to be remembered fondly.

By the same token, I often explained my vision for the retail component of Tuscan Square using imagined people to help bring it to life: the clothing line was summed up by a Tuscan gentleman I envisioned, a dashing man in his forties who lived in the old city of Florence. Because the countryside was just a stone's throw away, his look was both cosmopolitan, expressed in the quality of the fabrics he wore, and country, demonstrated by a certain degree of informality. This guy might wear a *filo di cotone* cotton shirt, a chocolate brown vest, a corduroy jacket inspired by the boar-hunting season, with 1920s-style side pockets for his cartridges, and heavy slacks cut wide at the bottom to make way for his boots. I would never compare myself to Ralph Lauren, but in many ways he was my inspiration: I wanted to create a Tuscan wardrobe not unlike his idealized vision of American style.

My goals for the kitchenware and tableware were inspired by the same notion of city and country, antique and modern, with everything from classic pewter tabletop items to stylized, contemporary flourishes like you might see in a modern restaurant. In addition to the clothes and the housewares, there would be a wide range of merchandise that reflected the artisan traditions of Tuscany, from hand-blown glassware to leather-bound agendas and diaries that showed off the exquisite paper-work of the region.

Was all of this a bit over the top? Of course it was. But in the time in which I was operating, it seemed right at home. There was so much cash around in the 1990s, surely there'd be no limit to the number of customers willing to spend heaps of money on food and furnishings. And the taste for all things Tuscan was exploding as well, not just because of my restaurants, but also because of the others that had sprung up in the almost fifteen years since Il Cantinori had debuted, and because of books like *Under the Tuscan Sun*. In keeping with the times, it wasn't just one store I envisioned, but many. I saw Tuscan Squares in other big cities like Boston and Los Angeles, and maybe even in certain affluent suburbs.

As the construction proceeded and I watched the place come to life, it was almost enough to make me forget my Sfuzzi woes. There was just one nagging concern: whenever I left the premises and stepped outside, I'd look to my right and see thousands of people coursing down Fifth Avenue, but almost none of them turned onto Fifty-first Street. I'd never really thought about it before, but Rockefeller Center is like its own little enclave in the heart of Midtown and you just didn't venture within without a purpose. I began to wonder if foot traffic, the lifeblood of most retail operations, would be a challenge for us.

In addition to the enormous construction job, I had to generate an entire retail line from scratch. I assembled a team of friends and consultants to help me put out feelers all over Italy, mostly in Tuscany, and find all those artisanal products we'd need. My man on the ground overseas was Marta's husband at the time, Gianni Salvaterra, an Italy-based restaurant and lifestyle consultant who I hired to canvass Tuscany, make first contact with vendors whose wares he thought I might respond to, and set an itinerary for me when I would go over on buying trips. He produced a dizzying schedule for the first one, in April 1997, arranging face-to-face meetings with about forty-five companies in two weeks. I asked a good friend of mine, Gary Wolkowitz—the president of Hot Sox, who had impeccable taste and a house in Chianti—to travel with me and serve as my American alter-ego, offering feedback on what he thought people would best respond to here.

It was rare to spend two weeks back home. I made some time to visit my parents and my siblings, but for the most part all we did was travel up and down the corridor from Florence to Siena to Pisa to Lucca, meeting with artisans to see what distinguished each one's products from the others and to select and contract for Tuscan Square exclusives, negotiating terms and telling them how, if at all, we wanted things altered.

The range of products we discovered was breathtaking: blankets, throws, and runners made from exquisite baroque fabrics; antique-looking pewter tabletop items; soaps, candles, and fragrances made with basil, lavender, and sage; a dozen different lines of glassware; terra-cotta plates, bowls, and mugs; and Casentino wool apparel, made from a cooked, singularly curly wool and named for the area to the south of Florence where it's produced.

Tuscany was becoming one huge cottage industry for us as business owners referred us to others they knew. Sometimes I would just stumble upon something and find out how to get it, like the day I dropped into a collectible arts store in Florence and saw resin chargers (underplates) that suspended herbs and leaves within a plastic casing. I thought they were the ultimate expression of seasonality at the table, and I became obsessed with having them for myself. I asked around town like a private eye. Finally, the clerk in a neighboring store told me that the family who produced these plates lived fifty kilometers west of the city. He didn't know the name or address, but in the countryside, you often don't need those details: "You go past the train tracks and there's a little industrial development. They live there," he told me.

The next day I drove myself out to the town and after some more asking around, found the father. When I told him I was from New York, he looked at me with extreme skepticism, but I began telling him my story and he eventually invited me into his shop and demonstrated his technique: he heated the resin and poured it into the bottom plate of a mold of an oversized dish. When it dried and hardened, he created a collage of wheat on its surface. He then poured molten resin over it, and let it cool so that the wheat was suspended within the charger. It was fascinating.

We sat down and began talking business. I told him I wanted

hundreds of chargers of fall leaves, representing autumn, and green spring wheat, and golden wheat, which stood for summer. I also wanted marine-themed chargers, a nod to my love of the beach. He was hesitant about this, telling me that he'd have to forage for the shells, starfish, and pebbles himself, but he agreed to do it. Meeting him, and countless others like him, was a look into a creative aspect of Tuscan life that I had always admired but had never experienced at the source. As we got a close-up look into the lives of the often very humble artisans who made all of these products, and saw their painstaking craft, I felt enormous pride in where I came from, and couldn't wait to share it all with the city of New York.

I'D COME BACK from these exhilarating trips, and by the following morning, Tuscany would seem like as much of a long-lost dream as it had when I had first arrived in the United States. As my own little Tuscany was coming together in Rockefeller Center, I'd be constantly pulled away to focus on sprucing up Sfuzzi. I gave it my best shot under the circumstances, but there was simply no joy in it, so I turned to two of my most trusted employees, Jack Weiss and Joe Essa, assigning Joe to everything east of the Mississippi and Jack to everything west, and sent them on their way to kick some ass and whip the restaurants into shape. I tried to confine myself to isolated spot visits to sign off on places before they re-launched with my quickly diluting Coco Pazzo name on the door, and I brought the chefs to New York, one by one, to work with me and Marta in a kind of culinary boot camp, giving them a ten- to fourteen-day crash course in how to cook real Italian food—not that they, or their customers, were really all that interested.

Adding to the stress of the situation was the fact that the $6.1 million we'd borrowed from the Tuscan Square funding to finance the purchase of Sfuzzi still hadn't been replaced by the promised influx of cash. As a result, in order to keep Tuscan Square on track, we'd had to secure three new loans, with the attendant interest, over the first half of 1997.

By May, addressing the most urgent units in order, we had converted five of the restaurants: the two in New York and the ones in Dallas and

Addison, Texas; and the sold-off one in Atlanta. Fewer than half. (Under a separate deal with the landlord who had taken it over, we had also converted a former Sfuzzi in Union Station in Washington, D.C.) The work seemed without end, and the more Sfuzzis I visited, the more uphill the struggle became. No matter where I went, I realized that the various units were each operating independently, a chef doing his own thing with a malfunctioning support structure. I began to feel like the Martin Sheen character in *Apocalypse Now*, winding his way along that Vietnamese river and encountering ever-stranger sub-communities and soldiers gone renegade. It never occurred to me that I might be identifying with the wrong guy from *Apocalypse*; maybe by the time it was all over, I'd be more like the demented Marlon Brando character, Colonel Kurtz, sitting in that dark room, muttering nonsense and waiting for somebody to put him out of his misery.

MEANWHILE AT TUSCAN Square, Marta and I collaborated on the menu. All the memories unlocked by the buying trips put me in mind of home cooking, and we made our theme the rediscovery of the less well-known home-cooked dishes of Tuscany, such as ricotta and chicken meatballs (*polpette*), *pappardelle al pepolino* (a long, broad pasta with summer tomato sauce, pecorino cheese, and oregano), *calamari in zimino* (squid in spinach and tomato stew), *strozzapreti* ("strangled priest" pasta, so named because if you eat them too fast you might choke on them) with butter and sage, and *fritto misto di coniglio e carciofi*, a Tuscan fried rabbit and artichoke classic. Because the lower level was right on the underground concourse of Rockefeller Center, where office workers breezed past on their way from the subway to the elevator in the mornings, we'd be serving breakfast at the espresso bar, and so for the first time in ages, I found myself thinking of one of the quintessential Tuscan breakfast indulgences, *bomboloni*, or Tuscan doughnuts, lightly fried and sugared and filled with either pastry cream (*bomboloni con la crema*) or chocolate (*bomboloni con cioccolato*). As a boy, I had eaten them on the beach in the summertime, and I decided that we'd make *bomboloni* at Tuscan Square as well.

By the late summer, all of those products were rolling in from overseas and we were having a ball dressing the retail department, which had swelled from an initial goal of about one hundred fifty different items to more than *five hundred*, with each collection evocatively displayed: runners and throws were draped over chairs and settees; fragrances and soaps made from herbs and olive oil were artfully arranged on a sixteen-foot eighteenth-century Tuscan credenza; several lines of pewter, dinnerware, and glassware were presented on tables or shelves; the apparel, evoking weekends in Tuscany, with suede pants, cashmere sweaters, and coats, dressed an old-fashioned mannequin; a small library featured travel books and journals. There were even chairs, couches, credenzas, and armoires for sale, all that one could ever want to bring a little Tuscany into his or her life.

There was just one thing missing, and I had to have it: I located a company in California that knew how to install something I'd wanted in one of my restaurants since Il Cantinori: a cypress tree. They created a concrete trunk that began at the foot of the staircase on the concourse level and shot up along the stairs and up to the ceiling of the main-floor dining room, and adorned it with real cypress branches. The cost for this touch was twenty-six thousand dollars, and I thought it was worth every penny.

Tuscan Square had a soft opening on September 16, 1997. My publicist, David Kratz, whose larger firm had replaced my friend Susan, pulled off a minor miracle by getting the city to allow us to shut down part of Fifty-first Street so we could really go to town with our Florentine marketplace theme. We laid sod over the sidewalk and the street, brought in trees and rocks, and erected a platform stage for live music. As much as a city street could, it felt like the Tuscan countryside.

There were more than four hundred fifty guests, and they were positively blown away by the merchandise and the food. The purpose of the party was to generate press, and it succeeded magnificently with articles in the *New York Times*, *New York* magazine, and elsewhere. In the subsequent days, we hosted some friends-and-family dinners to get the kinks out, then we opened on—you guessed it—September 23. Though I still had opening-night jitters before every restaurant launch, Tuscan Square began with the same big crowds as my last few places had, and my team held up to the stresses magnificently.

It was one of the high points of my career up to that point, so much so that it was nearly impossible to imagine what might top it. It didn't occur to me at the time, but that also meant that the only direction for me to go was down.

MY JUBILATION WAS interrupted when I opened the *New York Times* on October 10 and read the "Diner's Journal" column penned by restaurant critic Ruth Reichl. In it, she said that Tuscan Square seemed "not very Tuscan," referred to the "sheer stupidity" of the silk aprons we sold, and concluded by considering whether she'd prefer to eat in a restaurant or a theme park. I was royally offended by the idea that somebody who had spent years celebrating a restaurant machine like Wolfgang Puck on the West Coast before she came to New York could refer to what I did as a theme park. (Furthering my sense of a double standard was the fact that she'd given Churrascaria Plataforma, an all-you-can-eat Brazilian rodizio complete with rolling capirinha carts, two stars earlier that year, and would go on to give Ruby Foo's, a highly stylized, vaguely "Asian" restaurant that combined Chinese and Japanese food in a dining room that was pure theme, two stars as well.)

Other critics would follow suit, offering similar opinions. A number of critics responded to Tuscan Square as though it were the Disney World or Epcot Center of Tuscany. We were so well received by our customers that I was a bit shocked by the cool critical reception. I was getting that old, familiar feeling again, the sense that colleagues and industry observers were trying to keep me down, that my ambitions to expand beyond the cubbyhole of a restaurateur and become a retailer were somehow out of line. I'll never forget the day that a well-known culinary travel writer was strolling the retail area when she caught sight of the soaps and candles and exclaimed, for all to hear, "Oh, my God! Who could have lunch with soaps?" Of course, she wasn't going to be having lunch with soaps, the fragrances of which can confuse the palate; she was going to be escorted to the separate dining area and served lunch there, well out of range of the scents that so offended her. I guess she'd never been to some of the great department stores of

London, such as Fortnum and Mason, where you can have tea or a meal almost within arm's reach of a box of soap or perfume.

This was not an isolated opinion, though. For whatever reason, the consensus among journalists seemed to be that Tuscan Square was a gimmick, but for me a gimmick is something that's shallow or lacks depth. I guess the reviewers wanted me to be a plagiarist. I have nothing against Keith McNally—in fact, I like the guy, and I think that Balthazar is a magnificent masterpiece of a restaurant. But at the end of the day, what is it, really, other than a near-copy of places that already exist? It would have been a breeze for me to find a little square in Portofino, or even take the Piazza della Repubblica itself, and just re-create little pieces of it in a big Manhattan space. It would have been the easiest thing in the world.

I'm sure I probably sound defensive, but I truly believe that while it was fine for me to be the Little Busboy Who Could, and open Il Cantinori, even Le Madri, this level of audacity was too much for some people. How else to explain that while Reichl had no problem giving a lovely review to Mad. 61, *in the middle of an actual department store*, she suddenly found the proximity to retail offensive?

Despite all the resistance, Tuscan Square did pretty well, especially the restaurant, and we did about $6 to $6.5 million of business annually for our first few years, against a projection of about $8 million. I kept thinking that if we were just a few yards to the east, on the corner of Fifth Avenue, we'd have exceeded that by a mile.

Meanwhile, my new Coco Pazzos were not generating the amount per unit needed according to the projection to sustain the debt obligation to the lender. By June 1998, we had to sell Coco Addison, followed a few months later by Coco Dallas. There were nine of the former Sfuzzis left, plus eight of my own restaurants, but other closures would soon follow. The corporation was sick and we were amputating limbs, trying to prevent the infection from spreading.

The funny thing is that I probably could have made those restaurants profitable and earned a lot of money for me and my partners. It would have been very easy actually: take what I knew about consistency and service, add in my ruthlessly efficient approach to food costs, dress the servers in T.G.I. Friday's–type uniforms, and serve

Italian-American food. I could have just called the chain Pino's, and we would all have been rolling in dough.

So why didn't I just do *that*?

Because until just now, as I was recounting all of this, the idea never entered my mind.

BY THE FALL of 2000, I was despondent. Whatever pleasure I had taken in Tuscan Square and my original places in New York City and Chicago was overtaken by the day-to-day grind of administering the half-dozen or so remaining Cocos, which were slowly but surely driving me *pazzo*, not just because of the thankless task of overseeing them, but because they were dragging me down into a quicksand of mediocrity. It felt like every time I picked up a newspaper food section or a magazine somebody was taking a potshot at my restaurant chain, and the worst part about it was that they were right. People had said a lot of things about me over the years, some true and some false, but nobody had ever called me mediocre. I was mortified, and I was driven deeper and deeper into despair. For the first time since I had moved to New York, I found myself wandering the streets again. Even though I had a handful of restaurants and an enormous retail store, I felt like I had nowhere to go.

On one of these walks, I ran into a friend of mine on the Upper East Side. I tried to put on a good face, but he was perceptive and realized that I was in hell. We got to talking and he determined that I was depressed and offered me the phone number of a psychiatrist he knew. I was skeptical, but I made an appointment.

The shrink's office was a shabby two-room affair on the ground floor of a prewar apartment building. The doctor was a shlubby, chubby, middle-aged guy who carried himself as if he had the weight of the world on *his* shoulders. He led me into his private room and I took a seat and started talking, recounting my saga of the past few years. At one point, as the enormity of my situation washed over me, I stopped for a moment and looked off into the distance. He picked up a box of Kleenex and held it out to me.

It was like having a bucket of cold water splashed in my face.

"What is that?" I asked him.

"It's OK to cry here," he said.

A grown man holding out a box of Kleenex to me was an insult, but a useful one, because it made me feel ashamed. I wondered what I was doing there. Was I not the same man who had managed to overcome the handicap of showing up in the United States with little money and even less English? Who had built a restaurant group out of thin air? Was I not the grandson of the great fisherman Ettore, who had known torture? I thought again of *The Godfather* and of Don Corleone shaking the crooner Johnny Fontaine by the shoulders, slapping him and saying, "You can act like *a man!*"

"You know what," I said. "I'll be very honest with you. I feel bad. But sitting here, it makes me feel worse. Send me a bill. I'm leaving."

I stormed out and into the street. It was a perfect fall day, not unlike the one, almost exactly twenty years earlier to the day, when I had wandered around the Financial District marveling at the sights and sounds of New York. I breathed in the fresh air and looked around. I was only a few blocks from where I had started my long march down to Da Silvano all those years ago (and, a few years later, the walk to Il Cantinori) on which I had decided to stay in the United States.

I had come through so much, I told myself; surely I could survive this.

I hailed a taxi and went back down to my office and got to work solving my problems.

AFTER MUCH SOUL searching, I decided to do something counterintuitive: open yet another restaurant. I needed to flex my entrepreneurial muscle with something fresh and creative, to prove that the Chain Formerly Known as Sfuzzi was one giant abomination, and that the real me was still here, still able to create a great new restaurant. This wasn't about recapturing that old, addictive rush; it was about pride. I had to show people that I still had it. Most of all, I had to show myself that all wasn't lost, that the thing that had defined my life in the United States was still there and functioning.

The concept I had in mind was radically different from anything

I'd done before. Having re-created, as much as I thought possible, a little corner of Tuscany in Rockefeller Center, I found myself thinking fondly of my own first days here in the United States, my affection for the immigrant experience of America. As with Sapore, I was reminded of a song, about a young boy asking his mother for *centolire*, one hundred lire, so he can go to America. I was sometimes critical of the Italian-American culture, especially when I first got to the United States. But after so long here, I realized that there was much about it I could identify with, especially the core truth of what America meant to me. I decided that my new place would be called Centolire, and would celebrate Italian-American culture.

I wanted to get back to the Upper East Side, and when the space that housed Celadon, a handsome but failing neighborhood restaurant on Madison Avenue, became available, I pounced. I loved the space, especially the glass elevator available to shuttle guests from the small first floor to the spacious, rectangular second floor. The deal was so sweet that I was able to move on my own, without my corporation attached to my hip, and make this truly my own venture. I signed the lease just before the New Year. As we left 2000 behind, I had the feeling that 2001 might be the year that I turned it all around.

I OPENED CENTOLIRE in March 2001, with illustrations on the menus of cruise ships bound for America, and food divided into New World dishes such as chicken *scarpariello* (chicken breast braised in an aromatic liquid of white wine and broth) and spaghetti and meatballs and Old World dishes such as *spaghetti alla rustica* and *pollo martini* (parmesan-crusted chicken breast with lemon sauce). The approach to naming the dishes was consistent with our Old Word versus New World inspiration: using "chicken" for the *scarpariello* because that's how Italian-Americans refer to it (many Italian-American creations pair Italian and English words), and *pollo* for the martini because that's what it's called in the motherland.

For the first time in what felt like a lifetime, I was excited about a new restaurant opening. I had Marta in the kitchen and two of my most reliable front-of-the-house guys on the floor: Ariel and Gianfranco.

We were all a bit older than we used to be, but it was just like old times, especially when a lot of my longtime customers from the original Coco Pazzo found their way over, welcoming me back, welcoming me home.

He wouldn't get around to reviewing us for a while, but when he finally did, the *New York Times* critic William Grimes made my day, recounting my roller-coaster ride in America:

> When Pino Luongo burst on the New York scene nearly 20 years ago with Il Cantinori, he looked like a culinary Pavarotti in the making. His restaurants, by combining high quality with flashy presentation, put sizzle back in the steak Florentine. Italian food seemed exciting again. Il Cantinori begat Le Madri, which begat assorted Coco Pazzos, and before long, Mr. Luongo was running neck and neck with Mario Perillo for the title of Mr. Italy.
>
> Success led to mediocrity. Lately, Mr. Luongo has seemed more interested in cashing in than doing the hard work of preparing good food. This dubious track only adds to the appeal of Centolire, a surprise return to form by Mr. Luongo. The restaurant, in the two-level space that once belonged to Celadon, is a large, good-looking trattoria with a warm, beating heart. The food, doled out in substantial portions, is honest, well executed and deeply satisfying. Mr. Luongo is once again hitting his high C's.

It was an honest summation of my life in the restaurant trade to date, except for one thing: I hadn't "cashed in"; I was out of cash, or at least my company was. The same month I opened Centolire, we closed Coco Opera. (The landlord had decided to exercise his demolition clause, and we had to vacate.) Soon thereafter, after trying to salvage it as a Coco Pazzo Cafe, we shuttered Il Toscanaccio. Tuscan Square was still underperforming and so were the various restaurants around the country. I was in a state of perpetual regret: how could I have made such a poor decision by taking all of this on? Adding irony to the state of affairs was the fact that all of my original restaurants, Le

Madri, the original Coco Pazzo, and the Coco Pazzos in Chicago, were still doing great. But it was never enough. It wasn't that we couldn't pay our vendors, it was that we were in a kind of quicksand: no matter how well we did, we couldn't make our payments to the lender. The debt seemed more and more insurmountable every day, and we wanted to negotiate new and more reasonable terms.

I consulted with some attorneys and accountants and concluded that the only way out was to have Toscorp file for bankruptcy, which would allow us to restructure the corporation and separate out my original restaurants. I was resistant at first. Back in Italy, filing for bankruptcy was something shameful that called your personal honor into question. It meant that you'd be stiffing people for their bills and throwing in the towel on your business. One of Toscorp's attorneys showed me a little tough love when he pulled me aside and said, "Kid, you ain't in Italy anymore. This is America. It's just a business solution."

And so, on August 23, 2001, we held a board meeting and decided to file for Chapter 11, to refinance the corporate funding, and to reconstruct the ownership, all with the goal of protecting its most vital aspects in New York City and Chicago, the barely beating heart of this huge and dying beast.

It wasn't the end of my problems. We still had units in Philadelphia, Las Vegas, Austin, and Costa Mesa. We also still had Coco Marina in downtown New York, in the World Financial Center, which was perhaps the only one of the former Sfuzzis turning a respectable profit.

Of course, I couldn't know it at the time, but that one would be gone in less than two weeks, as well.

FOURTEEN

A Star Is Bored: Interview Questions for Young American Chefs

TRYING TO STAFF fourteen dysfunctional units of the Chain Formerly Known as Sfuzzi, not to mention my own original restaurants, put me in touch with a broad range of young chefs in the late 1990s. This was a transformational time in the American cooking trade because the first generation who had grown up watching celebrity chefs on television and in ad campaigns were coming into their own.

As a result, a lot of young men and women had entered a very old and noble profession for all the wrong reasons. Where their predecessors had fallen in love with food at a young age and tirelessly toiled in other people's kitchens for years, often for no money, traveled all over the world just to spend time in the birthplace of certain cuisines and techniques, and patiently waited until they had amassed a wealth of knowledge before even imagining that they might call themselves a chef, the new crop thought they had the chops to be a chef right out of cooking school. Many of the young cooks I met had no interest in *perfecting* their craft: they were simply looking to learn enough to get into a kitchen and then, as soon as possible, get out of the kitchen and in front of a television camera.

It's like I was saying about pasta before: you can't be told how to make a perfect *spaghetti alle vongole* (spaghetti with clams). You need to learn how to recognize the best fresh clams, and how to clean them. You need to know how to cook pasta right. You even need to know the best way to chop the parsley. Then you need the palate and technique to put it all together and make it taste good and then the teaching and management abilities to be able to teach others to do the same and ensure they get it right time after time.

It takes patience and humility, not just ego, to become a great chef. And yet I met a steady parade of kids who thought they were hot stuff, who really believed that they were going to be the next Food Network star, or reality-show winner, or supermarket product cover boy or girl. There was the young Italian-American kid who showed up in an Armani T-shirt and designer jeans, his muscles betraying the fact that he clearly spent more time at the gym than he did thinking about food; or the mad scientist with cotton-candy hair and polka-dot tie who fashioned himself a molecular gastronomist, proud of all the foams and jellies he could create, with no appreciation of the fact that the two most important functions of food are, *and always will be*, to taste good and to satisfy.

Over the course of my career I've gotten pretty good at interviewing chefs. One of my many tricks was to meet them anywhere but a restaurant, to take them out of their natural habitat and see them a little more nakedly. My first question was always, "How did you learn to cook?" I was looking for some sign of passion, of a lifetime of cooking at their mother's side, or their grandmother's, or of how they'd fallen in love with cooking unexpectedly in their first job. I was almost shocked at how many chefs had made the decision at the end of high school and seemed to have little love of food or of cooking.

To save myself time and disappointment, I developed a number of questions designed to cut to the quick, and I'm pleased to share this helpful quiz for interviewing young American chefs:

1. Who were your last three employers?
   a. A Michelin three-star restaurant in France, an unheralded but locally famous tavern in Greece, and David Bouley.
   b. Alice Waters, Jeremiah Tower, and me (in my own forty-seat restaurant).
   c. They were all before cooking school; do you still wanna hear 'em?

2. *Top Chef* is . . .
   a. what I push myself to be every day.
   b. an OK reality show.
   c reviewing my audition tape . . . *again.*

3. What's your favorite technique?
   a. Grilling in the summer; braising in the winter.
   b. The right one for the dish at hand.
   c. I can't decide between *sous vide* and freezing with nitrogen.

4. What's the mood like in your kitchen?
   a. It's not my kitchen; it's the owner's kitchen.
   b. Calm, cool, and collected, just like me.
   c. Whatever my mood *du jour* is; the kitchen is just a big, stainless steel reflection of whatever I'm feeling. Deal with it.

5. Do you go to the gym?
   a. I get enough of a workout on the line every night.
   b. I don't have time, working six or seven days a week.
   c. Of course, gotta stay trim; the camera adds ten pounds.

6. What's your ideal Saturday night?
   a. Every table turns three times and we put out at least four hundred dishes.
   b. They're all different, but it's my favorite night of the week, the one that lets me know that I have what it takes.
   c. My sous chef covers it; he does all the real work anyway.

7. What's your philosophy of management?
   a. It's all about hiring the right people.
   b. I try to be supportive, but firm.
   c. They take 10 percent right?

8. What about purchasing?
   a. I phone my vendors personally about an hour before we close the kitchen each night.

b. Food cost is my priority.

c. You talking to me?

9. If most of the dishes on your menu weren't selling, what would you do?

a. Change the dishes themselves.

b. Lose some of the more esoteric stuff, keep the popular items, try some new things.

c. Write a letter to be included in the menu, explaining my philosophy to our customers in order to educate them.

10. Who's your role model?

a. Not Rocco DiSpirito.

b. Not Rocco DiSpirito.

c. Rocco DiSpirito.

Grading the quiz:

No C answers: When can you start?

1 to 3 C answers: You seem like a nice enough young man/ woman. Try back after you've worked in real restaurants for a few years.

4 to 7 C answers: We'll call you (not really), don't call us.

7 to 10 C answers: How much would you take to stay out of my industry?

FIFTEEN

The New Normalcy

ABOUT TEN DAYS after that fateful board meeting, I flew to Spokane, Washington, with Jessie, Marco, and Jacobella for a family trip, leaving our youngest son, Lorenzo, back home with our nanny. It was good to be away in the Pacific Northwest, where we got lucky and caught a break from the notorious perpetual gray drizzle of the region and instead were awash in sunshine and cool breezes. New York City, and all of my problems back there, seemed like a distant memory. Unfortunately, the days blew past quickly, and when the end of the trip came, we all packed our bags and went to bed early so we could wake up at the crack of dawn, return our rental car, and board the plane back to my own circle of New York restaurateurs' hell.

It was September 10.

Before I even opened my eyes the next morning, I could feel that I was coming down with something: there was a tickle at the back of my throat and I was more tired than I usually am when I wake up. I hoisted myself out of bed and turned on the television set. The first thing I saw was the image of the north tower of the World Trade Center, with a crater in its side and dark gray smoke billowing out into the blue sky over New York City. The newscasters were explaining that an airplane had crashed into the tower, discussing it as though it were an accident. But I remembered well that the World Trade Center had been attacked by car bomb in 1993, and I had always been concerned that the buildings might be attacked again. And, of course, my worst fears were confirmed moments later when a second plane sliced through the south tower, sending up a huge fireball and more clouds of smoke.

As horrific as the scene was, I have to be honest: my first thoughts weren't of the people in those buildings; they were of the people who worked for me at Coco Marina, in the World Financial Center just to the west. I unplugged my cell phone from its charger on the nightstand and speed-dialed the restaurant but was met by a persistent and unusual busy signal, so I called Pearl, the comptroller of my company, in the offices above Le Madri, about two miles uptown. She told me that she was getting nothing but busy signals as well. I could hear panic in her voice, and I told her to stay cool and just take it one step at a time, and that I'd be in touch.

I hung up and just sat there on the edge of my bed, watching the towers bleed smoke on the television screen. Jessie came over and sat down beside me and we didn't say a word. We didn't have to. We were both thinking the same thing, both watching along with the rest of the country between Spokane and New York. I must have been in a state of shock, because I was definitely not thinking straight and now that I had a moment to consider what was actually transpiring, the enormity of it began to sink in. I told the kids to get showered and dressed so we could leave for the airport, but then it occurred to me to call the airline and of course all the flights had been grounded.

I forced myself to focus, to think, but it only made things worse. I began to envision the repercussions of what was playing out, a historic event on par with Pearl Harbor. It also occurred to me that I probably knew people who had perished, customers and the parents of my kids' schoolmates who worked in finance, and surely former employees who worked at Windows on the World restaurant on the top floor. I also flashed forward in my mind, wondering about the ripple effect in world politics, picturing how security would probably change. And then, of course, the profound business impact. I guess it's selfish, but it occurred to me that I had just filed for Chapter 11, with an eye toward reorganizing my business around the life-support system of my restaurants in Chicago and New York. I felt gut-punched.

The only thing I knew for sure was that I had to get back. I loaded up the car, ushered the kids into the back, and we drove to the rental-car office at the airport to tell them that I was going to be returning the car in New York. I definitely wasn't thinking straight because normally I'd have just done it, just driven back east and sorted it out when I got there. Sure enough, my hesitation cost me: the agent at the desk said that we had to bring the car back to the Spokane location. I insisted, explaining that my business was in Manhattan, and she rented me another car and we got on the road.

It was already afternoon by the time we hit Interstate 90, which would be our means of passage to the east. The roads were sparsely populated and the contrast between what I'd seen on television and the tree-lined asphalt around us was stark. Compounding the sense of disorientation was the fact that I was clearly coming down with something worse than a cold; my dry cough was turning wet and my head felt like a fishbowl with liquid sloshing around its confines. To make matters worse, my kids were bickering in the backseat and I was getting aggravated, not just by them, but by the fact that for long stretches of time, I couldn't find a news station on the radio because we were in the middle of nowhere. When I could find a station, we got intermittent reports about the extent of the damage and the early piecing together of what had happened and the profiles of the terrorists who had carried out the plot.

We went in and out of cell phone range as well, but whenever we had service, I got Pearl on the line and had her conference in the managers of the various restaurants. I kept Centolire and the original Coco Pazzo open but closed all the others. I would later hear that Mayor Giuliani was instructing people to go out to dinner and forge on with their normal lives, but I had to do what I could to protect my already-fragile interests. I knew that the places in Midtown and downtown would be empty that night.

Apart from those calls, we drove in a silence that was punctuated by the kids' occasional flare-ups. With nothing in sight but the frontier, all the thoughts I'd been keeping at bay during our holiday came seeping into my head and I was reminded of my original voyage to the United States. In many ways, I felt just as lost now as I had then, just as adrift and unsure of what lay before me. At the same time, the attacks activated a sense of American patriotism in me, made me feel as though I myself had been violated, and that all the souls who had perished when those towers fell to the ground were members of my own extended family.

We stopped for the night in Bozeman, Montana. The only thing that could have made this town seem smaller was if tumbleweed had come rolling at us down the desolate main street. We checked into one of the budget hotels interspersed along the road, and I was struck that the entire place was run by one person who did multiple duty as check-in clerk, night manager, and "concierge," describing our local dining options, which in this case consisted of the vending machines on each hallway and the restaurant across the street. We chose option B and walked across the dusty, deserted road to have dinner in the local bar and grill. We were the only people there to eat, but there were a bunch of dudes in blue jeans and flannel shirts clustered at the bar drinking beer and watching some local baseball game on two wall-mounted televisions. I excused myself from my family and asked them to switch the channel and the bartender stared at me coldly and said, "Why?"

I told him that I wanted to see some news about the attacks. The man groused and changed the station to CNN. I stood there watching that endless looping of the planes crashing into the towers and listening to the updates, which were mostly speculative at that point. After a few minutes, they went back to the ball game and I returned to the table for our dinner: cheeseburgers for me and Jessie; grilled-cheese sandwiches for the kids.

September 12 was Jessie's birthday. We continued our beeline across the United States. Again, I worked the phone whenever I could, checking in on the restaurants and trying to reach a few of the workers from Coco Marina who were unaccounted for, especially a young steward who had worked for me for a long time. I finally caught up with him on his cell phone.

"Mr. Pino," he said to me. "I run and I run and I get on the train and I go to Philadelphia!" He wasn't kidding: he had fled to Penn Station and gone straight to the City of Brotherly Love. He would never come back to New York.

Talking on the phone aggravated my increasingly sore throat and left me hoarse and depleted, but I kept it up for as long as I could, gathering as much information as possible and making decisions about which restaurants to open and which to leave closed. I was also dying for details about the physical condition of Coco Marina, but they were impossible to come by as the entire neighborhood of the World Financial Center was cordoned off to everybody except emergency personnel.

We made a marathon push that day, driving more than twelve hours. I was no fun to be with but Jessie understood what I was going through and, in her distinctly Southern way, let me have the space and time I needed to process my thoughts. Even when I was short with her or the kids, she was very sweet and calm, keeping the family together and never pressing me to adjust my attitude.

By late that night, we made it to a small town—I can't for the life of me remember the name—near Sioux City, Iowa, checked into a Comfort Inn, and walked around the corner to a local restaurant. It was just like the day before—a drive through barren highways that ended up in a small town, a largely unmanned hotel, and a perfunctory meal in a restaurant permanently perfumed with nicotine.

We ordered Caesar salads, lousy burgers, and a wine I'd never heard of. I asked the waitress what they had for dessert, and Jessie, reading my mind and imagining a slice of day-old chocolate layer cake with a candle sticking out of it, turned to me and said, "Don't even think about it."

When we woke up the next day, I was determined that we were going to make it to Chicago. My cough had become a dreadful, hacking thing, and I was trying to reach my doctor, but he hadn't resumed normal business hours since the attacks and was nowhere to be found. I did reach Jack Weiss, however, and I asked him to arrange a hotel room for us, and when we got to Chicago on Thursday night, we checked in and went straight to Coco Pazzo. My business was in a desperate state, my adopted home was facing a historic crisis, and there was nothing I could do. All I could hope for was that a familiar meal in familiar surroundings would make my family feel more secure than I did.

When we got to the restaurant it was almost completely empty. The staff were there in their starched black and white uniforms, and the antipasti table was all set up, but there were just a few diners scattered about, some of them no doubt stranded away from home themselves. We sat at a round table in the corner of the massive dining room and had a full view of the sad spectacle. Coco Pazzo Chicago was framed with blue curtains that usually imbued the scene with extra energy, but it felt as though the life had been sucked out of the space and it reminded me, more than anything, of an empty stage, a theater glimpsed on a dark night. It was the most depressing evening I'd ever spent in one of my own places. I'd made it back to civilization, only to learn that civilization had changed.

In the car on Friday, I finally got through to my doctor. He offered to phone a prescription into a pharmacy so I pulled off the highway in a rundown postindustrial Indiana town with angry-looking teens prowling streets that looked more like Beirut than America.

"Do you have a gun?" Jessie asked, and we laughed nervously.

I found a drugstore, parked outside, and told Jessie to lock the doors.

It was like the drugstore that time forgot, with picked-over shelves and a little makeshift pharmacy in the back set off by walls of unfinished plywood and a little hinged door through which I guess the pharmacist could come and go. A fiftyish black man with a colonial British accent (how he ended up in this town was anyone's guess) appeared in the window.

"What do you want?" he asked, and for a moment I actually wondered if he lived in that little room and perhaps I was trespassing. After three days driving cross country, anything seemed possible.

"Are you the pharmacist?" I asked

"Yes."

"My doctor wants to phone in a prescription," I said and began to hand him my cell phone.

He pushed my arm away and said, "You have to use our phone here."

Through the window he passed me an oversized plastic telephone like something out of *Pee-wee's Playhouse*. It was the perfect, surreal flourish to the visit. I had my doctor call him and, miraculously, I procured my meds, got on the road again, and after many more hours of driving, we hit the outskirts of New York City. Passing it from the northwest, we could all smell the smoke in the air. I looked across New Jersey at the skyline. The first thing my eyes always went to were the twin towers, one of the beacons of my life here since the 1980s, the visual cues that told me if I was walking north or south. But they were gone, replaced by smoldering remains and the glow of searchlights; and sure enough I felt lost, and unsure of which way was up.

WITH THE EXCEPTION of Coco Marina, which would remain closed forever, we reopened all of our restaurants by week's end, but New Yorkers were not in a fine-dining mood. Many people who lived in and around the city were too busy burying the dead and grieving all that we'd lost to think of anything else. I myself found it hard to function and make even the most basic business decisions amid all the funerals we were attending for departed friends in the city and Westchester.

But life went on, and over the following few weeks, I had to come to terms with the fact that gross revenue across the company's restaurants was down by 50 percent. With a lending company to satisfy every month, and units outside the state that were underperforming as well, I began thinking about letting people go, but then I had an epiphany: what if everybody on salary were to take a 20 percent pay cut, starting with me because, after all, I was an employee as well. I figured things had to turn around sooner or later. This was New York, after all; people would have to start coming again at some point, wouldn't they? And when they did, we'd all still be together, with a stronger bond formed by our shared sacrifice.

When I came up with this plan, I began to embrace a phrase that had previously been something of a private joke to me: *self-help*, which I'd always associated with the American pop-psychology industry. There's no Italian phrase for *self-help* because in Italy it's a given that you take care of yourself. But I came to think of what had to be done to save my restaurants as self-help, pursuing avenues I wouldn't normally take in order to simply be alive the next morning. *Self-help* meant doing whatever it took, and doing it on my own, to survive. I had to help my-self, because no one else could. It would become a mantra.

I called all my managers, chefs, and executives to a morning meeting downstairs at Tuscan Square and made my pitch, explaining how the hourly employees were already suffering because they were work-ing fewer shifts every week, losing both their baseline income and tips, and that now it was time for *us* to take a hit. We all needed the money, and there were no other jobs to run to. We were on a sinking ship, and this was the only maneuver that might keep it afloat.

"Don't give me your answer right now," I said. "But I will need to know by tomorrow."

By the next day, everybody had agreed, some more grudgingly than others. One manager had the temerity to suggest that we dismiss all the waiters and let the GMs wait the tables, keeping their current ex-ecutive salaries and making tips, to boot. My unspoken response was that maybe I didn't need any managers. The most amusing part of this and similar dialogues was that the ones who pushed back were the same ones who, whenever I asked them to roll up their sleeves and put in some extra time, would look at the clock and say, "My day is done. I gotta go."

When all was said and done, we took my suggested pay cut, and it was the right thing to do, and much as I love America, I must say that it was the Italian thing to do; the textbook American corporate tactic would have been to trim off the expendable employees like fat from a side of beef. That would have been the clean way to handle the crisis, the ruthlessly efficient decision that would have best preserved the health of Toscorp. In the long run, my creative solution turned out to be a poor choice, because the business would continue to lose money, plunging deeper and deeper into the red.

But I'm still glad I did it.

LESS THAN A month later, Centolire was reviewed by the two major publications of the day: both the *New York Times* and *New York* maga-zine described my latest restaurant as a return to form.

It hardly mattered. Business was in the toilet for me, same as it was for everybody else in town. At eight P.M., you could look out the window of Centolire and Madison Avenue was as desolate as it usually was at three in the morning.

That October, I attended a meeting organized by NYC and Company, an organization created by the mayor's office to promote tourism and business in Manhattan, in a Midtown conference room. All of the usual New York City restaurant characters were there: Danny Meyer, Drew Nieporent, Steve Hanson, Tim Zagat, Tony May, Giuseppe Cipriani, Keith McNally, about thirty in all. The purpose of the meeting was to see what we could do to help each other as the holiday season approached. It was noble in its intent, but for me the gathering had the opposite of the desired effect: it became clear that there was nothing to be done but to ride out the storm. It was a powerful reminder that for all of our combined influence in the restaurant world, for all of our friends in high places, at the end of the day we were what we had always been, since our days as busboys and waiters: people who served food. And if nobody wanted that food, there wasn't a damn thing anybody could do about it. There it was again: *self-help*. If I wanted to survive, I'd have to find a way on my own.

As if all of this weren't enough to bear, later that month, Carlos, the beloved maître d' of Coco Pazzo, died. At the funeral I sat next to his young son, just ten or eleven years old at the time, and watched helplessly as he stared at the urn containing Carlos's ashes and at the photographs of the man surrounding it. Shortly thereafter, his widow decided to take the kids and move back to South America to be with her family, a sad ending to what had been a happy immigrant success story.

As winter approached, the days grew darker earlier, and I was plunged into a deep, deep depression, far worse than any I'd ever experienced. I'd say that I went crazy, but to me, becoming depressed seemed like the most sane reaction possible.

One Saturday in November, I was sitting on the steps of my front porch. The advent of autumn is always a special time for me, but I was preoccupied with the swirling anxieties in my head, not the leaves blowing around our yard.

My son Marco, thirteen years old at the time, came up to me.

"Papá. Can we go paintballing this weekend?" he asked.

"You know what, Marco," I said. "Leave me alone."

He was beyond confused, his eyes utterly blank. When he snapped out of it, he asked: "Are you OK?"

I felt so terrible that I began to cry. It was as if he were the adult and I was the child. I was ashamed, and rightfully so. It's never all right for a father to speak to his son that way, and to break down and cry before him was almost worse. I pulled him close and gave him a hug, told him I was sorry.

Despite that awful display, it was actually my family that kept me going: in the mornings when they were all getting ready for school, playing in the kitchen and running up and down the stairs of our house, I'd look at them and think, "I have to get through this. For them."

After that blowup with Marco, I resolved to put on the best possible face for my family, but I felt that there was nobody I could turn to, nobody who would understand or could help. I began looking for new ways to compartmentalize what was happening. Sleep became precious to me, the only time that I could put everything out of my mind. I don't know why it wasn't interrupted by nightmares—maybe because nothing I could dream up could be worse than the reality of my life—but it wasn't. I also took refuge in the culture of the Italy of my youth: I'd sit in my study, playing the music of my adolescence on the sound system and reading the plays I had acted in.

I was so lost, so eager for answers, for signposts, that when a friend put me onto a woman who did astrological charts out in California, I didn't hesitate. I phoned her up and gave her all the essential information, such as my date of birth.

She crunched the numbers and called me a few days later: "You're going through hell," she said.

"Yeah?" I said. "Tell me something I don't know."

"You didn't do anything wrong," she told me soothingly. "You didn't make any bad decisions. This scenario occurs once in a lifetime and you've been caught up in it for three years and will continue to be caught up in it for another year or two."

I swear on my children that I accepted everything this woman told me. Although she was wrong about my not having made any bad decisions—had I simply said no to the Sfuzzi proposition one last time, I wouldn't have been in this predicament—I latched on to her advice. There was no point in nitpicking and analyzing what had gone before. No sense in agonizing over the lost money and time and the damage to the Coco Pazzo brand. I tried to put it all in perspective: just as I had come to believe it was my destiny to become a restaurateur, this was my time for bad luck. It was the flip side of my swift ascent to the top of the restaurant ladder. It was, belatedly, time to pay my dues.

The next installment came due in December. We had long planned a life-altering holiday season for Tuscan Square, preordering several new lines of exquisite and very expensive merchandise months earlier. The store was stocked with a beautiful collection of glassware, china, and housewares, all cast in the elegant glow of a new lighting scheme. It was the very picture of my original vision for the store. I would stop by at night, putting things in the perfect place, picking up a beautiful plate or blanket just to feel the reassuring weight of good craftsmanship in my hand. But most times, there was nobody in the store but me. The country was in shock, and no one wanted luxury, no matter how simple and honest. The big holiday push ended up costing us more money than we took in and putting us even deeper into the red.

OF ALL THE businesses under the Toscorp umbrella, the one that would never get back on its feet was Tuscan Square. After doing almost $1 million in retail sales the winter of 2000, the winter of 2001 showed just $350,000. By June 2002 we had no choice but to shut down the retail program, and we held a huge liquidation sale. It was cold comfort that so many of the people who turned up for the first time seemed to truly love the merchandise, because it was too late to make new fans. We turned the entire space into one huge restaurant and cafe.

Other steps were taken to conserve money and reduce losses: I closed my laundry facility, which had been a tremendous source of pride for so long, and started using a rental company. We closed the

Coco Pazzos in Austin and Philly that year, and sold the lease in Vegas back to the landlord.

And that fall, as the New York restaurants started piling up debts and I began sensing anxiety among our primary lender, I shopped around for investors who would buy the note at a steep discount and step in as a new lender, buying us more time to get back on our feet.

The final streamlining, or at least what I thought would be the final streamlining, took place two years later, in 2004, when I invited Jack Weiss to create a new investment group to take over the ownership of the Chicago restaurants and license the Coco Pazzo name from me. I was glad to see him benefit from his years of hard work, though it was, I must admit, a very painful decision. But I was in perpetual triage mode; if any given decision simplified my life and provided the money for another day's survival, then I did it and moved on.

WITH JUST FOUR restaurants left in New York City—Le Madri, the original Coco Pazzo on East Seventy-fourth Street, Tuscan Square, and Centolire—I was finally able to focus on running them the right way, on rebuilding my name and reputation, and also trying to redis-cover the joy I once had felt at being a restaurateur. For the most part, this went fairly smoothly, but in 2004, I began to receive calls from Gianfranco at Centolire, all of them beginning the same way.

"Pino," he'd say, with a mixture of bemusement and concern, "you have to come see the specials tonight."

Marta had left Centolire a year earlier, and with my attention fo-cused on the business of my restaurants, the new chef had begun tak-ing extreme liberties. I'd ask Gianfranco to tell me what the problem was and words and phrases like "verbena" and "sushi" and "fish in a tomato coulis" and other culinary terms that have nothing to do with Italian or Italian-American food would come pouring out of his mouth.

I saw an opportunity to get back in touch with my long-lost joy and installed myself as the chef of Centolire. I began creating a new menu and working with the guys in the kitchen. The moment I first put on a chef coat and an apron, I knew I was doing the right thing. It was energizing to get back in a kitchen; I'd been surrounded by kitchens for the past few years, but I'd been so preoccupied with other concerns that I had never had time to spend in them. Now, as I filled myself up with new experiences, I found myself able to let go of the past, to stop beating myself up for all the pain and loss I'd caused, for all the drama that had come about by taking my eye off what was important to me: food and cooking, the two things that had always given me the most pleasure in life. It put me back in touch with the Italian at my core, that guy who—as we liked to say back home—lived to eat (rather than who ate to live), who would be eating lunch and already thinking about what to make for dinner.

A FEW MONTHS later, on April 1, 2005, one of my sisters called to let me know that my father had died of complications resulting from a stroke. Jessie and I made plans to fly to Italy the next day, but our flight was canceled due to a brutal storm in the New York area. We would have been reassigned to another flight the next day, but that happened to be the day that Pope John Paul II passed away and the flights all filled up and we couldn't get to Italy until April 3. On the flight, I thought back to my trip to America back in 1980, of how angry and afraid I'd been. It all came rushing back, no doubt because I associated those feelings with my father. I genuinely wanted to be there for the funeral, but missing it was the perfect bookend to our ill-fated relationship: he wasn't there to welcome me into the world and I wasn't there to see him out of it.

When we finally arrived at my parents' home, it was a day and a half after the funeral. All of the visitors had gone, leaving just a few family members: my sisters Anna and Rita were there, and my brother Ricardo. My mother was sitting in an armchair in the corner, holding my father's light blue cardigan in her arms. I apologized to her for being so late and she just shrugged. I didn't know if she was angry or not; I'm not sure she did herself.

I sat down and my siblings recounted the funeral to me, describing how many long-lost friends and military buddies had shown up and what nice things everyone had to say about my father. I listened, but couldn't take my eyes off Má, caressing that cardigan, holding it close to her face and rubbing at its fabric, and then it hit me: his smell was still on it. She was embracing him in the only way she could anymore, holding on to his physical presence for as long as possible.

It was one of the few times I can recall when she didn't cook for the family. My sisters made a simple lunch and we all sat down to eat. My mother sat at the table with us, but still didn't speak, just picked at her food and stared off into the distance.

She was so despondent that I felt obligated to say something: "Má," I whispered to her. "Papá is gone, but you still have so much family around you. Your children, your grandchildren. We all care about you so much."

"Pino," she said, speaking to me as though I were a child. "Right now, I don't care about any of that. I am missing my companion. I am missing my lover."

I felt like an idiot. It should have been obvious to me. Before she was a mother, she was a woman. I had never thought of my father as an object of anybody's affection, but she had adored him from the moment they met, from long before they had children. And now, she was alone. I was trying to make things better, but I had only succeeded in making them worse.

Curiously, since my father died, I call my mother less frequently than I used to. Even though I never admitted it to myself, I think a part of me was always secretly hoping that one day, while calling to check in on them, Papá and I would have a true reconciliation. No matter what transpires between them, every boy wants a good relationship with his father, even after the boy has become a man, even after the father is gone.

SIXTEEN

Closing Time

I N RESTAURANTS, AS in life, death is inevitable; in its own way, every establishment is as perishable as the ingredients that go into its food. As a result, every once in a while, a restaurateur's world is dismantled—the employees dismissed, the paperwork packed up into boxes, the windows smeared with soap.

The locations become other restaurants, or they turn into something completely different: spaces where I once welcomed diners have been converted into everything from pharmacies to office buildings, with no evidence of what we accomplished there, no lasting echo of the nightly party we hosted.

It's a natural part of the process. Places that people once clamored to get into become taken for granted. Ideas that were once new grow tired. Diners have never been faithful to one destination, but ultimately they are worse than polygamous: they are heartless. Those you entertained on a nightly or seminightly basis will desert you and watch as you die a very public death, and they won't give it a second thought.

There are restaurateurs who take this personally, but not me. I always understood my place with my customers. It's not their job to keep me in business; it's my job to make them want to come back. If I failed at that, then it was time to shut down and move on to the next project.

This was easy for me to say, because for the longest time, the only closings I was involved with either had an upside to them, or were simply unavoidable: dropping all those faux Cocos was like breaking out of prison, and Mad. 61 was simply out of my control. It occurs to me that there were closings I haven't even mentioned, like when Ian Schrager bought out my leases in New York and Los Angeles in order to sell his hotel company, or when I myself sold Sapore di Mare in 2000. I was so busy in those days, always moving forward to the next new thing, that I didn't linger on these losses. Those restaurants had outlived their relevance, or their usefulness, and it was time to say good-bye. As simple as that.

But I've had some more painful closings to contend with over the past few years. In 2005, my landlord at Le Madri decided that he wanted to demolish the building in order to erect condominiums on the site. He bought me out, which was a good business deal, but he also dropped the curtain on the longest-running restaurant I had left in my portfolio, one of the few remaining connections to my first years in New York and my first successes here. That building, where Fred Pressman and I had that fateful midday meeting in 1988, where I spent those hours with "the mothers" and later passed my time running Toscorp upstairs, is no longer a part of our physical world. It is, literally, just a memory now.

In 2008, unable to reach a renewal or extension arrangement with my landlord, I was forced to shutter Tuscan Square. All long-term leases, at least in New York City, allow for options and extensions subject to so-called fair market value. Landlords tend to overreach and if you're not careful, you end up signing on to more than you can cover and still make money. At the time of this writing, I've heard of restaurateurs in Manhattan agreeing to pay one hundred dollars per square foot, which is insane.

Though it had been years since we sold merchandise at Tuscan Square, the restaurant was still close to my heart, like a beloved relative who's in a coma but on whom you can't bear to pull the plug. Often in moments like those, people say it's a blessing when the patient finally goes, but I didn't feel that way in this case. If it had made any kind of financial sense, I probably would have held onto Tuscan Square for at least a few more years.

Like most death-related ceremonies, the closing of restaurants has a public and a private side. The public side is the press release, the "thank you for your patronage" sign in the window. The private side is messy. Closing a restaurant entails the management of the remains and the transference of property and possessions: the first order of business is, or should be, the employees. If you're lucky enough to have other restaurants, you make an effort to retain whomever you can; the others are left to fend for themselves. The next decision is how much you can take with you; if you have any use, personal or professional, for the liquor, cooking equipment, and sundry other items, then you make arrangements to have them delivered to the appropriate locations.

That leaves the items you *can't* use, usually the furniture and large kitchen equipment. If you can't take these things with you and use them elsewhere, there are three remaining primary options: just leave on the last day of the month and let the landlord deal with the mess; sell all or some of them to the restaurateur taking your place; or hold an auction.

When I closed Tuscan Square, with only Coco Pazzo and Centolire left, for the first time in my career I held an auction to get rid of the surplus merchandise. In addition to the usual things one amasses in ten years of doing business, I had held onto some of the unsold Tuscan Square merchandise for use in the restaurant that had survived the retail store: chargers and pewter tabletop items and oil paintings of Tuscan landscapes. I didn't know any auctioneers, so I opened up the *New York Times* and hired one. He scheduled and advertised the auction, which was set for a day in January 2008. On the day before the auction, he showed up, a short man who, though well dressed, had the air of a huckster about him. He and his team organized all my equipment and merchandise, everything from the pots and pans to the furniture and electronic equipment, into lots arranged by category, affixing numbered tags—I thought of them like toe tags on a corpse—to everything.

On the day of the auction I was introduced to an aspect of doing business in the restaurant industry that in a quarter of a century I had never encountered before: the first people to show up were movers and truck drivers, eight guys in jeans and T-shirts who sat around, clearly very practiced at the art of waiting. It struck me that by the end of the day, they were probably going to make the most money of anybody because once something was purchased, it had to be carted away almost immediately.

As the time of the auction approached, the bidders began to arrive: restaurateurs who were there out of curiosity, people who were planning to open restaurants and were looking for equipment and decoration, and opportunists looking to buy cheap and resell.

It was my first look at a strange subculture of my industry. These people reminded me of the guys who magically appear on street corners during rainstorms selling umbrellas. I had no idea where they came from or where their places of business were. I didn't really want to know. I thought they were vultures.

The auction began uneventfully as the auctioneer led the crowd from lot to lot. He carried a little collapsible stepladder and set it up at each lot so that he could be seen by one and all. And though there were only a few bidders, he actually went through the stereotypical auctioneer routine: "How much do I hear for this roasting pan? Can I get one dollar. I got one dollar. Can I get three? I got three dollars. Can I get five? Five? I have three. I have three. Going once. Going twice. SOLD!" And that's how it went as they moved around the store bidding on stainless-steel sauté pans, point-of-sale systems, the sound system, and so on. But when the auctioneer got to the stacks of seasonal chargers, the same ones I had personally commissioned, and the best bid he could elicit was three dollars per item, I was outraged. He was about to accept the offer when I ran up to him and whispered in his ear.

"These are no longer for sale," I said.

"Mr. Luongo . . ."

"These people are criminals," I said. "If you saw what went into making one of these, you wouldn't sell it for three dollars, either."

I walked away and the man made his apologies to the bidders and they moved on.

Next up was the pewter tabletop items, little trays and salt-and-pepper shakers, and water pitchers. Again, the bidding was insufficient and before accepting the measly offer on the table, he looked at me. I shook my head from side to side. No way.

The auctioneer came over to me and was surprisingly calm. I think he must have encountered similar reactions before.

"Listen," he said. "I know you're upset, but we either need to shut this down or you need to let me do my job."

I sighed hard and nodded. In addition to the chargers and the pewter, I told him to not sell any of the artwork. I walked over to the movers and hired them to pack up that stuff and deliver it to a storage facility I keep in New Jersey. I didn't have anywhere else to take it, but I'd be damned it I'd let these strangers make out like bandits.

Then I shook the auctioneer's hand, took a final look around, and left the building. I walked east to Fifth Avenue, where all the people had always been, and left Tuscan Square behind for good.

THEY SAY THAT bad news comes in threes, and the third recent closing was Coco Pazzo, again due to landlord issues. Unable to negotiate a new lease that made sense for me, in July 2008 I decided to move on.

It was the last remnant of another chapter of my life. We served our final dinner on July 30, then I spent the next day, the final day of our lease, getting the place cleared out. At the end of the afternoon, after all the employees and moving guys had pushed off, I sat there in the dining room that had once seemed so beautiful to me. Now it just seemed dingy and old. All the life had gone out of it with the tables and chairs and menus and barware.

It's funny. I guess I should have been upset, or moved, but I just felt empty. Some restaurateurs believe that when one of their places closes, they leave a piece of themselves behind, but my feeling has always been that you take yourself along wherever you go. Whatever you did there and learned there carries over to your next place. In a strange way, it made sense that the only restaurant I'd be left with was Centolire, because it was the one that most reflected who I was at the moment, my current feelings about Italy and America and food and hospitality.

I thought of that sensation I had when I first came to New York City, that Manhattan could be whatever you wanted it to be, and that the world changed every few blocks. That's as true for me today as it was back then. I left the space that used to be Coco Pazzo and walked over to Madison, then eleven blocks up to Centolire, where the night was about to get started and we had more than one hundred fifty reservations on the book for dinner. Life, as always, went on.

INTERLUDE

THERE WILL BE *follow-up questions, lots of them, and then pages to review and to edit, but Pino and I leave it there for the night. We don't really have a choice: the restaurant has cleared out, the kitchen has fallen into silence, and the lighting has been dimmed. The only person left is Gianfanco, who's closing out the credit card receipts for the evening at a little computer next to the bar.*

"OK, buddy," Pino says as he stands up out of his chair. I click off my tape recorder and rise, stretching. It's been a long night.

Pino walks over to the computer and rests a hand on Gianfranco's shoulder. He looks over the numbers, then punches something into the keypad. I've known Pino for ten years, but I'm not sure exactly what he's doing over there. I never ask about his business. I think it's why we've stayed friends for so long.

"I'll say good-bye to you outside," he says.

I head downstairs and out to the street. He goes to close up his office—just a little room situated under the kitchen, midway between the two dining floors, almost within the walls, a cramped space and a far cry from the three floors of offices it used to take to house his empire above Le Madri. He says he likes it this way, but sometimes I wonder.

I wait for him out front. It's dead silent on Madison Avenue, and my Subaru is one of just about six cars parked on the block. Finally he emerges, a leather work bag slung over his shoulder.

"I'm glad you're working on the book with me," he says as he locks the door behind him.

"Well, you had your options," I reply. It's a running joke between us because although we'd written two books before, and had talked about this project for years, Pino had interviewed another writer at one point. It didn't make me feel great, but I long ago made peace with Pino's separation of personal affairs and business transactions. He's not the only one who's seen The Godfather.

He laughs. "OK. You're entitled to say that. But the truth is that you know me better than almost anybody in New York."

I'm surprised by the comment. How could I, a writer fifteen years younger than Pino, who came to Manhattan five years after him, who grew up in Miami, Florida, travels in different circles, and only met him ten years ago, possibly know him that much better than all the people he's been seeing regularly for so long?

"Get out of here," I say.

"It's true."

I just shrug. We shake hands and say good night and he walks off down Eighty-fifth Street toward the garage where he parks his car. I get in mine and drive through Central Park to the west side, then turn left and head down to Chelsea.

I think about his statement again. On reflection, it makes sense. For all of the people who have come and gone in his restaurants, the vast majority of the conversations he's had there have probably lasted two minutes or less, and most of them were probably about the customer, not about him. He'd never say this, of course, but no restaurateur really knows who among his customers are the true friends; most relationships formed in a professional dining room are like those acted out in a play, and have no meaning outside the confines of the stage.

But Pino does make one mistake, I think. He might not socialize with many of them. They might not have been to his house, nor he to theirs. He might not know the names of their children or where they grew up. But if food is for him, as it was for his mother, the ultimate means of self-expression, then there are plenty of people who know him just fine.

EPILOGUE

Cooking at Last

FOR THE FIRST time since 1988, I've got just one restaurant. I'm not in the papers on Wednesdays the way I used to be, and I don't run around town every night, dropping in on each of my empire's principalities. It's been ages since I took a prop plane out to Long Island or even thought about opening a restaurant in another city or state.

I'm more anonymous than I've been since the days when I was a busboy. Many young chefs and restaurateurs haven't heard of me, or if they have, it's because they read about me in *Kitchen Confidential*.

I'm not a mogul anymore. I'm "just" a successful restaurateur. My restaurant Centolire does a great business, mostly from the Upper East Siders around us. I might have had my differences with the critics of the world, but I've always put my customers first, and in return they are loyal. Long-timers still have their regular tables and once in a while a new luminary takes a liking to us. I won't lie: it's still thrilling to meet the people in the arts who I've admired from afar all my life.

It's been twenty-five years since I opened Il Cantinori, but my life these days has come full circle. I spend my days at Centolire, supervising the prep work, and at night I divide my time between the kitchen and the service floor, still feeling a bit like a modern-day Rick Blaine. The customers are known to me from all times in my adult life: there's my Tuscan Square *consigliere* Gary Wolkowitz and his wife,

Sarah; Christie Brinkley and (separately) Billy Joel; and Glenn Dubin. Former mayor Ed Koch sometimes shows up in the winter. Some have been with me since Il Cantinori, or before: once in a while a customer will tell me that he or she remembers when I was a busboy at Da Silvano. More often than not, I don't recognize these people; that was a long time ago, and at some point all of the faces, so distinct once upon a time, begin to blend together.

But I remember most of the others: on almost any night, I can gaze around the room and see faces familiar to me from over the years. Often, I feel like Joe Gideon, the Roy Scheider character in *All That Jazz*, in that scene at the end when all the people from his life come to his final, farewell performance. There's also food from all the times of my life at Centolire: we'll make your Caesar salad tableside, the way we made salads in my uncle's restaurant at Porto Santo Stefano; we'll also make carbonara, the one I perfected in my theater days, that way. There's *rigatoni alla buttera* from Il Cantinori and *spaghetti alla rustica* from Sapore di Mare, and on and on, as well as new specials, some of which make it onto the menu and some of which fade into my past along with other honorable mentions.

What do I call this stage of my life? It might sound a bit anticlimactic, but the truth of the matter is that I'm happy. In many ways, I'm happier than I ever have been, and the reason is that, at long last, after all the pain and distractions of my youth, I've come to realize what it is that makes me happy.

Cooking.

I exhale every time I say that to myself.

Cooking.

Sometimes, I want to cry. Cooking has always been there for me. From the earliest moments of my life, when my mother fed me that *pappa al pomodoro*, or barley coffee, or taught me how to shop for fruits and vegetables at the market, or let me stand beside her in the kitchen as she showed me how to panfry those ravioli.

Let me say it again, for my own benefit: Cooking makes me happy.

Why has it taken me so long to realize this? Is it an oversimplification to say that this is what life is all about? Just like the editing of a novel or the refinement of a play, or the honing of a restaurant concept, those of us who are lucky learn to strip away what doesn't belong and are left with the essence of ourselves, the thing that makes us who we are.

Even though it's taken me a half century to figure it out, I consider myself a very lucky man to finally comprehend that it's not the business deals or the money that defines me, it's cooking. The pleasure of draining a perfectly al dente pot of pasta, slicing a tender *stracotto*, or even the simple pleasure of tearing basil leaves, unlocking their summery fragrance.

How simple my life would have been if only I could have known that twenty-five years ago. Maybe I'd still be down there on Tenth Street, running Il Cantinori with Steve and Nicola. The restaurant is, after all, still there—a quarter century after it opened, it's still there—that's how solid the concept was, and the food. I was the one who moved on to build an empire, have it crash down around me, and end up living the same professional life twenty-five years and seventy-some blocks away.

Now, more than ever, the kitchen is my sanctuary. With the cooking of any dish, I can take myself to any time and place in my life, and I can take my customers there, too. I've been mining my memories of home for a quarter-century, but I still unearth a new one once in a while. Just last year, I remembered how my mother used to make pasta with smoked herring roe. I worked my network of purveyors until I found one who promised that his smoked herring roe tasted like the one I described. I waited for the sample to arrive with rapt anticipation. When it showed up, I dropped everything and headed into the kitchen. I sautéed the roe with olive oil, butter, and garlic, then tossed it with linguine and finished it with a pinch of pepper flakes. I walked it with great ceremony over to a corner of the dining room and sat with my back to the staff. I wafted in the smoky, briny aroma, then twirled some pasta and roe around my fork and, closing my eyes, took my first bite. It carried me right back to that kitchen table in Grosseto. For a moment, I was a boy again.

For about a week I ate that pasta at least once a day, and sometimes twice.

I don't chew out my staff the way I used to. People think I've mellowed with age, but that's not really the case. I've mellowed because I have shed my addiction to opera and am in love with the size and scale, with the sheer *manageability*, of my life: my restaurant and my wife and three kids, and coaching my youngest son's soccer team and playing squash a few times a week between lunch and dinner service, and driving into Manhattan each morning, then back home at night and going to sleep in our big pillowy bed with the darkness of suburbia enveloping us.

I don't have the same highs I used to have, but I don't have the lows, either. It's a good deal.

But I have to be honest. Having shared my life with you, I'll let you in on a little secret: I just took a look at a new restaurant space the other day. The first time I went to see it, all the old juices started flowing again. I saw it transformed into a restaurant in my mind, and I began to envision myself walking in every morning, a paper cup of coffee from the local deli warming my hand, the smell of sawdust catching in my nostrils.

Is this a healthy sensation, or the early warning signs of a junkie about to relapse?

Cooking makes me happy.

I don't know. But after all these years, I would love to prove that I've still got it. I would love to know that I can create a restaurant that would lure all the younger diners, the ones who maybe have never heard of Pino Luongo.

Cooking makes me happy.

For the first time in years I'm in the grasp of an irresistible idea, a lighting bolt of inspiration that I need to bring to fruition.

Cooking makes me happy.

I'm just about ready to sign the papers, and I can't wait to get started on the build-out.

Cooking makes me happy.

Doesn't it?

One of these days I'll figure it out.

Recipes, My Way

Here are recipes for some of the dishes that have most informed my palate, and my life. I'm sharing them in the same way I presented recipes in my first book, *A Tuscan in the Kitchen*, without quantities, and with only a few cooking times for guidance. I know that you have the common sense to buy the right amount of ingredients to serve the number of people you'll have at your table, and that if you're a little off, you'll find something to do with an extra carrot, or a few slices of left-over pot roast. Moreover, I have always believed that cooking should be an instinctual act and that food should express the taste, experience, and even the mood of the cook.

I urge you to try a few of these recipes. Trust your sense of sight, smell, and taste. The beauty of them is that, thanks to their fundamental simplicity, even if they are not made perfectly the first time, they will still be tasty. And as you tinker with and adjust them the second and third times you cook them, you will sharpen your ability to cook intuitively, which for me is the only way to do it.

PASTICCIO DI DANTE (DANTE'S SWEET MESS)

One of the first dishes I introduced to New York diners, this can also be served as a starter or as a side dish to fish, especially white-fleshed fish like cod or halibut. For the most appealing look, use red, yellow, and green sweet (bell) peppers.

Olive oil
Red, yellow, and green sweet peppers (any combination, or just one),
    seeded and cut lengthwise into slivers
Black pepper from a mill
Capers, drained
Canned anchovy fillets in oil, drained
Fresh Italian bread

Preheat the oven to medium heat.

Heat some oil in a heavy, ovenproof pan over medium heat. Add the sweet peppers and cook over high heat until they begin to sweat and wilt. Drain the excess liquid from the pan, season with black pepper, and scatter the capers and anchovies over the peppers. Cook, stirring gently, over medium heat until the anchovies "melt" into the mixture.

Transfer the pan to the oven and cook, uncovered, until the peppers look and smell roasted and have shriveled a bit, turning them a few times to ensure even cooking and avoid scorching. Serve warm, or at room temperature, with bread for soaking up the sauce.

PAPPA AL POMODORO (TOMATO-AND-BREAD SOUP)

Of all the dishes my mother made for me, this is one of my favorites. It's also quintessentially Tuscan, because of its simplicity and because it uses ingredients that might have outlived their usefulness in other cultures: stale bread, which is important in attaining the thick consistency, and very ripe tomatoes. (If you don't have stale bread, you can break up fresh bread, lay it on a baking sheet, and lightly toast it.) It's also a very flexible recipe; the ratio of solid to liquid can be adjusted to personal taste, but a good rule of thumb is that the finished soup should resemble a bright red bread pudding.

Stale country bread with the crust removed
Vegetable broth
Olive oil
Few cloves of garlic, smashed and peeled
Very ripe fresh beefsteak tomatoes, coarsely chopped with their juice
Fresh basil, torn by hand into small pieces
Black pepper from a mill

Soak the bread in a bowl of broth.

Heat some oil in a heavy pot over medium heat. Add the garlic and lightly brown it. Raise the heat to high and add the tomatoes. Cook, stirring gently, then add the basil. Cook the tomatoes for a while, stirring, until the mixture has thickened. Lift the bread from the broth and squeeze it out. Shred the bread and add it to the pot.

Serve the soup in warm bowls, stirring in extra oil. Season at the last second with some freshly ground black pepper. If you have some extra basil leaves, you can garnish each serving with one or two. Serve.

SPAGHETTI ALLA RUSTICA (RUSTIC-STYLE SPAGHETTI)

The super-simple star of many nights at Sapore di Mare and other restaurants of mine. The name really does say it all: this is the essence of rustic cooking, making something distinct and special from a handful of the most familiar ingredients you can think of.

Unsalted butter
Olive oil
Red onion, thinly sliced
Canned tomatoes, crushed in their own juice
Spaghetti
Coarse salt
Parmesan cheese, grated

Melt some butter and heat some oil in a heavy pan over medium-low heat. Add the onion and sauté. Once you know from the smell and color that the onion is ready—not brown, but soft and golden—stir in the tomatoes. Let the mixture cook slowly, uncovered, until the liquid is gone, but do not over-reduce.

Meanwhile, cook the spaghetti in boiling salted water until al dente. Reserve some of the cooking liquid in a heatproof container, then drain the pasta.

When the sauce is ready, stir in a little more butter to enrich and thicken it. Add the pasta to the pan, and toss. If the dish seems dry or the sauce isn't quite bound, add a tablespoon or so of cooking liquid and toss again. Add the parmesan, toss some more, and serve.

PENNE ALLA SALVIA (QUILL-SHAPED PASTA WITH SAGE AND VEAL)

Here's a version of the veal ragù I began serving at Da Silvano. If you read that chapter and wondered whether a meat sauce for pasta could satisfy with no tomato, here's your chance to see for yourself. This is also delicious with rigatoni or *mezzi* (half) rigatoni. You can substitute ground pork or crumbled sweet sausage for the veal.

If you've never cooked with fresh sage before, keep in mind that a little goes a long way; just a few leaves will make a big impact here.

Olive oil
Ground veal
Prosciutto, chopped
Red onion, finely chopped
Carrot, peeled and finely chopped
Fresh flat-leaf parsley, finely chopped
Fresh sage leaves
Dry white wine
Beef broth

Coarse salt
Black pepper from a mill
Dry penne
Parmesan cheese, grated

Heat the oil in a heavy pan. Add the veal and brown it all over, breaking it up with a wooden kitchen spoon or a fork. Add the prosciutto, onion, carrot, and parsley. Stir in the sage, and add just enough wine to come to the top of the mixture. Turn up the heat and cook until the wine evaporates. Stir in just enough broth to keep the mixture from sticking to the pan. Lower the heat and simmer, partially covered, for about 45 minutes, adding more broth when necessary to keep the mixture moist but not runny. Season with salt and pepper.

Meanwhile, cook the pasta in boiling salted water until al dente. Reserve some of the cooking liquid in a heatproof container, then drain the pasta and add to the pan with the sauce. Toss. If the dish seems dry or the sauce isn't quite bound, add a tablespoon or so of cooking liquid and toss again. Add the parmesan and toss again. Serve with more parmesan on the side.

RIGATONI ALLA BUTTERA (PEASANT-STYLE PASTA)

One of the dishes that put me on the map at Il Cantinori. You can learn a lot about pasta making from preparing this dish a few times. The desired result is a pleasingly thick, creamy sauce but one that doesn't overwhelm the texture or flavor of the peas. It's fine to use frozen peas.

You can also make this with fresh tagliatelle or pappardelle. Never use a thinner pasta such as spaghetti; the rich sauce needs a substantial pasta for relief. You can also use just sweet sausage, but do not make it only with hot, or the heat will take over the plate.

Sweet and hot Italian sausages
Black pepper from a mill

Unsalted butter
Green peas, parboiled and shocked in ice water
Canned tomatoes, crushed in their own juice
Heavy cream
Parmesan cheese, grated
Dry rigatoni
Coarse salt

Peel the casings off the sausages and crumble the meat. Cook over medium-low heat in a heavy pan. (Don't use any oil; the natural fat in the sausages renders enough grease to keep them from sticking.) The sausages will crumble even more once the fat is released. When the meat is cooked through, drain the excess fat from the pan, season with black pepper, and set aside.

In a large, heavy pan over medium heat, melt a generous spoonful of butter and add the cooked sausage, the peas, and the tomatoes. Mix well and raise the heat. Cook until the sauce thickens and the peas are tender. Stir in the cream and reduce again. Stir in just enough parmesan cheese to thicken the sauce; it should be uniformly thick but moist.

Meanwhile, cook the pasta in boiling salted water until al dente. Reserve some of the cooking liquid in a heatproof container, then drain the pasta and add it to the pan with the sauce. Toss. If the dish seems dry or the sauce isn't quite bound, add a tablespoon or so of cooking liquid and toss again. Add more parmesan, toss again, and serve with more parmesan cheese on the side.

SPAGHETTI CON AGLIO, OLIO, E PEPERONCINO (SPAGHETTI WITH GARLIC, OLIVE OIL, AND PEPPER FLAKES)

This is one of my signature dishes, and also one of the simplest recipes you'll ever make, just five ingredients *including* the olive oil and salt. Timing is essential because the sauce cannot be held. For a different version, add a splash of tomato sauce just when the garlic turns golden. (The tomato version is very forgiving because the sauce cools down the contents of the pan and keeps the garlic from browning or burning.)

Don't serve this with cheese. Don't add anything. It's perfect just as it is; it's also delicious with a vodka martini.

Coarse salt
Dry spaghetti
Olive oil
Crushed red pepper flakes
Garlic, thinly sliced

Bring a large pot of salted water to a boil. Add the pasta and cook just until al dente, about 8 minutes.

Meanwhile, generously cover the bottom of a heavy pan with olive oil and set over low heat. Add a pinch of red pepper flakes and the garlic. Sauté until the garlic is golden. Drain the pasta (there's no need to reserve any cooking liquid in this recipe because there's nothing to bind), add it to the pan, and toss well. Taste for spiciness. If it isn't fiery enough, add more pepper. Serve.

IL CACCIUCCO (TUSCAN-STYLE FISH-AND-BREAD STEW)

I don't expect that most people reading this will have the experience (or the stomach) to clean and break down fish the way my mother used to when preparing *cacciucco*, or that you have a food mill, so here's a slightly different version from the one she made. You can vary the selection of fish and shellfish according to taste. If you have any extra, reheat it the next day, add a little water to open up the flavors, and toss it with pasta as a sauce.

Olive oil
Red onions, coarsely chopped
Few cloves of garlic, chopped, plus 1 clove peeled and left whole

Shellfish (clams, mussels, and shrimp), cleaned and left in their shells
Fish, a large variety, including eel and small fish such as striped bass,
  grouper, and/or red snapper, boned and cut into chunks
Coarse salt
Black pepper from a mill
Tomatoes, fresh or canned
Fresh flat-leaf parsley, chopped
Good Italian bread, sliced

Heat a large, heavy pot over medium heat. Add plenty of oil and let it get nice and hot, then add the onions and chopped garlic and sauté until golden.

Add the shellfish and fish: the juicier and stronger-tasting ones go in first, and you want to let each type cook briefly before adding the next. First, add the clams and mussels, then the chunks of eel and the rest of the fish, smaller pieces first. Finish by adding the shrimp. Raise the heat to high and let everything cook together briefly, then season with salt and pepper and gently stir in the tomatoes. (If using canned tomatoes, break them into chunks and add them with their juice. If using fresh, quarter them.)

Stir in some parsley, saving some for garnish. Let everything cook until hot, then pour in enough cold water just to cover the ingredients and stop the cooking. When the water simmers, lower the heat and cook, uncovered, until the fish is tender, taking care not to overcook. Start checking after 10 minutes; if you can penetrate a piece of fish easily with a fork, it is done. Use a slotted spoon to remove and discard any clams or mussels that have not opened.

Meanwhile, toast 1 slice of bread for each person. Cut the whole garlic clove at one end to expose the interior. Impale it on a fork and gently rub the cut side on each slice of hot toast, releasing the pulp and juice into the bread. Sprinkle the bread lightly with oil.

Once the *cacciucco* is done, put a piece of toast in the center of each bowl. Spoon the stew over it, shells and all, and garnish with parsley. Serve with empty bowls alongside for the shells and extra bread for mopping up the stew.

TONNO ALLA LIVORNESE (TUNA STEAK, LIVORNESE STYLE)

One of the dishes I used to make for Silvano after service, and which later went on the menu at Sapore di Mare. You can also make this with swordfish.

Olive oil
Tuna steaks, 1 inch thick
Dry white wine
Canned tomatoes, chopped, in their own juice
Capers
Green olives, pitted and sliced

Preheat the oven to high.

Cover the bottom of an ovenproof skillet just large enough to hold the tuna steaks without crowding with a small amount of oil and sear the tuna on both sides over high heat. When the tuna turns a light color, add wine to the skillet until it comes halfway up the sides of the steaks. Cook over high heat until the wine simmers and reduces by half. Add the tomatoes, capers, and olives. Cover with a lid or snugly with foil and place in the oven. Start to check the tuna by prodding it with a fork after about 10 minutes. The dish is done when the steaks flake easily.

To serve, transfer the steaks to individual plates and spoon sauce over them.

FEGATO ALLA SALVIA (CALF'S LIVER WITH SAGE)

The liver in this dish should be sliced so thin that it cooks when you look at it. If possible, buy the liver from a piece no larger than six to eight pounds, which means it came from a young animal; any larger and it may have a sour taste.

All-purpose flour
Calf's liver, very thinly sliced

Unsalted butter
Fresh sage leaves

Sprinkle some flour on a plate and dredge the liver on both sides, gently shaking off any excess. Melt a generous scoop of butter in a frying pan and brown 4 or 5 sage leaves. Let the sage cook until it starts to burn. Add the liver to the pan one slice at a time and cook for 1 minute on one side, then 30 seconds on the other. As the slices are done, transfer them to plates. When all of the slices have been cooked, pour the butter and sage over them. Serve at once.

STRACOTTO ALLA FIORENTINA (POT ROAST, FLORENTINE STYLE)

One of those long-cooked cold-weather dishes that made my childhood home smell so wonderful in the fall and winter. To this day, when it gets cold every autumn, this is one of the dishes I can't wait to cook and serve. For an even more tender result, do as the mothers did at Le Madri (and as I still do at Centolire) and make this with brisket.

If you have leftover pot roast, there are a number of options: mill it and serve it over polenta or as a sauce for fresh fettuccine or pappardelle. It's also wonderful tossed into scrambled eggs for a decadent version of steak and eggs.

Note: The meat will throw a lot of smoke when you sear it; you might want to open your kitchen window and turn off your smoke detector. (Just be sure to turn it back on when you're finished; the lawyers made me say that!)

Eye round of beef, trimmed of most excess fat (ask your butcher to do this)
Coarse salt
Black pepper from a mill
Olive oil
Red onion, finely chopped
Carrot, peeled and finely chopped

Celery, fibrous outer layer removed with a vegetable peeler and finely
    chopped
Fresh flat-leaf parsley, finely chopped
Few cloves of garlic, finely chopped
Red wine
Beef broth
Dried porcini mushrooms, soaked in red wine
Canned tomatoes, crushed in their own juice

Preheat the oven to medium.

Season the beef with salt and pepper. Use a snug ovenproof oval
pan if you can; otherwise, you'll need to use a lot of liquid. Moisten the
bottom of the pan with a little olive oil, using your finger to spread it
around. (The olive oil is just to keep the meat from sticking to the
pan.) Set the pan over high heat and preheat it, then add the meat and
brown it on all sides until practically burnt. The bottom of the pan will
start to turn a dark color thanks to the fat and extra liquid, which is the
honey of the dish.

Transfer the meat to a plate.

Put a thin layer of onion, carrot, celery, parsley, and garlic in the bottom of the same pan. Brown them over high heat, add a little wine, and
stir to loosen any flavorful bits of meat and vegetable cooked onto the
bottom of the pan. Return the meat to the pan along with any juices
that have collected while it was resting, keep it over high heat, and let it
absorb the scent and taste of the vegetables. After a minute, when you
see the vegetables sticking to the meat, add enough wine or broth—or
a combination of the two—to cover the meat. (Use about 1 bottle of
wine for 4 people, because a lot of wine evaporates in cooking.)

Add the porcini and the soaking wine to the pan and bring everything to a boil. Cover and put in the oven. Cook for about 2 hours, or
until you can penetrate the meat with a fork.

Transfer the meat to a cutting board and let rest for a few minutes.
Add a scoop of tomatoes to the sauce and boil for a few minutes. Slice
the meat and put the slices in the pot. Let cook for another few minutes and serve it with good bread.

Acknowledgments

I'd like to extend my sincere thanks to the following people:

My coauthor, Andrew Friedman, who unselfishly used his writing skills to capture my voice and help organize my story;

Nick Trautwein, our editor, for his smart notes, honesty, and patience, and for having his heart in the right place at all times;

Karen Rinaldi, for buying the book and first believing in it. I miss you;

Kim Witherspoon, for selling the project and especially for her feedback and guidance down the homestretch; and

Sabrina Farber in Bloomsbury USA's marketing department, for getting the word out.

—Pino Luongo

In addition to the people named above, my thanks to . . .

Pino Luongo, for his early belief and many pasta-filled nights;

David Black, for his always treasured counsel along the way;

Peter Bodo, for some crucial advice on Sunday, May 4, 2008;

Caitlin Friedman, for her unwavering support, both emotional ("You can do it!") and practical ("Sure I can take the kids for ice cream while you write for another hour."), and for keeping things in perspective for the two of us; and

Declan and Taylor Friedman, who went from babies to "real people" during the year this book was written; keep up the good work!

—Andrew Friedman

About the Authors

PINO LUONGO has owned and operated some of the most successful and influential restaurants in New York, the Hamptons, and Chicago. He opened his first restaurant, Il Cantinori, in 1983 and went on to open several legendary restaurants including Sapore di Mare, Le Madri, and Coco Pazzo. He is currently the chef and owner of Centolire in New York City. He is also the author of several cookbooks.

ANDREW FRIEDMAN coauthored the *New York Times* bestselling memoir *Breaking Back*, the story of American tennis star James Blake, and co-edited the popular anthology *Don't Try This at Home*. He has also collaborated on cookbooks with Alfred Portale, Tom Valenti, and former White House chef Walter Scheib, among many others.